CALCIUM MADE INTERESTING

Jim Yoakum has kept the flame burning as the
US curator of the Graham Chapman archives since 1997.
He is also a writer and author in his own right and
lives in the United States.

This book is dedicated to the following apology

Highgate,
London N6.

Dear John Kenelm Bennett and Pat, sons and daughters of the Angel Inn, Highgate,

Words alone will have to express my profoundly abject apology for my behaviour in your pub last night. I will have the shelf repaired, and I have already bought a half pound of fillet steak for Dennis's eye. The genital exposure was regrettable, and the fact that I threw out some of your customers was naughty in the extreme. Douglas Adams will vouch that I did stand myself in the corner for several minutes this morning rapping my knuckles with a three foot, sorry, metre rule, whilst suffering from acute alcoholic poisoning. While this letter was written in the Duke's Head, it does not necessarily mean that I will not besmirch the Angel with my presence in the future, but hints such as 'I'm never allowing that drunken perverted bastard who thinks he's God in the pub again' will be taken in the spirit in which they are intended.

Yours with affection,

Graham 'Filthy' Chapman

PS Can I use this letter in the book I'm meant to be writing when I've sobered up?

Acknowledgements

My thanks go out to everyone who gave me help, encouragement and advice along the way, especially to Ed Sikov, Tony Hendra, Carol Cleveland, Martin Bergman, Mark Ezra, A. Lee Blackman and the Nilsson Estate, Bernard McKenna, Nile Southern, David Yallop, Terry Jones, Eric Idle, Jonathan Lynn, the New Yorker, Ceres Hill, Augusten Burroughs and David Sherlock. Thanks also go out in one way or another to Leigh Haber McKenzie, Kate Travers, Max Eilenberg, Susan Morrison, Shelly Schultz, Eleanora Tevis, Clem Turner and Richard Miller. Grateful thanks to Ingrid Connell and Jacqui Butler at Macmillan for steering me right when things took a wrong turn. Compiling and editing this book has been my great pleasure and I sincerely hope that reading it will be yours.

In memory of Graham and John.

Contents

Contents

Contents

Contents

Contents

Introduction: An Untidy Life

by Jim Yoakum, US Curator of the Graham Chapman Archives

In life, Graham Chapman was many things: a celebrated and successful writer and performer, a founder member of Monty Python, a qualified medical doctor, an experienced mountaineer, a pioneering Gay activist, a reckless daredevil, an accomplished lecturer . . . His was a full life. In fact, it was many full lives. But it was his work as a writer and a performer that made him famous and quite rightly so. Like his friend Ringo Starr, Graham was a surprisingly skilful and natural actor. He played the lead role of King Arthur in the film *Monty Python and the Holy Grail* with a startling strength and depth. The fact that he was suffering from alcohol-withdrawal at the time may have added to his haggard pathos, but it's disingenuous to give all the credit to a bottle of Beefeater's as some have done. In *Monty Python's Life of Brian*, it's Graham's pitch-perfect performance as the hapless and befuddled Brian Cohen, the would-be Messiah whose life closely parallels that of Jesus Christ's, that helped dull many of the critical barbs thrown at it by outraged Christians. It's interesting to note that, of all the controversy that has swirled around this film for the last twenty-five years, as far as I know, not one critic has ever made mention of the movie's most obvious flaw: that a six feet three inches tall blond portrayed a Jew from Nazareth. On paper it was a character better suited to Terry Jones, who is shorter and darker. But the role demanded both a commanding and sympathetic figure, an actor who could make you look beyond things like height, colour, and national origin. It demanded Graham Chapman.

I find it difficult to imagine, much less discuss, modern comedy without mentioning at least three people (alas, now all dead) without whom it simply would not exist as we know it. Spike Milligan, the brilliant illogician behind the *Goon Show*, Peter Cook, genius personified, and Graham Chapman. What these three have in common goes beyond their ability to wisecrack, their linguistic gymnastics, flights of fancy, or their capacity to mimic and perform (there were many others in their peer group who could do that just as well); what sets them apart is the fact that they shared an innate belief in absurdity as a way of life. To them there was no difference (or very little difference) between real life and the reel life. Humour, and the sheer joy of madness for its own sake, effortlessly flowed through their brains and through their veins and was as likely to find an outlet on the street as on the stage.

It's well documented that Spike Milligan was plagued with depression and suffered no fewer than ten breakdowns. His home was littered with 'No Smoking' signs, and a notice on his front door said: 'This door can be closed without slamming it. Try it and see how clever you are.' Even his gravestone bears the epitaph: 'I told you I was ill', written in Gaelic.

Peter Cook virtually abandoned the spotlight at an age when most comics are just entering the field and, in the last years of his life, took to anonymously calling a late-night radio talk show pretending to be a Norwegian fisherman named Sven.

Graham's exploits, especially during his drinking days, are legendary and include attending a Cambridge University student union function – where he was the guest speaker – dressed as a carrot, and saying absolutely nothing for ten minutes.

It's nigh impossible to envision many of their peers (with the possible exception of, say, Peter Sellers) doing any of these things without the cameras rolling. It was eccentric behaviour certainly but what's really interesting is that they didn't necessarily look at these as being antics or absurdities. It was just another day in the salt mines.

Most comedians do their bit then turn off the comedy switch and go home to the wife and kids, but Graham didn't seem to have a comedy switch. He was hot-wired to the source; an unearthed live wire from where much of Python's lunacy sprang. To hear his friends and fellow Pythons describe him you'd think that they were either discussing a man bound for the sanatorium or else an alien lifeform: 'Graham was a very strange planet.' – Eric Idle; 'It was some years before I realized he didn't work properly.' – John Cleese; 'As far as I was concerned, he had come from the moon.' – Terry Jones; 'Graham was just on another planet at times.' – Terry Gilliam. His fellow Pythons have said that just listening to Graham tell them about one of his wild evenings out was fodder for a dozen sketches. That's not hard to understand when one considers that a typical evening out alone, or with fellow loons-in-arms like Keith Moon, Harry Nilsson, and Ringo Starr, could stretch on through the night and into the next day (and often did). Fellow Footlighter, actor and future film director Jonathan Lynn, once described Graham as 'the only true Python anarchist'.

So, were Graham's incessant drinking, carousing and off-hand approach to schedules and the accepted normal rules of social and professional behaviour a liability and a problem? According to many the answer was unquestionably 'Yes.' Without a doubt, Graham held little regard for such niceties as schedules or deadlines and, for much of his life, was a disorganized, undependable, and unpredictable man. But he was also a highly complex and internally conflicted one who never totally trusted his comic or acting abilities until much later in life. A man who battled alcoholism and the growing awareness that he was homosexual (or at the very most, bi-sexual), at a time when admitting such things – even privately – was frowned upon by society and, in the case of homosexuality, carried the added weight of being a punishable offence. None of this is said in order to make allowances for his behaviour and there's no question that Graham's life was occasionally a mess, but he preferred it that way. 'I want to be a loony. It's quite an important thing,' he confided in the working notes for his autobiography.

Graham's upbringing certainly didn't give any indications that he was destined for comedy. He was born in Leicester on 8 January 1941 in the middle of a Nazi blitz ('They were confused,' he later wrote. 'They thought they were bombing Coventry'), to father Walter – a Police Constable – and mother Edith. His brother, John, had been born four years earlier. Graham didn't know a great deal about his parents' background and only a smattering of information about his grandparents. His maternal grandmother was made a widow during the First World War after her husband was gassed in the trenches. She was left to raise a family of thirteen in Hinckley. He described his mother as being somewhat stern and (according to him) 'a bit of a snob'. His father was physically distant, as his police duties meant working odd hours and shifts, but according to Graham they had a good relationship. Graham attended an infants' school in Wigston Magna although the family moved around quite a lot due to Walter's job. When Graham was five they moved from Wigston to Braunceston, a suburb of Leicester, where Graham spent a lot of time on a farm. 'It was a great place to be when you're six to ten,' he said. Walter's job also exposed Graham to the horrors of real life at an early age. One of his first memories is of seeing the remnants of several Polish airmen hanging from the trees, in Leicester, victims of an unexplained aerial explosion.

Graham: 'I remember various bits of police duties of my father. One day, when I was about four, a gentleman came to the door of the house with blood streaming down his face and a gash on his head. Apparently his wife had stabbed him with a carving knife.' He also recalls that one of the saddest side effects of his nomadic life was that he was never able to have a dog. 'We were always moving, so I never had one. But I always was next door to the police pound and I would get friendly with one and then it would be put down two weeks later.' When he was older he claimed that this led to his buying a house in Highgate. 'I didn't really need a house, I could have lived quite happily in the flat in Belsize Park, but I wanted a dog.' Subsequently he had two beagles, Towser and Harry.

The constant moves gave young Graham a feeling of transience; that nothing in life was permanent; there was always someplace else to go and new people to meet. In a way it was the perfect upbringing for a career in entertainment, as that's where his true passion lay – although he had no idea how one went about becoming an entertainer, or if it was even a proper job one could have. 'I think I wanted to be Dick Barton, or Biggles – especially Biggles. I still want to be Biggles,' he said. 'My early ambitions of being anything at all centred around the radio, listening to it, particularly comedy shows. Later on I watched the TV. We only had BBC then, and before we had a set we used to go and watch *Café Continental* on Saturday nights at Mr and Mrs Clements's because they were awfully rich and had a TV. I remember watching *Puzzle Car, Kaleidoscope, In Town Tonight*.'

He says that the radio shows didn't necessarily make him laugh, that he was more curious to see what made others laugh. Only a select few got a chuckle from young Chapman including Frankie Howerd, the team of Jimmy Jewell and Ben Warris, *It's That Man Again*, *Educating Archie*, *Take It From Here* and *Much Binding in the Marsh*. 'I especially liked Robert Morton, although no one else seemed to like him very much. He would do things like tell jokes the wrong way around and switch punch lines. He was obviously a very good comedian and was ahead of his time. The appearance of incompetence was wonderful. He was one of my heroes.' But the show that truly astounded Graham, and was a major influence on his comedy was *The Goon Show*.

Graham also became something of a voracious reader, devouring everything from Enid Blyton's *Famous Five* and (of course) *Biggles*, to anything adventurous. But no comics. 'My mother was a bit of a snob,' he said. 'And not being in the position to be one, she was. She thought comics weren't good, but I was allowed the *Children's Newspaper*. I didn't like that very much because it was like Sunday school, which I detested, hated. I only went twice and had to be dragged there.' When he was about ten years old Graham spoke to his father about the radio programmes that he'd been listening to and said at one point that he wanted to grow up and do something like that. Walter told him that that was ridiculous, complete nonsense and 'not a thing to do'. Graham responded, saying that he felt being able to make people laugh was a clever thing to do. It was the only time he recalls ever discussing the matter with his father. 'It was pointless,' said Graham. 'I was destined for the law, like him. My father thought I should be a solicitor because they had a better time of it than policemen; they didn't work shifts.'

Despite his father's adamant views on what career path he should take, Graham didn't recall his father as being an especially hard or strict man ('I very rarely got whacked'), instead he said that Walter was an extremely kind person who didn't like having to arrest people. 'He was of the school of thought that if you caught someone doing something wrong, you give them a cuff around the neck and say "Don't do it again" and send them home.'

*

Meanwhile, life moved on. At the Braunceston school he showed academic promise and was pushed forward a grade. But this proved to be a hardship on him as his end-of-term exams showed. Used to being in the top three of his class, he was suddenly 38th. 'I thought maybe 38 was good, I mean maybe they worked it the other way round, however my father pointed it out differently.' This came as a shock to Graham and for the rest of his stay at the school he began to develop a mental picture of himself as a bit of a dunderhead. Some of the teachers even picked him out as being the class idiot. The family moved again, back to Wigston, by which time Walter had made an Inspector. Graham took his eleven-plus, passed, and went to South Wigston Boys School. At the time, the Chapmans were living in the police station near the railway and Graham's only friends were the children of the railway workers. He discovered that one of the drawbacks of being a police-man's son was that you had to constantly show you were 'one of the boys', capable of being a bit naughty, but he was always careful to be the instigator rather than the perpetrator.

It was at South Wigston that he had his first taste of acting, sort of, when he got the lead in a school play about pirates. But one of the other boys became upset that he didn't get the lead and began to cry, so the part was taken away from Graham and he was instead given the 'extremely important' part of painting the scenery. This seemingly innocuous incident hurt Graham so deeply that, even years later, he recalled it with anger and vitriol. 'I swore all the way with all the words I knew, which was quite a lot. It was never an anger that I'd expressed openly before. That, above all else, is probably the reason that I'm doing what I'm doing now. In some strange way, I go back and say, "Sod you!" It really hurt. I knew I'd been betrayed. I didn't even get a walk-on, just got to paint scenery. I didn't mess up the scenery in revenge, I did a good job. I painted some really good canvases.'

Although he hated South Wigston ('It was a pretty poor school, a few cold taps and old coke stoves') he was a lot happier than he had been at Braunceston. Some stability at home was attained by Walter's promotion, his teachers were better, and he began to do well in school again. But that, like most things in his life, was temporary. Walter's job put the family on the move yet again and Kidworth Grammar School, where Graham went after South Wigston, was another set of trials and tribulations for him. He knew virtually no one in his new school and those he did know were hated by all the new kids he hung around with. Graham ended up in a fight on his first day of school and was put on detention, but since he didn't know what detention was he didn't show up for it. He was caught about a week later and was punished. He was also kept back a year. Typically, the misery didn't last long: less than a year later the family moved again, to Melton Mowbray. Walter had been made Chief Inspector.

By this time Graham had become used to the idea of constant change, the fighting, and of having to prove himself over and over again. However, this time he hit upon a novel idea in order to improve his lot: self-deception. He decided that at his new school he would pretend that he was brilliant. He decided that, because Wigston was closer to Leicester than Melton Mowbray, then that meant he was practically a local and therefore smarter than 'these country bumpkins'. Amazingly, the plan worked. He learned more and did better in school, coming top of the class in geometry. He then turned to maths and sciences and aced those too.

It was around this time, at the age of fourteen, that several things happened that for ever altered Graham's life, the first, and most surprising, being that Graham decided to be confirmed in the Church. It was an odd decision for a boy who professed that he had to be dragged to Sunday school, but Graham claimed he fell foul of *The Gideons' Bible*, of which there were copies distributed around the school. He actually read the New Testament about three times thinking that, if he did, it would make him good and everything he wanted would come true. 'I thought about it, considered all the possibilities and decided it was a good idea. It came as a surprise to my parents. Confirmation classes were great fun, quite a giggle.' Confirmation classes a giggle? 'There's no laugh better than a suppressed one,' he said. 'So confirmation classes were pretty good. The biggest hoot of all was the actual ceremony which, if you look at it, is a bit silly, all that mumbo-jumbo that surrounds it. So why not have a laugh?' He wasn't laughing at God, rather the solemnity and ceremony that surrounds the Church, something he would attack years later in the film *Life of Brian*. 'Why do you have to be so miserable? It should be fun if it's worthwhile. I'm interested in religion but not the Church. Formal religion is rather silly.' Graham was confirmed at Melton Mowbray by the Bishop of Leicester, but afterwards claimed that he didn't feel much different than before. 'I wasn't sure whether I believed in anything or not, but I was keeping myself covered. I haven't been to church since.'

Also at age fourteen he developed an interest in girls, although his first real experience with them was painful. One date with a girl took a quick downturn when Graham proved to be too slow at putting the moves on her – and she told him so. Graham was mortified ('The old "insulted my manhood" bit'). She became angry and went home. It had quite an effect on him. 'The episode put me off girls for a long time afterwards,' he said. 'I was all ready, I had gone out to get the condoms and everything. I couldn't have been more ready. It was so fucking annoying. Just the confusion over foreplay. If it hadn't been for that my whole life might have been different.' The episode did, however, spur him to pursue other interests ('To be a man,' he said) which included an odd mix of rugby and musical comedy, especially the works of Gilbert and Sullivan ('I knew them backwards and revelled in it. I belonged to the local dramatic society from about the age of sixteen onwards'). He was also in the chorus of *The Mikado* and played Bosun in *HMS Pinafore*.

He went on to play rugby for the town of Melton Mowbray (the school didn't have a team). He started as a winger because of his speed (he could run 100 yards in 10.6s), but then switched to a forward. It was also at this point that Graham began his long love affair with alcohol. It started with him going down to the pub with the boys on the team and having a couple of pints. Although he was only fourteen, he was tall for his age and he elaborated on his mature look by smoking a pipe. He had no problems getting served. On the academic front he got eight O-levels, although he admitted that he cheated in Latin.

The last major event that occurred in his fourteenth year was the night he happened to catch an excerpt of Cambridge University's annual Footlights theatrical revue on the television programme *Saturday Night at the London Palladium*. The Footlights revue of 1955 was called *Between The Lines* and the clip in question featured a young, rubber-faced, long-limbed performer named Jonathan Miller, later of

Beyond the Fringe fame. Those few minutes spent in front of the TV changed the course of Graham's life. It verified what he'd thought all along, that people could actually make a living by writing and performing comedy; that it was as much a real profession as being a solicitor, a doctor, or even a Chief Inspector. The only thing he was still unsure about was how to get a job doing it.

He took note of the title of the revue, the performer, and the name of the university: Cambridge. His brother was at St Bartholomew's Hospital training to be a doctor. 'I thought, if he was able to do medicine then, perhaps, Cambridge might be possible for me.' Armed with this information Graham began to subconsciously formulate a plan whereby he could attend Cambridge and join the Footlights club. To him the only path that led there with any degree of certainty was medicine. 'Attending Footlights was the sole reason I wanted to go to Cambridge. Medicine was just the excuse.'

He was interviewed at Emmanuel College, and it went well, although he was left uncertain as to whether or not he'd actually been accepted. There was no doubt, however, about his acceptance to St Bartholomew's Hospital, not once they learned that his brother John attended and that Graham played rugby. Hedging his bets, Graham was also interviewed at St Mary's Hospital. 'They gave me an intelligence test,' he said, 'and were stupid enough to leave me alone in the room and so I cheated for the second time. I also altered the clock, giving me five additional minutes. I must have come out with some incredible intelligence quota.' He was accepted at Emmanuel and brotherly loyalty took him to Bart's to finish his medical degree post-Cambridge, though St Mary's offered him a place too. However, getting into Footlights – his sole reason for attending Cambridge – proved harder. 'They had a stall at the Societies Fair and I went straight to it. Behind it was David Frost, who was club secretary. He pointed out that you couldn't just join Footlights, you had to be elected. I asked him the point of the booth then.'

Graham met up with a fellow Footlights hopeful named Tony Branch, who seemed to know the secret of getting in. You had to hold a smoking concert, invite the committee and ply them with plenty of cheap claret and sandwiches. Attending their smoker were Frost and club president Tony Bellwood. They were sufficiently impressed to invite Graham to audition properly, which he did, with little hope that he'd actually get into the club. At the Footlights audition he met another man who was to play a large part in his life from then on out, a tall bearded writer named John Cleese. 'I had no idea how John got an audition, perhaps he knew someone. He did attend a better school.' But Graham and John Cleese met over coffee, and played around with a few sketch ideas, although by Graham's admission most of them were imitative of Peter Cook, with whom they were both infatuated. They were both elected and joined the Footlights club in 1961. 'We immediately felt a part of the privileged few and consequently treated everyone else abominably,' said Graham.

It was at Footlights that Graham got his first real experience in performing for people, doing as many as two smokers a term, cabaret once a fortnight, and the annual end-of-the-year Footlights revue. 'Footlights was my real college,' said Graham. The Footlights revue in Graham's final year was called *Double Take* and was the first one ever to perform at the Edinburgh Fringe Festival, where it received good write-ups. (In addition to Graham and John Cleese, the show featured Tony Hendra, Trevor Nunn and Tim Brooke-Taylor.) After *Double Take* had run its course, all that he'd been striving for since he was a child – getting into Cambridge, into Footlights, becoming a performer – it was all over. At twenty-one he graduated, and now faced the daunting task of hospital life. He'd also rediscovered an interest in sex (still with women) – not that he had a lot of luck with it. 'In those days it was more difficult. I didn't really get anywhere, although I do remember fearlessly attacking my brother's wife's sister at a wedding reception. I was getting a bit desperate then. I didn't win.' He'd also developed a now fairly serious relationship with alcohol. 'I had learnt to become a pretty good drinker by then,' he says. 'I had started drinking with the rugby club and then at school; when doing productions we'd smuggle in VP Sherry, miniatures – anything. Of course I'd done a fair bit of drinking at Cambridge, claret and beer.' Graham left Cambridge on the best of terms with Cleese (who still had another year of university to go) and they had hopes of seeing each other again.

There's a distinct possibility at this stage of his life that Graham may not have entered show business at all if it hadn't been for the meagreness of his student grant. To earn some extra money he teamed up again with Tony Hendra, and took a five-week job at the London nightclub called The Blue Angel. It wasn't exactly the Palladium. The team of Chapman and Hendra did a half-hour routine, mainly pratfalls and duologues, in front of drunken guardsmen and ladies of the evening. They went over well and later moved on to the more upscale Edmundo Ros' Dinner and Supper Club on Regent Street.

It was tough on Graham having to spend all day in medical school and then performing at night, sometimes not going on stage until as late as two-thirty in the morning, then getting back to his quarters by 4 a.m. only to have to rise at eight-thirty for a nine o'clock ward round. But the showbiz bug bit him hard and so he continued his extra-curricular activities, even going so far as to get a Footlights show to perform a smoking concert at Bart's, which he directed. (Graham continued to direct ward concerts at the hospital well after he left and, on several occasions, they included his Cambridge friend John Cleese.) The late hours eventually did take a toll on his studies and he frequently ran foul of hospital staff, who took a dim view of his part-time job as a comic.

Meanwhile, as Graham toiled away in medicine, Cleese's final Footlights revue, *A Clump of Plinths*, moved up to London and into the tiny Arts Theatre, thanks to a financial investment from impresario Michael White, and underwent a name change, to *Cambridge Circus*. American rights to the show were snapped up by Ed Sullivan (who hosted a very successful Sunday night TV variety show), with the idea of putting it on Broadway with an American cast. British humour was 'in' that year. The American rights to David Frost's satirical television programme, *That Was The Week That Was*, had also been purchased and an American version was produced. It featured (among many others) 'special correspondent' David Frost, Woody Allen, Buck Henry, Bill Cosby, and Alan Alda (later of *M*A*S*H* fame). It lasted one season.

Meanwhile, when one of the cast of *Cambridge Circus* (Tony Buffery) had to leave, Cleese called up Graham to take his place. Even though he had a heavy load already with school and exams, it was his chance to get back on the boards and Graham took it. 'They all knew me, and my drama coach skit fitted in well. Suddenly we were on the West End and then a six-week tour of New Zealand.' He took six months' leave from school, which he told his parents had been a 'Royal Decree' after the Queen Mother (who'd been visiting the school to dedicate a new lab) said he 'simply had to see New Zealand'.

The New Zealand tour was a muddle with poor publicity, meagre turnouts, ramshackle theatres, and equally dicey accommodation. Just as they were ready to throw in the towel, director Humphrey Barclay received an offer to do it on Broadway. So the troupe tramped over to New York City and performed it twenty-three times at the Plymouth Theatre. Despite a shot in the arm when Ed Sullivan showcased the cast on his programme (and Graham performed his one-man wrestling bit), it was a mixed success. A review in the *New York Times* (the only review that really mattered) effectively killed the show and it was soon transferred to a small cafe/theatre in Greenwich Village. But like Tony Buffery, Graham too had to leave the show. ('I'd been given six months' leave and I had already been gone nine.') He returned to Bart's to take his final exams.

Cleese stayed on in America and did a turn in *Half a Sixpence* and wrote briefly for *Newsweek*. While there he also met actress Connie Booth, who would later become both his wife and co-creator of *Fawlty Towers*. After returning to London, Cleese often took up residence in one of the rooms at Graham's medical college that had been abandoned by a vacationing student. He pursued a job at the BBC, writing skits for various people, including Dick Emery; this soon led to a job as a writer/performer for the radio show *I'm Sorry, I'll Read That Again* (ISIRTA), to which Graham began to contribute sketches (Graham also contributed material to *The Illustrated Weekly Hudd*, starring Roy Hudd).

The ISIRTA programme was somewhat based on *Cambridge Circus* and featured many of the same performers. This eventually led to Chapman and Cleese writing for *The Frost Report*, and the film *The Rise and Rise of Michael Rimmer* (co-written with, and starring, Peter Cook). It was while on a working holiday in Ibiza to write this movie that Graham met David Sherlock, a man with whom he shared the rest of his life in a committed relationship. It was also in Ibiza that Graham learned that he'd passed his medical exams and could finally attach the title 'Doctor' before his name. 'I finished as a doctor in 1966,' says Graham, 'but that didn't mean I could set up a practice in Willesden. I would have to have done a house job (at the hospital) for six months. Then I could have been a General Practitioner.'

With *Frost* and *Rimmer* under his belt, Graham took John Cleese up on the offer to write and perform with him in the TV series *At Last the 1948 Show*, with Tim Brooke-Taylor (who had also appeared in *Double Take*) and Marty Feldman (who had been script supervisor on *Frost*). Graham also began to write (with Barry Cryer and Eric Idle) a TV series for Ronnie Corbett called *No That's Me Over Here*, as well as scripts for the BBC-TV series *Marty* (starring Marty Feldman), and the medical comedy, *Doctor in the House* (whose scriptwriting team resembled a Footlights reunion and included at times Bill Oddie, John Cleese and Jonathan Lynn). A life in showbiz was now looking like a definite possibility and it was around this time that Graham began to consider the possibility of giving up medicine. But there was another reason for that decision, one that had nothing to do with the busy and glamorous life in TV versus the mundane and plodding one in medicine. It was the dawning realization that he was a homosexual. He knew that there was no place in the staid institution of medicine for an admitted homosexual, not only because of the unspoken (or, indeed, spoken) insinuations and liabilities that having a gay doctor on staff would bring, but also because he'd have no one to take to medical functions – no 'Mrs Chapman' – who could bundle off with all the other 'Mrs MDs' whilst the doctors talked shop. This was the mid-1960s after all.

With Sherlock's support, Graham decided to tackle the whole 'I'm a homosexual' situation by throwing what he termed a 'coming-out party'. He invited many of his friends from television, and a select few from medical school as well as . . . his fiancée. It's not often mentioned, but while still at medical school Graham (and before he'd met Sherlock) had met a very attractive and intelligent woman who was also attending St Bart's. They hit it off and she became his first steady girlfriend, by his own admission the only one he ever had. She was mostly responsible for Graham passing the exams as she frowned on his drinking (which at this stage was fairly regular) and forced him to study. 'I did it for her,' Graham said. 'She was the closest woman to me that any woman had ever been. We were mentally close and sexually compatible. Wonderfully so.' But the idea of marriage, or the idea of anyone telling him what to do, didn't suit Graham. It was while in Ibiza, after he met David Sherlock, that he realized he had to break it off with her. He phoned her up in London and said that they'd have to have a chat once he returned. Which they did at the party. He'd already told David Frost, and Cleese, but it was news to her, and she understandably flew out of the room in tears. 'It was a bit of a full-in-the-face way to do it,' Graham admitted, 'short and quick. It was also a rather thoughtless thing for me to do. There were a lot of tears.'

The news had come as something of a shock to John Cleese. 'I would describe John as my best friend,' Graham once said. 'He's the person I suppose as far as comedy goes I respect most. I know him pretty well and indeed him me. We don't share problems — we're far too British to do those things — nothing emotional. We just didn't communicate that way. So this made it a bit of a shock to him when I told him I was a poof. He was surprised that this "pipe-smoking, rugby-playing mountaineer" should decide to live with another gentleman, and had been doing so for a year. He had no idea.' Cleese also admits that he was surprised, and that he also felt a bit like he'd been misled by all of Graham's overt 'butchery'. Graham's mother Edith was distraught and cried for the better part of a week. She pleaded with Graham to not tell Walter as 'it would kill him' and, although he didn't think it would, Graham kept it a secret. He was surprised to receive a phone call from his father a week or so later where Walter merely said that 'women don't understand' this sort of thing and to not worry about it.

In 1968 Graham and John Cleese were asked by Peter Sellers to work on the film script for *The Magic Christian*, based on the novel by Terry Southern. The book told the story of the world's richest man (Sir Guy Grand), a man who liked to see what lengths people would go to for quick money. It had long been a favourite of Sellers' and after he'd optioned the book he had a script commissioned by Southern, but in typical Sellers fashion he thought it could be improved with a little 'new blood', and Chapman/Cleese were hot property. According to Graham, the film company basically needed additional funding and they thought that if they could write in a part for Ringo Starr (who had begun his solo film career a year previously on another Southern property, *Candy*) as Grand's son, then it would be easier to get the production made. Southern was reluctant to change the storyline (there was no son in the novel) and so Chapman and Cleese were tapped for the job. It was ultimately an unsatisfying assignment for them (as outlined elsewhere in this book), although it was their first, real, introduction to the movie business. (*Rentadick*, their first foray into film, had been so appallingly bad that they petitioned to have their names removed from the credits, and although *Michael Rimmer* was a much better film it received very limited release.) The film did give them future fodder for material though, as the character of 'James McCretin' in an episode of the *Python* TV series (played by Cleese) was loosely (and unfairly) based on *Christian*'s director Joe McGrath.

By 1969, things were looking up for Graham on both the personal and professional front, which was underscored when he and John Cleese were given the go-ahead to write and perform a new TV series with Eric Idle, Terry Jones, Terry Gilliam and Michael Palin for the BBC, originally called *Bunn, Wackett, Buzzard, Stubble and Boot* . . . It eventually went out under the title *Monty Python's Flying Circus* on 5 October 1969. A new era of comedy was born that day.

Monty Python (the troupe) has often been referred to as 'the Beatles of comedy' and, in many ways, Graham held the same position within Python as did John Lennon within the Beatles. Not the unchallenged leadership role (that belongs to John Cleese) but the same natural absurdity and irreverence that, while it often chafed and created unwelcome controversy, sparked the others to achieve greater heights.

Graham's open support of, and association with, the British newspaper *Gay News* led to more controversy when in 1976 the paper printed a poem by James Kirkup entitled 'The Love That Dares to Speak Its Name', which was an explicit description of a homosexual affair between a Roman Centurion and the crucified Jesus Christ. The publication of this poem led to a legal battle between the paper and moral-reformer Mary Whitehouse, on the grounds of blasphemy. The

Gay News case proved a legal precedent when the publisher, Denis Lemon, was prosecuted under the English blasphemy law and found guilty.

Controversy again surrounded Graham when he and David Sherlock became the legal guardians to a troubled runaway teenage boy named John Tomiczek. Eyebrows were raised, but Graham and David felt they were only doing the right and sensible thing, as he needed a stable home life and they supplied it – as unconventional as it may have been. Besides, they had the full support of his father. (John grew up to become a well-adjusted man who, in later life, became Graham's personal manager and married a lovely young American woman before heart-related problems claimed his life in the early 1990s.)

But to just focus on Graham's sexual beliefs misses the point. Except for a very brief period, he wasn't a rampant pro-homosexual zealot – nothing infuriated him more than to be confronted with a fanatic of any sort, for that usually signalled inflexibility of thought – he was, instead, a dedicated proponent of frank and open-minded discussion on all issues, sexuality included. Unfortunately, a lot of the rest of the conventional world didn't share his philosophy, hence the controversies – but then railing against orthodoxy was the one thing Graham was fanatical about. If that sounds like a contradiction of character, then it is. He was a qualified medical doctor who held the accepted practices of the medical establishment in low regard. A man who disliked sentimentality, but appreciated sentiment. A raucous and boisterous wild man who was, at the core, an extremely shy man.

He was also quite aware of the state of his often precarious (and sometimes overwhelming) financial predicaments. 'Life is a complete laugh,' he once said, 'and sometimes a hollow one. That's not to say I don't take things seriously, I take a lot of things seriously. It's like Billy Bunter, constantly waiting for a postal order.'

Graham decided to write his autobiography around the age of thirty-six as he was certain that his years of alcohol abuse and hard living were taking their toll. In fact, he was utterly convinced that he was going to die at the age of forty-two. The book, which he joked at the time would be 'the first autobiography ever written by two people' (it ended up being written by five), was begun with writing friend David Yallop. Graham later expanded the line-up to include new friend Douglas Adams, Alex Martin and David Sherlock. Graham began writing while still deep in the throes of drink, so it was initially a slow slog full of false starts, periods of idleness, illness and drunkenness followed by sporadic bouts of frantic activity. It eventually culminated with Graham suffering a severe case of delirium tremens and being rushed to the Royal Northern Hospital. It was at this point, facing certain death, that Graham made the final decision to live. He promptly stopped drinking (a promise that he kept until the end of his life) and once he was well again, at least well enough to resume work, he finished off the autobiography with no problem. In 1980, *A Liar's Autobiography* was published to worldwide acclaim and critical plaudits. It was reprinted in paperback in 1999.

It has been levelled at Graham that he was the author of his own financial misery; that he simply lived beyond his means. Certainly Graham lived well when he could afford it (and even when he could not), but he never rested on his laurels and moaned of his plight. Instead, he went to work. When financial concerns came calling in the early 1980s, Graham and family moved to Los Angeles for a year, breaking new ground by becoming the first of the Python group to test the waters of Hollywood. For Graham it wasn't just a financial move, it was to be a career shift.

Newly sober, with *Life of Brian* still racking up the numbers, and the newly filmed *Monty Python Live at the Hollywood Bowl* set for release, it was no surprise that the acting offers came rolling in almost as soon as his feet hit Sunset Drive. Whatever trepidations Graham may have had about his talents, they weren't shared by the movers and shakers of Tinseltown: He was a star. Better than that, he was a Python; a walking, talking, living comedy legend. And what better way to treat a legend than to toss him feet first into the Hollywood star-making machinery.

Graham was offered an assortment of roles, from the good to the bad to the downright unmentionable, and Graham took most of what was offered and made the best of them. In 1980 he had a recurring role on NBC-TV's *The Big Show*. It was a throwback to a genre thought long dead and one that Graham, working within Monty Python, had helped bury: the comedy/variety programme. He also spent a week guest hosting on *The Hollywood Squares* game show, appeared in *Saturday Night Live*, and did a fairly impressive dramatic turn as a police inspector in an episode of *Still Crazy Like A Fox*, among other things. He managed to break through to middle-America as a solo artist and pay the bills, but although the California climate agreed with Graham and family, the Hollywood mentality did not sit as well. So he returned to Great Britain.

It was then that Graham became involved in the Dangerous Sports Club, an ad hoc collective of 'adrenaline junkies' who did mad things such as attempt to hang-glide over active volcanoes and ski down mountain slopes on grand pianos. Today this would all be labelled Extreme Sports, but at the time it was considered sheer insanity. It suited Graham. According to David Sherlock, Graham's adventures with the Dangerous Sports Club provided him with the rush he missed from alcohol. While he was never an official member of the club (you had to participate in three DSC events in order to be a proper member), Graham was inspired enough by their antics to form the idea for an adventure movie and write a pseudo TV documentary about the club, which is included here (see p. 192). But what really set Graham off in a new direction wasn't skiing down black runs on a wooden gondola, it was touring American colleges.

The idea for this came about totally by accident. He was attending a screening of *Monty Python's Life of Brian* at Facets Multimedia in Chicago in the early eighties when, to his horror, he discovered that the promoters had billed it as 'An Evening With Graham Chapman'. He soon realized that he was expected to speak to the audience and even take questions. Totally unprepared, and never the most comfortable of people before a large group, Graham was panicked. He managed to stumble his way through the evening unscathed and, after reviewing a video of the performance, discovered to his utter amazement that he actually quite liked it. He decided to repeat the experience.

As the tours developed, the 'comedy lectures' (as he called them) became more polished. He incorporated Python clips, stories of his life, of his encounters with the Dangerous Sports Club, and adventures with his dangerous friends, like Keith Moon. The lectures were a rousing success, SRO affairs, and Graham was feted and feasted by the students – many of whom were too young to have experienced Python first-hand. Once again it was Graham who paved the way in new creative directions. (In later years both Eric Idle and John Cleese would do similar-type affairs.) The transcripts from these tours form the mono-logues chapter.

Once back in the UK, Graham ploughed into a number of new projects, including a film script called *Ditto*. This project had been floating around both his office and his brain for several years, having begun life in the late 1960s. Peter Sellers had given Graham and John Cleese an Italian screenplay to adapt titled *The Future Began Yesterday*. Sellers saw it as a vehicle for himself and his unrequited love, Sophia Loren. But that project was quashed by Loren's husband, film director Carlo Ponti. Graham and John Cleese took a few passes at the script, and then Cleese moved on to other projects. But it never left Graham's mind. He toyed with it and tweaked it with other writing partners (including David Sherlock) for the next twenty years, and was actually getting it set-up to film (with Hal Ashby to direct) when he died.

Another project that came his way (and was the last project he was ever to work on) was a proposed series for American TV called *Jake's Journey*. The series was initiated by a phone call to Graham from Allan McKeown at Witzend Productions, and was going to be a television milestone: the first original prime-time American sitcom ever written and produced in another country. 'I never had fantasies about writing an American sitcom,' Graham once said, 'but then I thought, "Hang on, if they want to pay me that much money to write twenty-three minutes of material which probably won't get made anyway . . . why not?"' Loosely based on Mark Twain's book *A Connecticut Yankee in King Arthur's Court*, the series starred Graham as a wise medieval knight and had guest appearances by the late Peter Cook. Although several scripts were written, and one episode was filmed, it was not picked up by the television network and languishes in the vaults to this day.

*

Graham remained busy and productive in the last years of his life writing scripts, performing, touring, having adventures with the Dangerous Sports Club and actively pursuing his career with a determination unseen at any other point in his life. To a large degree this had to do with his finally getting sober and healthy. As dedicated as he'd previously been to drinking, smoking, and carousing, the latter-day Graham Chapman was just as adamantly opposed to such things. In fact, he became something of a health nut. He had seen the readouts of his liver-function tests when he stopped drinking and he was originally given six months or less to live, unless he stayed clear of alcohol for the rest of his life. As a good chemist, he was dedicated to undoing the damage he knew he had done to himself and survived a further ten years. Like his friend Keith Moon, Graham had managed to cheat death on numerous occasions so it came as a shock in 1989 to learn that he was dying.

It all came to light when he made a routine visit to his dentist and the assistant accidentally scraped his throat with a dental instrument. Some dead skin fell away. A biopsy was taken and the results were not promising, he had throat cancer. Within a few months it had spread to his spine, leaving him dependent on a wheelchair and, on 4 October 1989, he died in Maidstone Hospital, just a few miles from his home in Kent. At his death Graham was surrounded by friends and family, including Peter Cook and an inconsolable John Cleese. Graham held on until his adopted son, John Tomiczek, could arrive from the States. When John at last appeared Graham smiled, said 'Hello', and then passed peacefully away. In typical Graham fashion he went out like he had come in, in the middle of a blitz. But this time it wasn't Nazis, rather a blitz of publicity surrounding the approaching twentieth anniversary of Monty Python. The celebration would have been the next day, on 5 October. Terry Jones called Graham's passing 'The worst case of party-pooping I've ever seen.'

Graham Chapman lived an untidy life and, in some respects, this book mirrors that. Inside you will find everything from humorous essays on serious topics near and dear to his heart (over-population, a common-sense approach to good health, sexuality), as well as comic flights of fancy that serve no other purpose except to elicit a laugh. Some things were written strictly for his own private amusement, some to amuse his friends, and others were created in the hopes of having them produced. Unfortunately, most were not. That fact bothered Graham both artistically and financially, but it didn't unduly worry him. 'I used to worry about things, about money,' he said. 'But I don't anymore. You're always living on what you've got coming in the future. I follow the path of least resistance.' That may not be a groundbreaking philosophy, but it does sum up the personal philosophy of the man fairly well.

Dr Samuel Johnson had his Boswell, Dr Livingston had his Stanley, but Dr Chapman had no such secretary to chronicle his work during his lifetime. Taking the Boswellian position is something I do with distinct pride, yet at a distinct disadvantage, too. Graham's life was spent in a flurry of activity and he was not a great one for always labelling or dating items. At his death, his personal papers were hurriedly and haphazardly jumbled into boxes with little or no clue as to what bit of paper went with which other bit of paper: things from his days at Cambridge might be in the same folder as his manuscripts for *Yellowbeard*. Over the years (and especially during the course of compiling this book), I've become fairly good at piecing together his work through a series of deductions and pure educated guesswork — but it's an imperfect science and, as you will see, I've not always been able to pinpoint exactly the source of every item within. But this should in no way affect your enjoyment of the material, for no matter when it was produced it was still created by one of the most inventive minds ever to silly walk his way out of Leicester.

When Graham was a little boy he once dragged a chair across the kitchen floor, placed it in the sink and then sat on it for several hours in order to gain a different perspective of the room. That's sort of what this book attempts to do through his essays, monologues, thoughts, notes, scripts, letters — and even ideas for silly games and such; put the chair in the kitchen sink and try to gain a different perspective of a man who was, without a doubt, one of the most original and effortlessly funny thinkers, writers, and actors of late twentieth-century humour. But if all it does is make you laugh, then that's okay too.

MONOLOGUES

ABUSE
D.S.C.
VIDEO
BALLOONING
KEITH MOON - MEETING
                    - SHITTIES
        QUESTIONS
                    - LONDONDERRY
BRIAN NUTTY   O
- FILM
~~CENSORSHIP~~
                    INTERVAL
~~HARD ROCK~~ - P.P.S. ~~DRUGS~~
~~BRIAN NUTTY~~

QUESTIONS -
~~CENSORSHIP~~   ~~SHIT SHIT SHIT~~
FILM   UNDERTAKERS
HARD ROCK/PPS DRUGS
GRAIL DRINKING/ MOON DOR
GEORGE MELLY
- FILM
    END

        GRAIL DRINKING
        MOON + DOOR

Introduction

In the mid-1980s Graham took to touring US college campuses, speaking about his life, and his life in Monty Python. It was something that initially surprised his fellow Pythons as Graham had always been known to them as a man of few words who shied away from speaking before crowds, especially the type of large, wildly enthusiastic crowds that he always encountered whenever he spoke. The 'lecture tours' (as he called them) were funny, intimate affairs and were liberating for Graham, allowing him the opportunity to connect to the fans and, to some degree, demystify both himself and Monty Python (the alienating superstar aspect that came with his fame never rested easily on his shoulders). This is not to say that the thousands of 'Chapmaniacs' who thronged to see a real live Monty Python in the flesh cared about any of that, they just wanted a good time.

His shows followed a fairly standard routine, although the audience Q&As were always different each night. Graham would touch on his career, tell a few tales about filming, speak out about his drinking and homosexuality, his famous friends such as Keith Moon, and then wrap it all up by showing a montage of classic Python clips. Although the shows appeared to be loose and spontaneous affairs, his 'talking points' were worked out well in advance and he seldom varied from his written notes. Of course, it being Graham, he couldn't help but speak frankly about events and people and would often say things that, on paper, could appear indiscreet, but in his heart he had nothing but affection and high regard for his colleagues and peers. What follows, includes transcripts of Graham's notes discussing his early collaborations with John Cleese, and the Python experience. Interested in how the other Pythons viewed Graham's own take on the group, I emailed them some of Graham's ruminations on the topic in early 2000 and include their replies here.

The Dangerous Sports Club

A couple of years ago I was sitting at home, trying to write, when I had a telephone call from a British newspaper called the *Daily Mail*; not one of our better newspapers, not the worst, either, sad to say. But they irritated me in that they wanted to know what I would do if I won their £1 million bingo competition. I immediately replied that I would give it to John Cleese so that he could take the afternoon off.

They thought that was quite funny, but a little cruel, and so printed a watered-down version of the joke in the newspaper the next day, which annoyed me intensely. But they also mentioned that I would like to go to the Andes. Now I had in fact mentioned the Andes in talking to them, because I used to climb a little bit, and they saw fit to publish that. Well, the same day that this article appeared I had a telephone call from a gentleman called David Kirke, who said he was the chairman of the Dangerous Sports Club, and he wondered if I would like to go hang-gliding over active volcanoes in Ecuador. I said, '*Ummmmmnnnno . . .*'

But I *was* kind of interested in that I hadn't had many phone calls like that before and so I chatted with the man a little bit. All I knew about the Dangerous Sports Club at that point was, I'd seen excerpts of some of their activities on television, and it appeared that they were people who liked to jump off bridges on pieces of elastic. Well, I chatted with the man a bit, and got to know a little more about the group, and subsequently *did* agree to go to Ecuador with them. I realized at the time that I was probably being used as some sort of a useless mascot, perhaps to gain a little extra sponsorship money, that sort of thing, and so I agreed that I'd go for only one week. I'd arranged lots of important meetings that I said I had to attend after one week. It was all totally fictitious, but

4

I wanted to make sure that my time there was going to be limited, so that the chances of my having to do anything dangerous were also limited.

Now Ecuador is quite a tall sort of place. Quito, the capital city, is some 10,000 feet above sea level, and I found that bending down to tie-up shoe laces gave me quite a headache. And I imagined that climbing any of the mountains around there to hang-glide off would involve a little bit in the way of acclimatization to altitude because a lot of volcanoes in that country are 20,000 feet or so in height. But, of course, the Dangerous Sports Club don't believe in acclimatization. They would prefer to do things with the headaches.

Towards the end of that week I thought I was going to get away with not having done anything at all dangerous, but they did suggest that perhaps I should climb up one mountain with them, a mountain called Cotopaxi, which is somewhat over 20,000 feet in height. It is a volcano, so it has that sort of shape; it's not particularly, *technically*, difficult as a climb, but it is rather tall. Also the other problem about climbing this mountain is you have to climb it at night because it's on the equator and if you're on the mountain after about, ooh . . . eight o'clock *in the morning* . . . then the sun tends to melt the snow and ice above you and it tends to fall on you.

We set out from our mountaineering post at about 15,000 feet, with considerable headaches, at about eleven o'clock at night and climbed on up. I must say that it was one of the most physically exhausting things I've ever attempted. It really was a matter of taking six *incredibly* deep breaths every step, that kind of thing, because none of us were acclimatized, and indeed had wonderful thumping headaches. We got to within about 1,000 feet of the summit when suddenly one the members of our party of four developed altitude sickness, so obviously the sensible thing to do was come back down again. Particularly as the leader of the group had lost his way. The reason for this little jaunt, really, was to find out just how difficult it was going to be to carry hang-gliders up there – and obviously the answer was 'very'.

Well, we came back down again and shortly after, I left and returned to England. The group did stay on though and subsequently *did* get to the top of Mt Chimborazo, which is somewhat higher. And they did manage to carry some hang-gliders up there, although they found out when they reached the summit that the snow was well above waist deep and, consequently, you couldn't really run to take off. So they merely hung around up there long enough to get frostbite and then came back down again.

As that expedition was not really particularly successful from a hang-gliding point of view, they do intend to go back in a year's time. There is one mountain that they have their eyes on called Sangay that conveniently erupts every ten minutes or so . . . That's very much the place the Dangerous Sports Club are aiming for, they're interested in the kind of conceivable updrafts you would get from this volcano. It is a bit of a problem to climb up because every ten minutes or so red-hot boulders roll down . . . I don't know whether I shall join them on that expedition.

Anyway, I arrived back in England and found that I felt guilty that I'd been made a member of this club and hadn't actually done anything dangerous. A curious sort of guilt. But I had got to know the group of people and found that they were a very varied crowd, really. On the one hand was the usual out-of-work English person, and on the other, a member of, well, a member of the British aristocracy in a way, I suppose, in that he was kind of a third cousin or something of Queen Elizabeth, with the extraordinary name of Xan Fitz-Allen Herbert. Quite a loony. A very nice loony, but a loony nonetheless.

And in between those two extremes, quite a variety of people; anything from farmers . . . stockbrokers – all sorts of people – but they all had one thing in common, and that is they all liked to do things which scared them a bit. They liked to do things to which there is an unacceptable risk attached. They were adrenaline junkies, basically. Anyway, feeling guilty that I'd been made a member of the club and hadn't done anything dangerous – you're supposed to take part in three official Dangerous Sports Club events, really, before becoming a proper member – I did decide that I would go with them to St Moritz for their winter sports that year. In the knowledge that I would be adult enough to say no if it looked too stupid or too dangerous. I wasn't going to succumb to peer pressure and take part in something which would end in an injury, or worse.

I arrived in Switzerland to find that the Dangerous Sports Club had already had difficulty getting into Switzerland; at the border, they'd been prevented access because David Kirke hadn't paid his hospital bill from the previous year. Once that was squared-up they were allowed in and I arrived to find them at the top of a snow slope. Now the rules for the Dangerous Sports Club's winter sports are that it is an uncontrolled descent of a snow slope; there has to be something interposed between yourself and the skis, thus rendering control impossible, the normal method of stopping, of course, being to crash. Points are given for imagination in terms of what it is that's placed between yourself and the skis. It can be anything from a wheelchair to a grand piano.

Anyway, I found them at the top of this slope grumbling to the organizers that they'd been given too gentle a slope. Now it looked fine to me . . . ! I had no problems with it, but no, apparently it wasn't steep enough, or not bumpy enough, or interesting enough for them and they insisted and the organizers unfortunately agreed to give them another slope; in fact gave them the end of a black ski run. Now a black ski run is the nastiest kind of ski run, and the most senior sort. Indeed it *was* a lot steeper with a lot more bumps on it and also there was no run-off area at the bottom, just a sort of drop with some trees poking up . . .

I was getting ready to be very adult about this.

The item they had chosen for me to go down the slope on – I suppose they thought it was appropriate because of my medical background – was an operating table on skis. Now I don't know how much you know about operating tables but they are rather heavy, metallic objects – this was no exception – and the idea of lying flat on my back on this thing, staring up at the sky while hurtling down a black ski run did not appeal. So I was very adult about that and said, 'No, I won't go down on that thing, thank you very much.'

But that made me feel guilty again and so I thought I ought to go down on something, so I looked around for the safest-looking vehicle that afternoon, just in case I decided eventually to join in. The slowest-looking vehicle was what I was looking for, and in fact that turned out to be, in my mind, a 15-foot-long wooden Venetian gondola which they'd borrowed from some Italian restaurant. If I was going to go down the slope that was going to be good because it looked *slow*. And also there were no nasty metal bits sticking out or anything . . .

Anyway, the first ten or so members of the Dangerous Sports Club set off down the slope on wheelchairs on skis, and only one of them was lucky enough to reach the bottom. And he was very fortunate in that he hit a tree. The next item down the slope was a full-scale replica of a Cruise missile. This had two people on board, and because of its design it was very aerodynamic. That successfully reached the bottom of the slope, and they were very fortunate too in that the front of their machine merely crumpled up on impact with a tree . . .

No real injuries so far, just a few bruises and minor scratches and so on, but the next person down the slope was not quite so fortunate. As his vehicle he had a Formula 3 race car. This didn't have its skin, its outer shell, but it was basically a Formula 3 race car and of course these machines are designed to withstand impact. But he didn't want to wear the harness, he thought it would be much better for him if he was thrown out of it. He also wasn't keen to wear a safety helmet either, but all of us thought that was sensible and persuaded him eventually to wear a helmet. Anyway, he set off down the slope and did gather up considerable speed unfortunately about two-thirds of the way down he must have caught on some projection or other and he promptly turned three or four cartwheels and he was indeed thrown out. Unfortunately part of the steering wheel passed through his left thigh as he was thrown out and he came to rest in a heap on the ground and didn't move for several minutes.

About four minutes later, I suppose, the paramedics on skis

arrived at the scene and by then he was beginning to stagger to his feet. But he subsequently had loss of memory for some five days after this event, and it occurred to me at the time that that's probably why he turns up every year. He'd completely forgotten what happened to him last time . . .

Anyway, this little crash had cast quite a pall over the proceedings, particularly among the spectators, and I suppose David Kirke, thinking of this, decided that he ought to go down the slope next just to cheer everyone up, as chairman of the club. His vehicle was a C5, which is a little electric car developed by a man in England called Clive Sinclair. Not a very commercial success at all, in fact *not* a commercial success, but on skis it was very aerodynamic. David really shot down the slope and he too must have hit some projection or other and came to an abrupt halt halfway down the slope and didn't move for several minutes. When he *did* get out and stagger around there was a trickle of blood coming from his left temple and—

It was my turn next.

It's a curious thing this peer pressure, but I found myself for some reason or other sitting optimistically in the back of this gondola. Optimistic is the wrong word really . . . worried. Sitting next to me was Xan Fitz-Allen Herbert. Not much comfort there. Xan turned to me at that point and said, 'Looks like a bit of a brown trouser job this afternoon.' Which did little to improve my state of mind . . .

And sitting in the front of the gondola was Eric.

Now Eric is the Dangerous Sports Club's mascot and he is in the shape of a man totally bandaged from head to foot, with eyes that swivel, he always smokes a little cigarette and, for some reason or other, wears a pair of boxer shorts beneath which is, what can only be described as, an erection. A rather *mobile* erection. They use Eric to annoy people in restaurants, at which he is singularly successful.

Anyway, Xan, myself and Eric were pushed off from the top of this slope in this gondola, and by the second bump we were airborne. The thought 'broken leg' immediately went through my mind and I soon found myself flying over Xan's head. And then I noticed Xan flying over my head, and then we were both pursued down this slope by this wretched wooden gondola, which we were trying to kick away to avoid further injury.

We both finished up badly winded but ALIVE! And that felt GREAT! I mean I was thoroughly elated, totally full of adrenaline, I suppose, and it really did put the whole world into perspective for me suddenly. I mean the bank manager was no longer important, I could've rung him up and told him he was a fool. The whole world was in perspective and I felt good for two weeks after that event. I was beginning to realize what a charge these people got out of their weird activities.

Later on that afternoon I was glad that one event didn't take place that Xan rather hoped would. He had brought along with him that afternoon, for the downhill event, a London double-decker bus for which he'd had enormous skis made. He suggested it would be a great idea if, at the end of the afternoon, we all piled into this bus and . . .

I thought not.

In fact the local mayor thought not as well, as there was a local election that week and he was worried about an ecology issue in that damage might be caused to certain trees – and hotels.

But anyway, I got back to England after this event and while I certainly knew about the buzz you could get from these activities, I was by no means an adrenaline addict . . . Yet. In fact it was another year 'til I agreed to take part in another one of their activities, which happened to be in the nature of a catapulting event.

Now this was for charity and it was held in Hyde Park in London as part of Bob Geldof's 'Sport Aid Day for Africa'. I decided this time to arrive late. I didn't really want to hang around and have to put up with a lot of 'brown trouser' talk, so I arrived late in the hope that they would be absolutely ready for me – and indeed they were.

I arrived in Hyde Park and was put into this climbing harness and then an enormous 150-foot crane lowered down three strands of aircraft carrier elastic; the sort of heavy-duty stuff they stop aircraft going off the end of aircraft carriers with. That's attached to the front of my flying harness, and then from behind I was attached by another rope to a large concrete block set in the ground. The crane then raised itself up to its full height. The man standing next to me then said, 'There are one or two things you ought to know . . .'

He said, 'You will be experiencing a force of some 6Gs, so you'll have to hold your hands behind your head like that otherwise you will get whiplash. Not might, will. When you get to the top of your flight (he said) you'll notice these coils of rope sort of floating around beside you; don't get tangled up in those otherwise you'll strangle yourself. And then, when you get to the bottom of your flight remember to hold your arm in front of your face like that, otherwise the rope could smash you in the nose and one of our guys lost partial sight in one eye the other week.'

And with that he said, 'Count to five.' I don't remember getting any further than four when the decision was taken out of my hands and the rope behind me was slashed with a knife and I just went . . .

ZIIIIIINNNNNGGGG!!!

. . . and I don't remember much about the way up, either.

It was all so very . . . quick. But I do remember arriving at the top of my arc and floating around for what seemed like an age! I suppose I was so full of adrenaline by then, and sure enough I saw these coils of rope floating around beside me and I thought, 'Well, *surely* by now I should be—'

And then I was.

And being so full of adrenaline I certainly did remember to hold my arm in front of my face preventing any possible damage that way, and then I found myself merely bouncing up and down on the end of the rope and I was able to do kind of moon hops on the ground and everything, and again I felt *thoroughly exhilarated*! It was like the best fairground ride I'd ever had! It really was quite amazing.

They'd been quite kind to me, in fact 6G in their eyes wasn't too bad and I'd only gone up to a height of about 130 feet or so . . . They quite regularly exert far more than 6G, even going up to 11 which is practically black-out time. But they were kind to me, thankfully. However, I haven't yet taken part in my third activity, which I suppose I will have to do at some point. And that will be a jump on a bungee cord from a bridge.

I did go along with the thought that I might take part in that event one afternoon to a village in Oxfordshire, a little local charity event. David Kirke had a huge crane there again and was going to do bungee jumping from a bucket suspended from this 150-foot crane. I went up in the bucket with him to see what the ground looked like from up above, and to me it looked like concrete. I began to have doubts at that point. I descended and David went up again with a sack full of bricks weighing about the same as himself, just to test out the rope, and he threw that out from the bucket and the thing promptly smashed on the concrete. And I thought, 'Perhaps this isn't the afternoon for me to do that particular event.' So that is still sometime in the future for me. And I've insisted that it will be over water. I've decided that the Dangerous Sports Club would make a very good subject for a full adventure movie, and I've in fact written a movie script about the Dangerous Sports Club.* I think it will be the first adventure movie without special effects. Or insurance.

David Kirke has had a little bit of bother in that he had a court case that he was obliged to attend. The Civil Aviation Authority in Britain prosecuted him for travelling between England and France in the pouch of a 25-foot-high inflatable kangaroo. He evidently didn't have the appropriate licence for this . . . it was decided at the height of some 10,000 feet by a passing airliner pilot who duly felt obliged to report him as a near miss.

I subsequently went along to a courtroom in eastern England to act as a character witness for Dave, thus perjoring myself. Another

---

* Actually, Graham wrote a film treatment, and not a complete film scrip. Graham did, however, write a half-hour television script/documentary about his involvement in the DSC titled *Above Them, The Ground*. This script (never filmed) would have incorporated actual footage of the DSC's adventures intercut with new footage of Graham doing comedic set-ups. The script for *Above Them, The Ground* is on page 192.

member of the club, who works for NASA, is really keen to do a freefall jump from a height of 150,000 feet, which is quite a height, and somewhat of a record, should he do it. But he's very keen, he's worked out all the mathematics, the physics, for the occasion. He will arrive at 150,000 feet suspended from the hydrogen balloon, he'll be wearing a full-pressurized space suit. He will sever connection with the helium balloon at that point and then merely plummet, and he's calculated that by the time he reaches the height of 50,000 feet he will personally be travelling at 1,100 miles an hour.

It should be an interesting afternoon out.

Paralysed at the Polo Lounge

There were a lot of outrageous things that tended to happen to me too, particularly in those sort of hazy, alcohol days . . . I remember once I went to the Polo Lounge in the Beverly Hills Hotel and for some reason or other, I don't quite know why, I decided that the people in the Polo Lounge didn't care all that much about less fortunate people in the world. I don't know *how* I got that feeling . . .

Anyway, it did get to me in my drunken state and I decided at that point that I was going to be paralysed from the waist down. I informed the waiter that I wanted a wheelchair, because I'd just suddenly become paralysed. He didn't believe me of course because he'd seen me walk in, but I told him, 'No this *is* a joke, but I'm playing it to the hilt! I'm not going to move from the waist down. It may be a joke but I'm not going to move from the waist down from this point on, so would you get me a wheelchair?'

He was somewhat reluctantly obliged to get a wheelchair and wheel me out of the Beverly Hills Hotel. Now because I was there publicizing some movie, I'd been provided with a limo and a driver who was waiting outside for me, but the waiter was, I think, rather annoyed. He thought I was up to something obviously, and we didn't get quite as far as the limo before he stopped and he wouldn't go any further. He wasn't going to go through with this 'joke' and help me into the car or anything, he just left me there, so I thought, 'Well, I shall take it through to its extremity . . .'

Fortunately for me there also happened to be a fund-raiser event for some political organization going on, so a lot of very important people were arriving. I then threw myself to the ground from this wheelchair and crawled into the back of the limo. I don't think it did much for the reputation of the waiter, or of the Beverly Hills Hotel.

I certainly hope not.

A Liar's Autobiography

At the age of 37, no I was 36 I suppose, it's been eleven years now since I stopped drinking, but at that point, 36, I thought I would start writing my autobiography because I didn't think I was going to last much longer. It didn't disturb me, it didn't *worry* me that I was possibly going to be dead in perhaps three, four or five years maximum. In fact I thought I'd die at the age of 42,* that's kind of what I thought then, it didn't worry me at all. Stupid isn't it? But there we are.

I started to write this little autobiography† just to get a few things down, really. The writing didn't progress very quickly, because I was drinking quite torrentially at that point. But after I'd sobered up, the writing progressed very much more quickly. It was quite a cathartic experience to write that and have to think back about my life and how this had all happened in the first place. It was also quite an enjoyable process.

I called it *A Liar's Autobiography* in fact because I realized very quickly, very early on, that it's almost *impossible* to tell the truth. Not because of reasons of libel – although a title like that certainly would help, I thought, to protect me in some measure – but because *truth changes*. I know that sounds like nonsense, but truth, which is truth to you, *can*; three or four years later when you go back to

---

* Fans of Douglas Adams take note. The answer to the question 'What is the meaning of life, the universe and everything?' as found in his *A Hitchhiker's Guide To The Galaxy* book, is also 42. Graham, a longtime friend of Adams', supplied the answer '42' when Adams asked him for the answer to the above question while writing *Hitchhiker*. For the record, Adams denied this years later.

† *A Liar's Autobiography*, first published in 1980 by Methuen, and reprinted by Methuen in 2001.

look at that same situation, you're looking at it from a different perspective and it actually *changes*.

I began to realize this while writing this. Certainly it changes from the point of view of someone else's perspective. I could write my version of what happened one afternoon and someone else who was there would have quite a different version. They'd agree on certain points, but it could be quite dramatically different even though both could swear they were telling the truth. Well, who's right? So I couldn't really swear that I was right, particularly with all that alcohol that had gone inside me, so I decided the truthful thing would be to call it *A Liar's Autobiography*.

I was contemplating writing it with other people, and therefore I thought that title would be a good way to get me out of the problem when writing an autobiography with several other co-authors.* When Douglas Adams turned up at my house one day, basically out of work, I asked him to join in with me on that project. The problem was, though, my autobiography kept turning into a space story. So we had to part company on that one, although we did write a sketch or two for *Python* together and a few other things.†

I'll talk about a couple of moments which had great impact on me personally. One moment of amazing embarrassment which occurred during the filming of *Life of Brian*. We filmed in Tunisia, which is, of course, in North Africa, and most people in Tunisia happen to be Muslim people, they're Mohammedan folk. I'd just spent the whole day as Brian, being chased by a whole load of followers which I have no wish to have, and then eventually managed to escape them and spend my very first night with my newly acquired girlfriend, Judith Iscariot.

---

* Co-authors include Alex Martin, David Yallop, Douglas Adams and Graham's longtime partner, writer David Sherlock.

† Other things include the never-produced television special for ex-Beatle Ringo Starr entitled *Our Show For Ringo Starr (a.k.a. Goodnight Vienna)*, and Graham's one-off post-*Python* television show *Out of the Trees*. The script for the never-seen, never-filmed second episode of *Out of the Trees* (although it was not written with Douglas Adams) is on page 150.

I'd had a wonderful night and woke up the next morning full of the joys of spring, and, totally naked, I threw open the shutters only to discover this huge band of followers waiting outside for me. Well, the matter of genital exposure was no particular problem to me, I am a doctor after all, but there was a problem in that we had a crowd of Tunisian extras – we had some 300 people posing as 600 – and half of that number were women. Muslim women were forbidden by Muslim law to see such things. It's absolutely forbidden. So when I flung open the shutters half the crowd ran away screaming! That had a profound effect on my psyche. I'd like to think it was the religion; anyway, I'm sure that it was . . .

Also in *Life of Brian* was a scene that affected me – perhaps not so much for its comedy, but for the impact it had on me at the time – which was the actual moment of crucifixion. We'd been filming for some seven weeks by that stage, in Tunisia, under really hot and bright sunlight, totally clear skies, and we went further into the desert for the crucifixion scenes. As soon as the crosses were in place, huge dark clouds suddenly rolled in. Although none of us said anything I think all of us felt, 'Goodness me, *have* we gone too far this time?' It really was quite a tense moment. Then, logically thinking it through, 'He' must have been on our side because that was *precisely* the effect we needed for that particular scene. And it's a very strange experience to be laid back on a cross, be hauled up into the air, and you hear a sort of 'THUD!' as it slots into place. Then the crew all sort of . . . go away . . . and you think, 'Well, *have* I been nice to them?' A very odd feeling to be crucified, and no doubt a very nasty death indeed.

One other moment which had great impact on me concerned a complaint. We didn't really have very many complaints about the *Python* television series, but I do remember one in particular because it concerned myself. It was written by a very very angry lady from Newcastle, England.* You could tell the rage in this person's heart

---

* Actually she was from Liverpool.

from the very rage in each word that she'd written in this letter. It concerned an appearance I'd made on a talk show in England hosted by a gentleman called George Melly.

Now George Melly is an English jazz singer, if that's not a contradiction in terms. A very good jazz singer actually. He's a full Renaissance man really, he's also an expert in fine arts, a very good author and general *bon vivant* ... His notion for this talk show was that he should only invite on to it people whom he knew. Not only so he wouldn't have to do a whole load of research, but also so he wouldn't have to have a clipboard full of notes or anything and he could just have a very casual conversation with his guests and thus hopefully bring the best out of them. And also to that end the hospitality before these shows was of *formidable* proportions. There were incredible quantities of alcohol freely available and also other things too, of course, because he *was* a musician ...

This meant that I appeared on his show in a *very* relaxed frame of mind. George had just been talking, while on the show, about a book he'd written called *Owning Up* in which he'd admitted taking part and indulging in 'certain practices' while he was a member of Her Majesty's Navy. Not that that sort of thing happens in the British Navy AND IT NEVER WILL!!! ... And neither does cannibalism.

Anyway, I had gone on in this relaxed mood to admit that I myself had taken part in similar activities in my past, and that was the substance of this lady's complaint. She wrote to the Python office, we had one by then, saying that 'Someone from *Monty Python* who hadn't had the courage to give his name—'

Well, that was monstrous really because obviously George had introduced me as Graham Chapman and had spoken to me as Graham throughout, and there at the end of the programme it said: TALKING TO GEORGE MELLY WAS GRAHAM CHAPMAN ... well, never mind, anyway ...

'—was evidently homosexual and therefore deserved eternal hellfire and damnation ...'

And it went on in similar fire and brimstone tone for about two and a half pages. And after she had finished there she'd included twenty-five sheets of paper on which were written prayers which 'if this person said every day for the rest of his life he might obtain some kind of purgatory'.

That was her best offer.

Well, Eric Idle had a wonderful idea, and he wrote back to her saying, 'We've found out which one it was, and we've killed him.' It's interesting to note that the next six programmes we did, the last six programmes we *ever* did, were the ones without John Cleese in them. I'm not sure *what* she made of that.

And I don't care.

Keith Moon

I seem to make a habit of getting involved with dangerous people in one way or another, and I remember a dear friend, no longer with us, a gentleman by the name of Keith Moon, who was of course the drummer for the group The Who. Quite a wild character indeed.

I first met Keith at a charity soccer match in England. It was in fact 'Monty Python Versus The Rest Of The World', and Keith was playing for the Rest Of The World. I didn't play soccer, I used to play rugby football, and I was rather bored with the way that the other people were taking the game, it was all rather serious and I thought that, on the whole, the audience had come out there that afternoon to see us all make fools of ourselves. That was the idea of the occasion, I thought, and with that in mind I'd gone along dressed as the Colonel figure from the Python series and just generally made a nuisance of myself walking around barking orders, shouting at people, standing in the goal mouth and generally being obstructive.

Keith must have felt similarly bored with the way the game was going because he left the field at one point and then drove back on in someone's car . . . and scored several goals . . . No one could catch him. That led to a kind of instant rapport between the two of us and we then went to a bar and drank very very very very very very very many drinks together.

The next time I met Keith he was staying at a hotel in London called the Londonderry. Not a particularly huge hotel, it was in fact the only hotel in London at the time which would allow him to stay. It was only about fifteen storeys or so, but Keith was staying in a penthouse suite. I arrived on the top floor and knocked on

Keith's door and Keith opened it and there were two or three Swedish girls – I don't know what they were doing, probably helping him tidy up or something – and Keith immediately apologized that he had no gin in the room. He knew that was my drink at the time, and he gave me a bottle of lager to get on with and then rang down to room service and asked them to send up a bottle of gin.

Well, some ten minutes (and about four or five lagers) later there was still no sign of this gin arriving in the room, and so Keith rang room service again and told them that if the gin didn't appear in his room within the next five minutes their television set would appear on the pavement. He was very strict like that.

Well, a few minutes later I was halfway through another lager and there was still no sign of the gin. Keith had wandered over to the side of the room and had climbed out of the window onto what I assumed was a balcony outside. I didn't know what he was up to but I was halfway through a lager so I wasn't too bothered – you know, he was a strange person . . . But you know, still no sign of him coming back in, so I wandered over to the window to have a look at what he was doing out there. And so I looked out – and there was no balcony. There was no sign of Keith either. There was also no mess on the pavement beneath or anything like that, all there was, in fact, was a ledge about four or five inches wide, no more, about four feet beneath the window. Evidently he must have climbed around the building on this ledge, certainly something I would never have contemplated, but it *was* Keith so I wasn't too bothered, so I sat back down, opened another lager and merely waited.

After I finished that lager Keith reappeared at the window carrying a bottle of Beefeater Gin! He walked in and plonked it down on the table in front of me. Evidently he'd burgled the next-door penthouse! And I thought, 'Well, now *there's* a friend!'

Keith often had strange incidents at hotels. In fact he was staying at one hotel in Los Angeles, the Hyatt House on Sunset Strip . . . He was returning home one afternoon after having rehearsed with the band in the morning, and was listening to a cassette recording of the rehearsal as he walked through the lobby. Evidently there was some kind of complaint about this and the manager therefore approached him and told him to 'Turn that noise off please.'

Well, Keith immediately obliged and turned it off and went back to his room, where he happened to have a large supply of detonator caps. He'd been saving these up for the act later on in the week, and he spent the next twenty minutes meticulously wiring these up to the back of his door. He then rang down to the manager's office and told the manager he wanted to see him immediately. So he waited . . .

He popped his head out of the door and checked that the manager had indeed just stepped out of the elevator and then went back in again. Subsequently the manager arrived outside Keith's door to see the whole door blown off its hinges and Keith stepping out of the rubble and smoke, holding up this cassette recorder saying, '*That* was noise, mate, *this* is The Who!'

He certainly had a way with authority.

Monty Python

I first met John Cleese when I arrived in Cambridge University and I was trying to join a club called the Footlights, a revue society, which I suspect is the real reason why I went to Cambridge in the first place rather than to read medicine. But I couldn't admit that at the time. See, from about the age of seven or eight I used to be an avid listener to a radio programme called *The Goon Show*. In fact, at that stage I wanted to *be* a Goon. But that didn't seem to be a very credible career, certainly not to my parents. Then, around the age of fourteen or so, I saw an excerpt on television of a revue produced by the Cambridge Footlights that had in it a gentleman called Jonathan Miller and I thought, 'That's very good! That's the university I'll go to, to read medicine!' The subconscious was working, quite obviously . . .

So, John Cleese and I both joined Footlights together, Eric Idle subsequently joined about a year later, and so three of us knew each other from Cambridge. We three then met two of the others, Michael Palin and Terry Jones, while all performing at the Fringe of the Edinburgh Festival one year, and we finished up working on the same television programme, writing scripts for a programme called *The Frost Report* hosted by a gentleman called David Frost.

A very modest gentleman, David Frost . . . His programme, if you noticed, was called *The Frost Report* and the credits at the end of the programme went: STARRING DAVID FROST in huge letters and WRITTEN BY DAVID FROST in huge letters, and then about thirty other names just went:

Brooooooouuuummmmppphhhh!!!

. . . and we five were amongst those thirty names.

Now, to be honest, I think I would have gone further *without* David Frost's flair and his introduction of me into showbiz. I don't think John Cleese would have gone as far . . . John was somehow latched onto by Frost. OK, that furthered my career too in that, obviously, John was doing *The Frost Report* and acting in it – whereas I was writing it and not acting. This annoyed me intensely because I'd gotten better reviews than John had in the Edinburgh Festival . . . I know Frost's a rat in a lot of ways, but I like him. I do. The thing is, he can't understand that he's liked by anyone, which is his big problem. He's an enigma because he's so insensitive about other people, and very selfish, and yet is very sensitive about products – about things that will work and won't work – I think I can say the same about John Cleese actually. Frost really doesn't give a shit about another human being – he *wants* to, he's *trying* – and he is surprised that nobody gives a shit about him. But he shouldn't be surprised, because that's the reason. Still, he's very clever in terms of show business and in knowing what to do at the right time.

Anyway, *The Frost Report* certainly did provide a basis for us all to get together and we got to know each other at that period really, and we were responsible for writing some of the better material. We also shared the frustration of taking along our scripts to script-meetings where they'd then be read out by the cast who would laugh at them quite a lot and then say, 'Oh we can't do that! It's too stupid.' Or 'it's too filthy' or whatever. They were worried about their image. Well, *we* weren't bothered at all about our image (not that we had any at the time anyway) and so, really out of frustration, the only thing to do was to do it ourselves, and so we subsequently did use quite a bit of the material that was written at that time in later *Python* shows.

John Cleese and I were asked by David Frost if we wanted to go off to Ibiza and write a movie called *The Rise and Rise of Michael Rimmer*. Well, I'd just spent two weeks standing in as a locum in ear, nose and throat surgery and the idea of going off to an island in the Mediterranean to write a film for three months appealed to me rather more than digging nasty things from the backs of people's noses. Consequently, it was a pretty easy decision to make, and I never really got back into medicine – it's a very nice hobby, however. I do still get a lot of medical literature pushed through my door every day and I read a bit of that and it does, occasionally, come in useful. But it has its hazards as well, in that, if you're ever discovered to be a doctor then you can feel obliged to help out . . .

Anyway, once in Ibiza, I was quite alarmed to discover that John – who at that stage would have been about twenty-five years old – had never ridden a bicycle. His parents had been very protective and didn't want him to ride a bicycle because then he would have mixed with all those 'rough boys' down the street . . . That led to some of John's peculiarities, another one of which I noticed when he and his first wife couldn't agree to get married until they'd both consulted their psychiatrist. He had to give the go-ahead to this marriage and I thought, 'Well, how romantic.' John does, I think, tend to work purely from the right-hand side of the brain – perhaps the left-hand side doesn't exist at all – he really does have a very clinical, analytical mind. He is the exact opposite of the other extreme in our group, Terry Jones, who is totally emotional in his thinking. Arguments often broke out between the two of them and John was always quite naughty in provoking Terry because whenever he got angry his voice used to rise in a high-pitched Welsh whine, which amused John.

And then we were joined of course by Terry Gilliam. It's interesting though with Terry Gilliam . . . John often used to rib him – well, we all did I suppose – about his use of the English language in that it was, well – limited. In fact John claimed that his vocabulary *stretched* to about thirty words. He was very good visually, extremely good visually as evidenced by his excellent direction in several movies, but the word department was not really his. John used to say that things with Terry would either be 'really great' or they would 'really piss him off'. Not many shades of meaning in between that. I remember on one occasion we were doing a stage tour of Canada and were flying over the Great Lakes one day, in fact we were flying over Lake Superior, and I remember Terry looking down at Lake Superior and then turning around to the rest of us and saying, 'Hey you guys, a whole bunch of water!' It didn't adequately sum up the lake . . .

Terry Gilliam originally comes from Minneapolis. He studied at Occidental College in California and met us via John Cleese. John Cleese and I were once in a stage revue called *Cambridge Circus* which was on in New York for a time, and Terry Gilliam saw this show and was looking for someone for a cartoon he was producing at the time for a magazine. He wanted in fact the ideal City Gent. He wanted the epitome of a London City gentleman: bowler hat, a tie, with pin-striped trousers and a rolled-up umbrella. And he thought John Cleese would suit this role exactly, and he asked John if he would pose. (Incidentally, the storyline of this photo montage was about a City Gent who has an affair with a Barbie doll. So there are in existence some rather nice photographs of John Cleese doing some naughty things to a Barbie doll – which I always cherish and keep locked away in a drawer just in case John gets stroppy . . .)

When Terry decided that he ought to avoid that rather nasty bit of business in the 'Vietnamish' area of the world, he came over to England. Very sensible, to avoid that. And John put him in touch with a few friends who happened to be called Michael Palin, Terry Jones and Eric Idle, and who were working on a children's television programme called *Do Not Adjust Your Set*. He worked with them on that programme and subsequently, with those three, joined John and myself when we were considering doing a new television programme, and that turned out to be *Monty Python*. So that's how it all happened.

I'm often asked how we got the name *Monty Python's Flying Circus*. Well, we were all busy trying to write the first thirteen episodes of the series – and weren't desperately keen (to worry about what to call it) as we were panicking to get everything done in time before we went into the studio. We *did* write everything in advance, there was never really any improvisation, there wasn't the money for that really. The BBC didn't give us much money. We only had an hour and a half to record each half-hour show in the studio – so we weren't keen to spend a lot of time arguing about titles. There'd already been suggestions, things like *Owl-Stretching Time*, *The Toad Elevating Moment* and *Sex and Violence* and Terry Jones came up with a nice one which was *A Horse, A Bucket and A Spoon*. I must say, I rather liked – never *understood* – but rather liked that one.

But we never had got agreement on any of these titles because, obviously, they were the ideas of individual members of the group and, being human beings, no one else liked them. But then the Head of Comedy, Michael Mills, came into our shed and told us

---

Terry Jones Replies

I sometimes think when I read what Graham thought about *Python* that it's a bit as if he'd read it in a book. I mean, all the stuff about me and John being opposites. But then, on the other hand, maybe it's in books about *Python* because Graham said it in the first place. Although I must correct Graham's memory on one thing; the title wasn't *A Horse, A Bucket and A Spoon*, it was *A Horse, A Spoon and A Basin*. Well, that's what *I* remember, and anyway, I'm sure it was Graham who came up with it and not me. But then things do get a bit misty.

The Toad Elevating Moment was Graham's, and was a favourite of mine, although it never stood a chance. *Owl-Stretching Time* was another one I was very fond of. It's odd that Graham doesn't mention the one title that we *all* agreed on (eventually) and which the BBC wouldn't allow us to use: *Bunn, Wackett, Buzzard, Stubble and Boot*, based on a fictitious football team of John and Graham's.

It's all a little bit as if Graham were looking at things from a distance. What do I think of Graham's assessment of my personality here? Well, I don't really know. And I don't know what *I'd* say about the others either. It's almost as if I'm too up-close and haven't got enough distance. It's why I didn't realize what was going on in the group dynamics until many years after the TV shows. But then I'm always like that.

that he wouldn't leave until we had given him a title, and that it had to include the word 'circus'. He wanted a title desperately because he had to have something to put in the TV magazine, and we had to use the word 'circus' in the title because the BBC had loosely referred to the six of us wandering around the building as 'a circus'. Kind of a BBC joke tee-hee-hee. This word 'circus' had appeared on contracts and inter-departmental memos and so on and in a bureaucracy like that it would have been a very expensive process to change all of that paperwork. It would have detracted from the budget of the next show.

So we thought, 'All right we'll swallow that, we'll use the word circus.' We added 'flying' to it to make it sound less like a real circus and more like something to do with the First World War, and then added 'Monty Python' because he sounded like a really bad theatrical agent. Just the sort of guy that might have got us together. And also the very hungry, huge, constricting snake wasn't a bad image either. So that was it. None of us liked it but none of us hated it so it was a typical committee decision, really.

There were two different directors involved in the early stages of *Monty Python*; one of them was called John Howard Davies – who was very much ex-public school and was once a child star, playing roles such as Oliver Twist in films – and the other was the mad Scotsman, Ian MacNaughton. Instantly on meeting them both, I preferred Ian MacNaughton. I suppose that's because, rather like me at the time, he drank a fair bit and is a jolly soul – but nevertheless he gets the work done. John Howard Davies was a rather serious person who tended to play squash quite a lot and keep fit, and so that suited John Cleese rather a lot. So, there were two possibilities, directorwise. In the end, John Howard Davies produced four of the programmes in the studio and Ian did the film inserts.

John Howard Davies's work for the studio programmes was very good – I have no complaints – except that he's not a very *human* person. He gets everything done, but it's all strict and to the letter and, consequently, rather boring. A bit too clinical in his approach, in that if you made a mistake of any kind, any sort of pause in speech, he would treat you rather as if he was a schoolmaster. No, give me a man that drinks, like Ian, who would say, 'Oh don't worry hen, everything's fine, it's OK.' Ian was more human in that he realized that people made mistakes because, well, he made them too – but he didn't make many in the box, in the control room. Which reminds me of the very first Marty Feldman television programme, which we all wrote for – that is, John Cleese and myself, and Tim Brooke-Taylor. This is immediately after the 1948 Show when Marty was becoming a star. The director came down after they had recorded the first sketch of the show and spoke to Marty while he changed for another number – Marty was obviously in a bit of a state, it was the first thing he'd ever done on his own – and he said, 'Relax, Marty, the show is only as good as you are relaxed', which screwed Marty up to such an extent that he couldn't carry on for some time!

To add to the directing drama there was also Terry Jones, who was busy being an embryonic director and who thought that Ian hadn't quite got the right angles and this sort of thing. On his side was Terry Gilliam. But it's my view of comedy that you can make the picture as pretty as you bleedin' well want to – but it won't make it any funnier. It might look marvellous, but be dreadfully unfunny, just like *Jabberwocky*. I don't think John Cleese is worried about pictures either; he's worried about words, and I think it's strange that films and television have those two angles (pictures versus words), but I believe the word is more important.*

There's something in *Python* that's liberating to the imagination. There were people who were prepared to give two fingers to

---

* Terry Jones seconds this: 'The chain-of-consciousness idea for the shape of the shows came out of an animation Terry Gilliam had done for *Do Not Adjust Your Set*. When we'd been setting up "Monty Python", I'd been very keen for it to have a different feel from any other programme on TV. I saw Spike Milligan's Q4 series once and thought "Shit! Spike's done it! He's broken the boundaries and shape of TV sketch shows!" I was especially impressed with the way he'd not even bother to finish a sketch but would segue into another one. Then I thought: "Wait a minute! Terry Gilliam did a cartoon called 'Elephants' for *Do Not Adjust Your Set* that was a chain-of-consciousness sequence. If we used Terry's animations as links, the entire show could be a chain-reaction – a dream – one thing flowing into another." So I immediately rang Mike Palin and Terry G. with my idea and they got it in one. But when we came to script meetings

authority and think 'I've got my life to lead, let me get on with it without too much of this bother.' I really felt that, and it was a good period to live through, because we'd been through the latter part of the forties and the fifties, which were fairly horrific because, even though everything was nice, we were young and didn't really know what was going on. We knew something was *wrong*, and then suddenly you find that you can actually play your own part in a community. That was a great revelation and I still live by the principle. It's very important, it's not living by rules. I'm right against rules.

I started out being a religious twit that read the Bible every night when I was fourteen, and was confirmed and all of that, and when I realized that I was actually giggling at my confirmation classes – certainly when the Bishop laid his hand on my head – I could hardly suppress the laughter. 'What are these grown people doing wandering around in these silly robes, trying to pretend they know more about life than I do? They bloody don't.' Canon Clark, who did the confirmation classes at Melton Mowbray Church, was proud – actually proud – of having known that there was a brothel in Port Said. That period, the flower-power and coming out and being gay and all of that, certainly permeated me. I listened to music perhaps a bit more than the rest of the Pythons. The Beatles helped me a great deal in terms of the sense of freedom I felt – *why don't we just go out and do it? Let's do it* – that helped.

---

the Cambridge lot (John, Graham and Eric) weren't so interested. It wasn't that they were hostile to the idea – it was more like it didn't mean anything to them. They didn't really get it. I remember John saying that the important thing was that the individual sketches should be funny. So the Cambridge set rather left it up to Mike and me and Terry G. to do the linking stuff in the first series. So I suppose, since Mike and I were running the LPs, it was inevitable that they should show more "flow".'

Partnerships in Python

I used to write mostly in conjunction with John Cleese; Michael Palin and Terry Jones used to write together – although quite often in different houses, I don't know how they managed that – and Eric Idle would write on his own and Terry Gilliam, of course, was responsible for the animations and so on. John's and my habit was to work out of my house or his and arrive about ten o'clock in the morning. I was usually about half an hour late, even in my own house, nevertheless we eventually started to think about working . . . well, really we were trying to avoid work. We'd sit there and drink cups of coffee, chat about the news, do the crosswords, read newspapers – anything to avoid that awful moment of actually having to write something funny down on paper. Sometimes during the course of that hour and a half or so of doing almost nothing, an idea would emerge that led us on to a sketch.

But on this particular morning nothing had really emerged. We had decided that we would resort to our final tactic which was to open up *Roget's Thesaurus* and merely stare at words. They sometimes sparked-off ideas, for instance the whole of the 'Cheese Shop Sketch' came straight out of *Roget's Thesaurus*. And I'm very grateful for it too. Anyway, we were just staring at words, and the word we were staring at that morning was 'anger'. Anger anger anger . . . We felt anger, what should we write about it? John was quite keen on this because it's an emotion he portrays particularly well. But we couldn't really see what to do with anger.

We had been talking that morning, however, about a minister in the government, the Wilson government in Britain at that time, who'd just been appointed to ministerial rank, cabinet rank, who clearly had no abilities at all. He hadn't actually been designated as Minister *for* something like housing or anything responsible like

Foreign Ministry or anything like that, so he hadn't got a title – until, fortunately for him, we went about two or three weeks without any rain. He subsequently became Minister For Drought; the first time we'd ever had one of those, but the man was completely incompetent so it was a reasonable sort of sinecure sort of job to give him. And he was very successful in this ministry because, of course, it rained. It rained so much he subsequently became Minister For Flooding. That sounds absolutely stupid, but it's quite true. His name's Dennis Howell. And that gave us the idea for some sort of silly ministry.

'Ministry Of Anger,' we thought. 'The Ministry Of Anger ... how could that go? No-no-no, that didn't really lead anywhere ...' And on this day we were working at my house, which stands on a hill, and at that moment, that precise moment, a gentleman I'd noticed the week before walk past my house up the hill, happened to do so that morning. He had a very strange ability. He was somehow able to walk uphill while leaning backwards! It was the most extraordinary angle. I don't know how he managed to do it, I couldn't see the footwork at all. I ran out to try and get a glimpse of the footwork but by the time I'd got outside he'd disappeared. But I came back in with a notion: 'Ah! Silly walks!' So, Ministry Of Silly Walks. That was the result. But by now it was very nearly lunchtime, so we rang up Michael Palin and Terry Jones and *they* wrote the sketch ...

As most people must know, a relationship between one person and another inevitably leads to conflict because one of them's thinking 'Am I being taken for a ride?' and the other one thinks 'Who the hell does he/she think he/she is pushing around?' Both of these points of view interact just like a chemical equation. And normally everything goes on happily, until you introduce a catalyst – for instance another human being – which can rapidly speed up the reaction in either direction without itself being affected in the process. In our case the catalyst was fame.

I don't suppose any of the rest of the group would agree to this 'fame' business as being any kind of motivating force, but knowing a little about human beings and the lies they tell themselves, I'm sure that it is. All of us were behaving paradoxically. We ran away from publicity while at the same time complaining that we weren't on the cover of the *Radio Times*. We eschewed (because it's a nice word anyway) any form of merchandising until several years later when we realized that we weren't actually making as much money as we thought we were. I can remember walking into a meeting – late as usual – to see Terry Jones, who of all of us was the greatest antagonist to commercialism, having abandoned his social principles – modelling a *Python* T-shirt. Perhaps he'd decided (as I had long ago) that it was perfectly reasonable to advertise a good product, but it struck me as an astonishing *volte-face*. (A French word for which we have no equivalent, except about-face.)

But I'm not being 'more Mohammedan-than-thou' over this: the reason I wanted us to make money was that I had a £26,000 overdraft. In the end, though, our decision came too late and we are now lumbered with 400,000 *Monty Python* T-shirts and 29,000 bowler-hatted Weepy The Wee-Wees that, when you press their heads, urinate and do the Ministry of Silly Walks (batteries not included).

Just as two people have problems in their relationship, it's hardly adequate to multiply those problems by three when you're dealing with six. Everyone, somewhere deep down (probably in the perineum, or perhaps in the pineal gland which, as yet, has no ascribed function) wants to be recognized as themselves. But then, like the journalists who were busily reporting the break-up of the Beatles (and still do), none of us really know ourselves – which is fortunate, because if we *did* we'd be latent suicides.

There are arguments in any family, and in any family – even a family of sea-lions – one member inevitably becomes dominant. For a few years. Welcoming the protection of the huge bull sea-lion, the less-dominant members of the family think 'I'm not getting enough of the action!' and they piss off to do their own thing – viz. Paul, George and Ringo; Graham, Michael, Terry, Terry and Eric; Harry Secombe and Spike Milligan. But all of the three groups mentioned above still work together, in different combinations, and even go round to each other's houses occasionally. John Cleese has been known to nip out specially to buy a bottle of gin and slimline tonic with ice but no lemon in. Eric talks to George Harrison. I occasionally have chats with Ringo and Spike. John Cleese talks to anyone important.

Writing and Reaction to Python

The *Python* series was not a hit in England at first. It received a good *critical* reaction, but the average elderly female-on-the-street generally didn't like the show. They said it was rubbish, that it didn't mean anything. It's the same sort of reaction that I'd had years before with my own parents when I listened to *The Goon Show*. I'd be chortling away, not really daring to laugh, and my mother would come in and say, 'You're not listening to that rubbish!' *Python* got much the same reaction. I don't know whether it says anything about the sexes, but it probably does. Perhaps it's that the female of the species tends to be more conservative and less free in her ideas – and it's a natural thing, it's part of biology – and therefore this kind of comedy, which they deem as nonsense, was impinging on their thought processes in that it might actually succeed in changing their minds on certain topics. To them, for instance, the Prime Minister wasn't a figure that could be made fun of, whereas (of course) he should be. This is a male angle. On the whole, the female likes the status quo.

Apart from a good critical reaction – which was perhaps a bit over the top – we weren't as good as we already thought we were being. There were cases where people would leave the pub early on a Sunday night just to come home and catch the show – most of them around at my place! And gradually, just as with *The Goon Show*, more and more people began to watch the show. Unfortunately, the BBC began to realize that we were a popular show and took a closer look at the scripts.

The programme was quite popular overseas, in the US and France and Japan especially, and there are, in fact, two fifty-minute television shows that we made for German television. That sounds bizarre, doesn't it? And it *was* quite bizarre actually. The first show that we did was totally in German. We learned it phonetically, which was quite tricky as German, we discovered, really wasn't a language designed for jokes on the whole. The structure of the language is somewhat cumbersome in many respects. Just one silly little example: I had a character to play, a Frau Mund* I think she was called, who was a contestant in a kind of *Stake Your Claim* panel game. People came onto this panel game to make the most monstrous claims such as they'd written the whole of Shakespeare and things like that – which was clearly not possible since it had been written some hundreds of years before this man was born. But my claim, as Frau Mund, was that I could 'burrow through an elephant'. That sounds silly enough in normal English, but in German it literally translates something like *'Ich durch einen elefanten burrow'*, or 'I through an elephant do burrow.' Which is kind of the wrong way round to me. It doesn't quite have the same sort of ring to it.

We then began offering *Python* to the Great American Continent, the northern part of it, the richest bit, and so a couple of people from the BBC came over to America with some *Python* tapes which they intended showing to an American broadcasting station. But, unfortunately, they'd brought the wrong sort of video which wouldn't play on the American system, and the high executive from the BBC couldn't sell the programme he'd come over to sell, but he didn't mind as he'd had a few free lunches, a dinner in the evening and a hotel. So we didn't really get on in the States until a Dallas, Texas, PBS station showed it. Which was great – except that PBS can't pay you very much money. But we thought it'd be a good idea if our programmes went out on PBS rather than CBS, or ABC, because they didn't edit them for commercials. We were foolish enough to say 'Yes, we like the idea of PBS. Let's flog it to them.' I think we got about £14 each for acting in each show – sorry, no, that was for a whole series of 13 programmes! Of course, if we'd been on a commercial network it would have been multiplied by a

---

* 'Woman Mouth'.

hundred – or certainly by fifty – but we wanted the show to be seen by lots of people and not be tampered with. And, consequently, it became very popular. It also laid the foundation for the films.

Sometime later, however, we had to sue ABC because they'd bought our last series (the last six programmes without John Cleese) and decided to make them into two one-hour shows. There was a fair bit of money involved, so we thought 'Well, yes, all right.' But what they actually did was unforgivable in that they cut out whole chunks for censorship reasons. Bits were cut out which, quite frankly, made nonsense out of the programmes. One of the most ridiculous instances was that of a cut made in a sketch in an upper-class setting; people were talking about whether words sounded 'woody' or 'tinny', in that there are 'woody' words like 'gorn' – which is the upper-class way of saying 'gone', and 'tinny' words like 'litterbin'. Towards the end of that sketch, I, being the father in the piece, suddenly get caught up in repeating lots of woody words, one of which was 'intercourse', and I carried on saying 'intercourse' until Eric Idle – who was playing my wife – tips a bucket of water over me. Now, they cut out that entire speech, but left in the end, so that I came into the scene drenched with water for no apparent reason.

I mean, 'intercourse' is not a bad word, is it? It means *talking* apart from anything else. Still, that was cut out. So we took ABC to court and we claimed one million dollars in damages and eventually, after the lawyers had taken their fees, we got about $30,000. That sounds like a lot but it isn't when divided by six. Still, it was a moral victory, and the courts upheld our views. Of course, they were totally bemused – the lawyers, the judges – in that here were six people who were suing to keep themselves *off* television! They didn't understand that, it wasn't part of their ethic. But we stood by our product and won.

Python Films and Music

So, after *Holy Grail* we all went to Paris for one day, to see what we all sounded like in French I suppose, and we went to a restaurant, in fact a Chinese restaurant, that evening, and chatted about what we would do next. What would the next movie be about? We thought perhaps they could find the Grail and we could take it on from there ... But then Eric Idle came up with a monstrous suggestion, a title for the next movie: *Jesus Christ: Lust For Glory*.

Of course we couldn't possibly do that, but it did give us the thought that something set in that period, in the time of Christ, would be a very good area for us to work in. Particularly as we'd done most of the research – I mean we'd all read the Bible – and originally that was going to be *The Gospel According to St. Brian*.* Brian was going to be a kind of 13th apostle who was always late turning up for a miracle, that sort of thing.

Well, it fell to John Cleese and myself to write some of the opening material for this movie, and we clearly thought at that time that we ought to write a nativity scene at some point or other. We couldn't quite see how to write a nativity scene because obviously that would involve Mr Christ, with whom we had absolutely no quarrel at all. I mean, he was a pretty nice person. We generally agreed with his teachings and felt he was a very good person indeed. Oh, he got a bit tetchy once when he caused a fig tree, or an olive bush, to be withered or something, but that was only a little fit of pique. Anyone can have an off day ... But otherwise he was perfect!

---

* An early draft reveals that this script was even titled *Monty Python's Life of Christ* at one point. In this draft Brian revelled in his fame and became something of a pop star.

The man was absolutely irreproachable. So no problem with him or his teaching. Wonderful wonderful . . .

That's really why I wanted to write the movie because we felt that churches subsequently had rather missed the central point of his arguments which was in fact that people should love one another, and got rather diverted into joining separate little clubs wearing different clothing and thinking of themselves as being rather special and those other people over there as not being worthy of going to heaven. We thought that this wasn't very Christian of them.

Anyway, we felt that this was a very fertile area, and our solution to writing a little nativity scene was that we thought of the three wise men going to the wrong manger, to Brian's manger, and therefore we would follow Brian throughout the rest of the movie, which is exactly what we did after *The Life of Brian* which turned out to be – unfortunately partly because of the bigots that complained about it – a very successful venture.* In a way it was very nice of them, they did all of the publicity for us . . . It was interesting to note that they felt quite capable of complaining, these various bodies of church organizations, about the movie without ever

---

* The Pythons even went so far as to draw up a generic form letter, on Python letterhead, to send out to complaining parties:

'Dear _____,

Thank you for your letter regarding the film *Monty Python's Life of Brian*. Whilst we understand your concern, we would like to correct some misconceptions you may have about the film which may be due to the fact that you have not had the chance to see it before forming your views. The film is set in Biblical times, but it is not about Jesus. It is a comedy, but we would like to think that it does have serious attitudes and certain things to say about human nature. It does not ridicule Christ, nor does it show Christ in any way that could offend anyone, nor is belief in God or Christ a subject dealt with in the film.

We are aware that certain organizations have been circulating misinformation on these points and are sorry that you have been misled. We hope that you will go see the film yourself and come to your own conclusions about its virtues and defects. In any case, we hope you find it funny.

Best wishes,
Monty Python

having seen it. But then that's the prerogative of a bigot, isn't it? As a matter of fact, I took the final script of *Life of Brian* along to a friend of mine in the clergy to see what he could make of it. I mean, we wanted to be sure that we were on good ground, morally speaking. He read it and loved it. In fact, he said that there were things in there that he'd been wanting to say for the whole of his life about the Church.

Anyway, because of the success of *Life of Brian* we were all gathered with a manager that we had at the time, a financial manager who happened to be George Harrison's manager, who made a suggestion which caused one or two people to change their minds about whether to do another movie or not.

At that moment I was thinking that there were other things that I wanted to do myself, I wasn't thinking we'd get down to writing another movie immediately, that wasn't the normal pattern of things. And John was usually rather reticent about joining in with future *Python* activities at that stage; you know, he'd got *Fawlty Towers* going and so I didn't imagine that he would be interested. But when this gentleman suggested to us that if we all went ahead and started work on another movie immediately then *none of us would ever have to work again* – John's eyes kind of lit up and he said, 'When should we start?'

So everyone kind of immediately went, 'Yeah okay then we'll start writing.' And we did begin writing what was later to become *The Meaning of Life*, but we wrote for two years in a complete vacuum. We had no idea what we were writing really. Some of us thought we were writing about the First World War, some the Second World War, some the Third World War, some thought it was about school, some of us thought it was about mysterious tiger hunts in India . . . After about two years of a *very* frustrating writing period – because who could tell whether any particular item was actually going to become part of the movie or not? I don't think any of us were anxious to repeat it – we'd still not come up with any sort of unifying theme – and we were then all shipped off to Jamaica for a couple of weeks.

*

The idea was that all six of us would stay in one house, with no wives, friends, or dental appointments or anything like that to interrupt us, and we would then come up with the notion that would unify this disparate material. After about five days of very hard thinking we still hadn't come up with any ideas at all. So we thought let's not bother, let's have a holiday. That kind of freed up the mind, particularly of Terry Jones, who then suggested, 'How about calling it "The Meaning of Life"?' We thought it was an outrageous enough title, and it also suited some of the better material that we'd written up to that point in that it slotted into a kind of 'seven or eight ages of man' theme. So that's what it became, *The Meaning of Life*. But I don't think any of us particularly need to go back to that process of writing. The most *important* thing as far as another movie is concerned is that we have an idea which we can all say, 'Ah yes! That'll be easy to write . . . !'

The songs in *Python* were most particularly the province of Eric Idle. He wrote a lot of the songs.* He wrote 'Look On The Bright Side' for instance for *Life of Brian*. The obvious exceptions though to me are things like 'The Lumberjack' which was Michael Palin and Terry Jones.† But more often than not you'd be fairly safe on betting that,

---

* 'I took school choir for about ten years, so I can read top lines and a bit of harmony – which meant I was able to bluff my way through opera when I did *The Mikado* with the English National Opera,' says Eric Idle. 'Then three of us formed a folk group at school and played spirituals and skiffle. Then when I was sick once (about the age of twenty-two) and confined to bed I studied the Mickey Baker Jazz Guitar course, which means I can read chords and play funky diminished and minor sixths, but sadly I got well and stopped at the daunting dots. I've always written funny songs, since my Cambridge days. It's part of revue training and background. This was quite a strong element in the Footlights in my day. I often wake up with a song in my head or a funny snatch of lyric. Or even a funny snatch. I like rhyming things. I like spontaneously improvising comedy parodies of existing songs. I have always found it easier to make up songs than remember them! I found the other day to my amazement that I have written around seventy!'

† Terry Jones: 'I can do about three chords on the guitar. I'm not musically very innovative – I tend to regress to British Music Hall circa 1900. I rely on someone else to make it musically interesting. I can't remember how (Mike and I) wrote "Lumberjack", for example. I couldn't tell you which part was mine and which was Mike's. All I

if there's a song there, it was Eric. I think he always rather wanted to be a pop star and that's quite possibly why he'd frequently be seen hanging around the likes of Mick Jagger and so on. Which led to Mick Jagger appearing in Jamaica at one point. It was an extraordinary evening in that we were in this isolated house and we finished up with nothing better to do than play charades, which is really rather strange. It was particularly memorable though because Mick Jagger was given the subject, the movie, *Shaft In Africa* . . . And his portrayal of that movie, on the floor, was really quite graphic. A very memorable moment.

Speaking of memorable moments, I wish there'd been more reaction to the song 'Every Sperm Is Sacred'. Really, *The Meaning of Life* didn't get promoted as much as it should have, I feel, because if it had been then I think we would've had a lot more bother about 'Every Sperm Is Sacred'. It *was* a very sweet moment to see rehearsals for that, to watch these little children singing the song. I hasten to say that they were given substitute words for some of the naughtier ones – not for the sake of the children but for the chaperones who were there and who would probably have objected to the real thing.* We used to actually self-censor quite a lot. We were quite responsible, although there was one sketch I remember writing with John Cleese which we actually felt guilty about while we were writing it. Consequently we laughed hysterically.

It concerned a gentleman who had a little problem in that his mother had recently died and he wondered how to dispose of the deceased. So he went along with his mother in a sack (we're giggling already) to an undertaker's establishment and was advised by the undertaker that there were only three things that he could do with his mother, quite logically: she could be burnt, buried or dumped.

Being burnt means (he explained) being put into the flames –

---

remember is that we wrote it together very quickly (in half an hour) at the end of a frustrating day of writing.'

* Terry Jones: 'When we were recording it we gave the children's parents the song to read so they could see what their little ones were up to. And – nobody objected! Except one of them was worried about Mike (Palin) saying "If I'd worn one of those little rubber things on the end of my cock." So Mike said "On the end of my sock" and we revoiced it later.'

crackle crackle crackle – which is not too nice, particularly if she's not quite dead. And being buried means being stuffed into the ground and being eaten up by lots of worms and weevils – nibble nibble nibble nibble – which is not too pleasant a demise for the departed. And then the third possibility is being dumped; merely being thrown into the Thames or some such. He didn't regard that as being really dignified enough for his mother. But then the undertaker came up with a fourth possibility, and that suggestion was that they could eat her . . .

Well, by now we were laughing hysterically. The man wasn't keen on this notion but the undertaker then went on to encourage him by saying, 'She'd be delicious with a few French fries and broccoli on the side!'

And the man said, 'Well, I am a bit peckish. But no-no . . .'

And then the undertaker suggested, 'Look, I'll tell you what, we can eat your mum and then we'll dig a grave and if you feel guilty about it afterwards you can throw up in it.'

By then we *had* gone too far. And the BBC thought so too and wouldn't allow us to perform that sketch unless we were attacked by the audience at the end of it. So we rather artificially had to arrange for the audience to attack us at the end of the sketch, which was a mystifying moment. Really a strange moment indeed.

Er . . . all quite irrelevant, but yes, Eric was responsible for a lot of the musical numbers, along also with Neil Innes, who was a kind of 'seventh musical Python' who took part in all the stage shows and indeed took part also in *Monty Python and the Holy Grail*. That film was originally going to take place in two different centuries, there was going to be the medieval story and also a modern-day section. In fact we were going to have the Holy Grail, in the modern version, discovered at a Grail counter in a department store. And also it was going to end with God driving the getaway car. But we gradually fell more and more in love with the medieval stuff, the atmosphere that we'd created, so most of the modern stuff disappeared except for the historian and the policemen who came along and we used that device to end the whole thing simply because we couldn't afford a final battle scene.

Economy was also the reason for the coconuts instead of horses. We only had five and a half weeks or so to shoot the entire movie and if we'd had real horses it would have taken at least ten and a half. So we avoided that and we tried to make something of it. So the *real* end, who knows, if we had written that, I think perhaps it would have been God driving the getaway car . . .

However, I don't know *what* was the reason, or significance, of the 'Find The Fish' sequence in *Meaning of Life*. I also don't quite know what I was supposed to be playing in that, I *was* dressed very strangely with forceps rather strategically placed . . . and that rather curious elephantine creature . . . Well, I can only say that it had absolutely no significance at all! I mean, it was obviously thrown in as a piece of absolute stupidity which we very much hoped would confuse one or two critics – and it may well have. I certainly hope so. No, it had *absolutely no significance* at all – which may very well be the meaning of life. I mean, you never know. We never got really close to solving that one. The problem with that is, if you *do* find out suddenly what the meaning of life is, you'd probably stop, wouldn't you? 'Oh, is *that* it? *That's* the meaning of life? Ooh, well, why bother?'

'Find The Fish' was a very silly piece of work, written in fact by Terry Jones – who also wrote another piece in that same movie (in which he also acted) about a rather *fattish* gentleman shall we say? A man who ate rather a lot and completely exploded. The filming of that scene wasn't particularly pleasant. It took place in fact over five days and we used Campbell's vegetable soup garnished with sweet corn as the, er, *required article* . . . And it sat in a catapult which can project ninety gallons of that stuff in any given direction. So if anyone has a need of such an object – it exists.

And Not Forgetting . . .

Speaking of comedic digestibles, I'm often asked if I like Spam. Um . . . not very much. There was a phase when I did, I suppose, but it was the end of the Second World War when we did get sent quite large quantities of Spam over to Britain to help us out. It was a very good thing too, there wasn't much else to eat, so Spam was certainly okay. But of course, we did go overboard about it in one rather *strange* sketch written by Michael Palin and Terry Jones.*

I've recently come into contact with Spam again, oddly enough. I went to Minneapolis, to give a talk at the Guthrie Theater, and obviously some advance warning had gone out about the asking for abuse at the beginning of these lectures because I didn't need to ask for it, I just walked out and it arrived. It was a whole lot of debris, including quite a lot of Spam. Some of it, unfortunately, still in the can. Which took a bit of dodging. But it was quite a pleasant evening nonetheless. None of it actually hit me.

The *melon* did.

---

* 'Spam . . . I can't remember,' says Terry Jones. 'I wrote the sketch originally, and then Mike and I worked it out together and the song was always kind of in there . . . with the Vikings. The great thing is there is now a "why" associated with the Vikings. I mean, that was the point of them.'

The Magic Christian and Rentadick

Recipe for Writing The Magic Christian Screenplay
by Graham Chapman

- Hire two famous scriptwriters to rewrite rewrite of two other famous scriptwriters, rewrite of the first and second drafts rewritten and rewritten by two famous scriptwriters, and then have the pleasure of ignoring everything they write.

- Go back to the original, or any of the other versions and, whenever the mood takes you, tell everyone that they have been fired and refuse to pay them, pointing out the ingenious small print which you must include in any contract which states that the company (being you) will pay only on the first day of principal photography which, being nominated by the company (being you), could be 2901 A.D.

- Have writers over a barrel, keep them in locked room from 9.00 a.m. to 5.00 p.m. and ask them for a synopsis before payment, which they will never get anyway, 'til you're home with synopsis.

- Serves no one.

My first involvement with movies in any shape or form was not a pleasant one. I suppose because of some writing that John Cleese and I had done on *The Frost Report*, we'd been noticed by Peter Sellers who then asked us to do a rewrite of a movie written by

Terry Southern, from his novel *The Magic Christian*. I read the book and liked it, although I thought it a bit episodic, then I read Terry's screenplay and both John and I thought that there were problems there. Anyway, what we were asked to do was a specific job, which was to write in a part for Ringo Starr so that the financiers could find the money to make the movie. That's the way these things happen.

So we wrote Ringo in as a kind of adopted son, an instantly adopted son, adopted by this incredibly wealthy man named Guy Grand who – I don't know whether you know the story but he basically liked to, well, *mess* people around who he thought deserved messing around, and he had the money to do it. He just had a great deal of fun doing absurd things to people. The whole thing's about the power of money, I suppose, and how people will do just about anything to get it. A bit too obvious a point, I thought. I mean, it's a fairly simple thing to say that people will do anything for money because if you give them enough of course they will. And I suppose to show how true that is, John and I each accepted £500 a week to write the script! We were supposed to do two weeks' work on it, and the idea of £1,000 for two weeks work was rather good so we accepted, largely for the money. Somehow or other we had to do another couple of weeks work on it, we thought, and so did it at the same rate of pay. We didn't intentionally do that, although it was quite good for the pocket, but I suppose that, subconsciously, there was something in the story that made us feel that way. Anyway, John and I changed the screenplay slightly in that we made it about a man going around showing people how basically cruel they were – not just how venal they were – which is a change of emphasis, I suppose.

As an introduction to movie-making it was a bit of an ordeal-by-fire. A number of writers toiled on it, and not all of them got credit (although everyone got handsomely paid). It turned into a great big sweat for John and me because after four weeks' work we found that we had written some pretty good stuff, which we were quite pleased with, and we really wanted *that* film to be produced, done our way, on the basis of the script we'd written. But then we discovered on the very first day of shooting that they'd gone back to the original script. Everything changed as soon as the money was actually got for the film – the whole thing's about bloody money actually – and when they *did* use something John and I had written, it was fiddled with.

For instance, there's one whole sequence we wrote involving Ringo and Peter which took place at Sotheby's, the auctioneering establishment in London, where some priceless exhibits were being auctioned and were also on show. And Ringo had quite a nice section with Peter at the beginning of this sequence; they were going around this place with a shopping trolley. Peter had decided that his character only liked the noses from portraits – very expensive portraits which he could afford to pay for – and he would just cut the nose out, much to the dismay of the art expert who loved them, of course for art, but also he loved money, he discovered, and so was forced to allow the man to cut just the noses out.

Well, this little sequence went rather well, particularly with Ringo wandering around casting these priceless exhibits into this shopping trolley as though it were a supermarket. And then we went into the actual auction sequence proper. Well, the very next day we all watched the rushes for that and it got a lot of laughs. But, mysteriously, the very *next* day it had to be shot again, leaving out the earlier sequence which John and I had added, and just leaving the auction sequence on the grounds that Peter thought he hadn't quite got his *character* right. But I subsequently suspect *maybe* it was something to do with Ringo getting a lot of laughs. These little things do happen. People are human. Peter was brilliant, a very very funny man. But all of us basically have feet of clay at one time or another and we do make these little human errors. The problem was, the whole thing wasn't an entity, there was no real central thought behind it. It was just a series of sketches joined together, really. I suppose Peter, thinking that the script wasn't working as well as it should, brought in all these stars – like Yul Brynner and Ursula Andress – and eventually the thing finished up costing a million whereas it should have cost half that.

*

The Magic Christian was a film where people did all sorts of bizarre things. Raquel Welch flagellates some women, dressed in leather. People wade into a huge vat of shit and dollar bills at the end. Wilfred Hyde-White is attacked by a gorilla. It was supposed to have been a big-budget success, but it turned out to be a big-budget non-success. It was a cult movie success. Not that that made the producers any happier. Everyone had fun making the film, except for John and myself, as we could see the whole thing slipping through our fingers. Eventually we gave up going to the set after a long argument. So that was a kind of a strange introduction to movies, and a lot of the stuff that we'd written for that movie bit the dust for quite the wrong reason, I think. We used some of it later on, and we did write – well, just to give you one little example:

John and I had written a little sequence, partly suggested by Peter, about a man, a very nervous man, not at all a social animal, who found himself at a party. He felt a little uneasy and sat down – but unfortunately sat down on the hostess's little Pekinese dog thus killing it, thereby having a bit of a difficult situation to explain his way out of. Peter read this scene and liked it very much indeed, I mean he laughed hysterically at it, but the next day when we came back to see Peter, he'd gone off it totally. He'd actually read this piece of script to the man who delivered his milk and he hadn't laughed, so it was out. And we thought, 'Is *that* the way we're going to be judged?!'

To be fair, Peter was in a very difficult situation. I mean, at that point he was regarded as the funniest man in the world, so who did *he* go to for advice? Well, the milkman! Why not? Who the hell *do* you go to when you're in that position? When people are put on pedestals I think they are in a very peculiar situation, and you've got to be *some brain* to think your way out of that problem sensibly and remain on an even keel.

Peter later commissioned John Cleese and myself to write a comedy/farce screenplay for him entitled *Ditto*. The story concerns a man who comes into contact with a machine that can make exact duplicates of anything – a device that he puts to immediate use when he makes an exact copy of his wife. John and I worked on this, off and on, for several years, and then John got fed up and moved on to other things and I've continued working on it for several more years. I hope to film it this September, on the cheap. Quite cheap. In fact, we'll probably be filming it in my house . . .

As bad as *The Magic Christian* was, from a writing point of view, there was one even worse. Originally it was called *Rentasleuth* but was released as *Rentadick*, which gives you some idea of the mentality. It was actually designed for John Cleese and myself, Tim Brooke-Taylor, Marty Feldman, Ronnie Barker and Ronnie Corbett to star in, and was eventually produced, against our will – John and I actually took our names off the script – because we'd already been paid by David Frost to write it. I do believe it was a very funny film, originally, but it was eventually produced by Ned Sherrin,* and because of the script changes – which trivialized and made it silly rather than funny – John and I refused to have anything to do with it.

It was about a firm of private detectives and security people who were constantly having squabbles and internal theft. The firm was run by an ex-Army major who really didn't have his finger on the pulse. Consequently, the firm was hired to both steal and protect a new nerve gas. In the end it was done as an Ealing comedy – not as well as that, really. It was a mess, a romp – and it wasn't designed to be a romp. I feel that you have to treat comedy seriously, the characters have got to be real, and they don't say things at odd moments just because, oooh, it might get that extra laugh. Anyway, the script was taken round and rewritten. People were now saying things that they shouldn't have said within the context of the film. As I said, it was a mess.

John and I did go to see the screening of it. I had hopes that, perhaps, the thing might still work – especially as we had invested two per cent each in it. But after we'd seen it we were so disgusted with it we just said, 'No, take our names off.' It's one of the few

---

* Noted producer and director. Sherrin directed the original *That Was The Week That Was* television series.

films which has gone out with credits which read something like 'Written by ... blank ... blank, additional material by John Wells', and someone else with a big nose. The full screen credit was 'Additional material by ...' We felt quite proud of that.

Graham Chapman

TO THE ~~HOUSE MANAGER~~

I would like

        to point out . . .

that you never write to me

Signature ...*Eric Idle*...

Room No. *127*...
(late 119)

The (Very) Late Doctor Chapman

by Eric Idle

Graham Chapman was a very doctory type of person. Lest that should inspire confidence in the unwary, never forget his caveat: 'Always remember,' he said, 'Doctors are only ex-medical students.'* You have been warned.

Graham has quite cleverly now become the youngest Python. As the rest of us soldier on into late middle age, the late Graham Chapman – he was famous for being late – is still, alas, sadly dead. But not forgotten. At the last Python meeting we even gave him a vote. 'All right, Graham,' we said. 'One knock for yes, two knocks for no.' He abstained. Which was fine. Since he never really abstained very much in his life.

Graham was a very strange planet. Since he was drunk so much of the time, he wasn't always the most accurate observer of people. In fact, he was desperately paranoid (probably about his gayness among all those tweedy doctory types), so that's why he got so paralytic. Since

---

* The following (intended for, but not included in, *A Liar's Autobiography*) underscores this statement:

'While at St Bart's, pranks were often played by student members of the medical profession in order to pass the time, and stave off inevitable mental meltdown. I remember when pissing seemed to be the 'in' thing to do. We all went outside and started a new competitive event called 'Pissing Up the Snake'. The idea was that the person who could piss up to the highest coil of Aesculapius' snake (the proud emblem of medicine that was set on the wall outside) was the winner. Most people managed about the second coil. One gentleman achieved 2½ coils, but his technique involved running up to the wall, part way up it, pissing, and then doing a kind of pirouette on one foot in mid-stream. I decided to try this technique, and because of my height and the fact that I could run 100 yards in 10.4 seconds, I took a 20-yard dash in full micturition, ran up the wall, just caught the fourth coil and landed with wet trousers. I don't think this record has been beaten since. When I tried recently, I had to be satisfied with coil two.'

he never said much and wrote even less, it was never easy to know just exactly what he was thinking. Whenever I read some of his work I noticed what a weird view he had of things.

The sadness of his early demise is still with us. The malady lingers on. At the twentieth anniversary of Python in LA I was with David Sherlock and said how much I missed Graham. 'I wish he was here now,' I said. 'Oh but he is,' said David. 'He is in my pocket!' And he produced his ashes! Next night he sprinkled them over the front row of the audience. Very Graham. He hated sentimentality. But not sentiment. So perhaps this is okay. He always looked on the bright side. He is still available on video and CD – and I believe David still has some ashes left. He was a wonderful chap.

Lemon Curry and All That

by Terry Jones

A few words about Graham. OK. The great thing about Lemon Curry, I'm sorry, *Graham*, was his (*with a melon?*) unpredictability. He would sit there through a Python group 'writing' session picking the odd spot on his shoulder (that was when he was going through his semi-nude stage) and puffing on his pipe and even – in the bad old days – sipping from a large glass of water which he always kept to hand. We all

GRAHAM CHAPMAN

14th April 1977

Most dreadfully dearest (blank).

What you've just been done sent is/are bits of Monty Python as heard on records over the last few years. I would like your views. If you feel that a lot of shit has been included, or that a vein of gold has been pissed on or passed over, I'd like to hear from you within 20 minutes.

Love,

P.S. I apologize for this not being a photocopy.

thought it was part of his obsession with keeping fit until we discovered it wasn't water. *Lemon Curry*. You see! That's exactly what would happen! Just when you weren't expecting it – out would come the non sequitur which somehow shouldn't have been there (being a non sequitur) but which somehow summed up the whole moment. Graham's writing, at its best, was like that too. It had that enviable quality of giving no evidence of where it came from.

He was like that too, except that we all knew he came from Leicester – but Graham showed not the slightest sign of having come from Leicester. As far as I was concerned, he had come from the moon – an amiable loony with the gift of conveying enormous reassurance. You always felt it would be all right while Graham was around – whatever 'it' was. And then he would be off round the bar of the King's House Hotel, Glencoe, determined to kiss everyone in the bar. Which he did. And got into a fight. And got banned from the bar.

I only saw one of Graham's lectures – it was in New York, and I went along wondering what on earth to expect. And once again Graham surprised me – this time with the warmth of his humour. It was a mellow Graham looking back happily with an audience of friends – well, they were all friends by the end of the evening.

Actress and comedienne Carol Cleveland was the unofficial Seventh Python who played all of the pretty girl roles in the *Python* television series and, most notably, the twin roles of Zoot and Dingo in *Holy Grail.* This celebration of Graham was written by Carol in July 2004 especially for this collection.

Underneath the Lunacy

by Carol Cleveland

I had not met any of the chaps before we got together for *Python* but I knew who they were and I was somewhat in awe. My background was totally different, no posh university for me, I was just a California High School girl, so I felt some trepidation at the thought of working with them. But it wasn't long before I felt quite at ease and relaxed around all of them – except Eric and Graham. I'm sorry to say that I never really did bond with Eric but happy to say, as time went on, I grew quite fond of Graham and I'd like to think the feeling was mutual. Even though I was twenty-nine years old when *Python* started I was still rather naive in some ways and I guess it was his outlandishness that I couldn't get used to at first and the fact that he did *everything* to excess.

Of course, I had gay friends but none so *overtly* gay as Graham. There were times when I found it a wee bit embarrassing and, on a couple of occasions, even frightening. I recall a day when we were on the *Monty Python First Farewell Tour* around England when Graham and myself were waiting for the others to pick us up. We were in some Northern industrial city and Graham suggested we wait in the corner pub, which was full of big, stocky workmen. Graham was wearing this rather large badge on his jacket proclaiming, 'Gay is Good' (or something like that), and one look at those guys' faces told me this was *not* the place for such a proclamation. They started closing in on us and one guy prodded Graham's chest and sneered, 'What's *this* mean then?' I was greatly relieved when Terry Jones popped his head through the door with, 'Car's here.'

On another occasion we were appearing at the New York City Center and were doing a live call-in radio broadcast. All was going well until Graham started talking about his homosexuality and then the whole tone of the show changed. This was New York in 1976 and most gays were still in the cupboard. The callers were getting more and more hostile. The interviewer decided we should perhaps not take any more calls but there was one waiting on the line. A very gravelly Brooklyn voice said, 'We don't like pansies here and the family's gonna get ya.' I wasn't sure which family it was – Manson or Mafia – but it sure frightened the life out of me. The guys of course just thought it was hilariously funny. Well, they would, wouldn't they?

As time went on I came to enjoy his outrageousness and one particular episode sticks in my mind. We were touring Canada with the stage show at the time and one evening after a boozy night out we returned quite late to the rather grand hotel we were staying at and decided to have a dip in the pool. We all went to get bathing suits and towels, except Graham, who just stripped off and jumped in. After a bit we got out and Graham ran naked and dripping wet along the corridor. Just as we reached the lobby, a couple in evening dress came through the front door and stopped dead in their tracks as Graham streaked past them and disappeared up the stairs.

Graham's drinking may have caused a few problems but it was also quite amusing at times. We used to end the stage show with a sketch involving Michael as a scruffy tramp, myself as a posh young lady and Graham as my daddy. Graham would have knocked back a fair bit of gin during those two hours and each night his entrance onto the stage got later and later, leaving me and Mike improvising like mad. One night John Cleese appeared in his place. Greatly relieved, I said, 'Oh, hello Daddy.' John replied, 'I'm not your daddy' . . . Bastard. We all collapsed . . . and so did the sketch. We cut it.

His 'alcoholism' did, of course, occasionally get in the way of the job at hand. I felt so sorry for him when I arrived at the location where we were filming the *Holy Grail* and found him sitting on the ground with his head buried in his trembling hands. I hadn't realized that he'd promised not to drink while filming and this was clearly proving difficult for him. This must have been very frustrating and worrying for the other guys and I believe John used to get quite angry about it but his anger was never vented in public. All the Pythons were gentlemen and underneath all that lunacy they were quite professional. I think they had a lot of respect for each other. Graham was a very funny and talented man and the others clearly admired that. My guess is that they also loved him. Why else would they have put up with his antics?

On the day we were about to celebrate *Python*'s twentieth anniversary with a big party I got a phone call from the Python's office to say it would have to be postponed. Until then, I'd had no idea how ill Graham was and I was devastated to hear that he was dying. I wish I'd been able to say goodbye to him. Graham was a lovely man: wild, outrageous, funny, very genuine and honest. A man who was not afraid to stand up and say 'This is me like it or lump it.' He was also gentle and kind-hearted, I think. He was always very nice to me and, although I never had reason to, I somehow felt that if I'd ever needed a shoulder to cry on, I could turn to Graham. I miss him.

GRAHAM CHAPMAN

Stocks,
Aldbury,
Herts.

22 December 1976

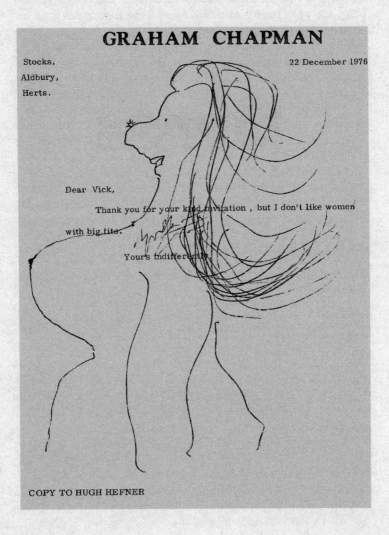

Dear Vick,

Thank you for your kind invitation , but I don't like women

with big tits.

Your's indifferently,

COPY TO HUGH HEFNER

LETTERS

Introduction

While not a voracious letter writer, Graham did enjoy working in the medium and could turn even the most mundane correspondence into high comedy (such as his letter of complaint about a faulty gas cooker, included here). There seemed to be no situation so dire that Graham couldn't attempt to diffuse it or infuse it with humour, whether it was a letter regarding overdue payment on his Barclaycard charge account, or one to friend Harry Nilsson (also included here).

Along with Ringo and Keith Moon, Harry Nilsson was one of Graham's dearest friends. They first met in the early 1970s via Ringo, around the time that Nilsson and Starr and Moon worked together on the horror comedy film *Son of Dracula*. Ringo produced the movie through the Beatles' Apple Films division and co-starred as Merlin, Harry played Dracula's spawn (the unfortunately named Count Downe) and Moon had a cameo as 'the drummer' in Nilsson's on-screen band. As fun as it all sounds, *Son of Dracula* didn't work as either a horror or as a comedy and after its disastrous premiere in Atlanta, Georgia (one of the movie's few public screenings), it was decided that what it needed was a new angle, so Graham was recruited by Ringo/ Apple to rewrite much of the dialogue. He also ended up re-voicing great chunks of it as well, going so far as to impersonate Starr's voice when Ringo was preoccupied elsewhere. Considering the talents involved the movie was a mess, both commercially and critically, and only exists today as rare (and badly dubbed) bootleg copies. Graham's version is even rarer, and was screened only once, by Nilsson himself, at a Beatles convention in the 1990s. And even that was by accident – he thought it was the regular print.

Despite their creative misfire, the Olympic drinking team of Chapman, Nilsson, Moon and Starr operated on all cylinders, sharing both a common love for ethanol and of flaunting the conventions of polite society. They simply had no use for it. Whether they partied in duos, trios or (the much-feared) quad form, they could out-drink, out-smoke and outrage anyone. So scandalous were their exploits that they even managed to shock members of their cloistered circle of peers. Such as the time that Graham appeared to collect a TV award from the *Sun* newspaper on behalf of the Python troupe. The highly inebriated Chapman assured the crowd that he'd do nothing to take away from the dignity of the occasion, then promptly began to yowl and screech at the top of his lungs, convulse and twitch, and then crawl on his belly like a reptile back to his table. Reaction was a mixture of stunned and mortified horror and convulsed laughter from the few that got the joke. The fact that the event had been nationally televised only added fuel to the fire.

Pub crawls often became pub brawls and habitually resulted in hurt feelings, injured people (usually Graham) and letters of apology and recrimination the next morning. The letters collected here run the gamut from the real to the imagined, the silly to the serious, and the ridiculous to the sublime.

A Letter to Keith

Keith Moon
C/o Cayman Islands
or Somewhere Else

Excrementally dear, nevertheless hugely, darling Keith,

This is a piece of paper – to accompany other pieces of paper
which are far more important – and I hope you find them
interesting although, in fact, compared with this piece of paper
they are incredibly boring. FUCK, SHIT, SPUNK, CUNT,
CUNT, CUNT!!! Wow – that was more interesting than
anything you will find on the other pieces of paper. WANK,
MUFF-DIVING – there we go again! This page just can't stop
being interesting.

Read all the other dull pages, if you can spare the time. The
script* seems to be going incredibly well and, of course, I will
be sending you a copy as soon as I have one.

I've promised to spend the rest of my life attempting to shit
on hydrangeas if this film doesn't take off.[1]

Not much more to say, really.[2]

Love,

Graham

1 This in no way constitutes a contract.
2 This page is more interesting than all the others. I said it
would be.

---

* The script referred to here was for the film *The Odd Job*.

This piece was one of the many written, but unused, for inclusion in *A Liar's Autobiography*.

To People that Aren't Quite Like Us

Hello!

I, that is we, would like to take this opportunity of pretending to apologize for the fact that most of this book, except for this bit, and – OK – a few other bits, is otherwise written totally in English. But apart from the Chinese, whose language is divided into so many different dialects, English is, after all, the most popular language. Sorry about that, Froggies, Eyeties, Russians, Spics, Dagos, Swedish Square-heads and, most of all, Krauts. In all honesty I can say that anyone speaking a language other than English is betting on a loser. So pull your socks up, pull your fingers out, and jolly well get down to learning English.

Yours,

Colonel G. Chapman, M.A.D. and bar.

P.S. We've gone to a great deal of trouble to write this section of the book, and have it translated, so if anyone is ungrateful we'll send round one of Her Majesty's gunboats – well, actually the only one (if it still exists).

A Letter to God's Parents

Dear Mr and Mrs God,

This letter is to inform you of God's behaviour in class. To be honest, God makes normal school life impossible as He/She/It is with all of us all of the time, everywhere. Not even the staff break room, or the study, is sacred. At this very moment He/She/It has the audacity to be inside every fibre of my body and, while it is not yet a criminal offence for someone so young/old, I think it shows tendencies better dealt with by more qualified authorities. I am therefore suggesting that you send your Son/Daughter/Thing to one of the many excellent state-run homes for such unfortunate children/young/old people.

I am sure that you appreciate that I have His/Her/Its best interests at heart, and am forwarding His/Her/Its name accordingly. I hesitate to mention this at such a time, but we are still praying for a new pavilion.

Yours,

J.H. Smallwood – Headmaster.

Overdraft

10 Rosslyn Court
NW1

Dear Mr Coombes,

Please stop writing these abusive letters about my overdraft.
I consider it to be quite a nice one and if you keep insulting it
with such wildly extravagant phrases such as
'couldn't support indefinitely', 'unsecured overdrafts', 'matter
of some urgency', 'extremely high-borrowing' and 'so far to no
avail', it will understandably, I feel, take offence and move to a
different house where it will be more comfortable.

Yours with 'real concern'

Graham Chapman

A quite different version of this piece appeared in the *Brand New Monty Python Papperbok*, titled 'How to take your appendix out on the Piccadilly line'. It was mocked up to resemble a London Underground map.

An Appendectomy on the Bakerloo Line

Dear Sirs,

I've had letter after letter after letter after one particular letter which asked 'What should I do about my appendix on the Bakerloo Line?' Well, Miss N., I can only assume you're talking about an acutely inflamed vermiform appendix. The answer simply is – take it out! I've no wish to give glib advice. I know there are bound to be difficulties for the inexperienced lay man or woman, contemplating auto appendectomy. One tiny hint here: have a good rummage through your handbag and make sure your Lane's Forceps are not caked with biscuit crumbs, bits of fluff, old bus tickets, etcetera. It could save an awful lot of fuss later on. I have set out some details which may help you in this, sometimes irksome, chore.

First, find yourself a diagram of Lines and Station Index issued free by London Transport, or go to your nearest Underground Station and ask. Remember, the stations marked with an 'O' are interchange stations. Stations marked with a 'star' are closed Sundays, and also remember to pick up a plastic bucket for the guts.

Now, having found any open Underground Station, study your diagram, or look at any of the conveniently placed maps of the Underground system and find the brown line clearly marked 'Bakerloo' in the key. Select a station appropriate to the severity of the inflammation. That is to say, for mild or grumbling appendicitis, you could start at Lambeth North – being careful not to change at Waterloo – and comfortably have incised your abdomen and exposed the inflamed organ by the time you are between Marylebone and Kilburn Park. You will then have up to Willesden Junction on the Bakerloo Line to complete your excision. And the six minutes between there and Wembley Central gives you plenty of time to be completely sewn up before the terminal at Harrow and Wealdstone – a very unpleasant place to be with a gaping abdominal wound and a plastic bucket full of smelling viscera.

Points to remember. One: If you are at all uncertain, please ask the ticket inspectors about gridiron incisions. They are fully trained public servants, and are most helpful. Two: The Bakerloo Line stops running at midnight. And three: For severe inflammation consult the London Transport Information Centre, and choose one of their longer journeys, arranging so that the actual excision of the inflamed viscus takes place somewhere along the length of the Bakerloo Line which, by means of considerable travel – say on the Circle Line, or by taking a shuttle up and down the Victoria Line for any pre- and post-operative treatment.

Finally, a few words of warning. Whatever you do, remain calm at all times. Do not throw used swabs onto the floor of the carriage as these can cause delay, or prevent the automatic doors from closing. Also, a purse-string suture should be inserted into the caput caeci, about half an inch from the base, and failure to surrender a valid ticket at the end of the journey could mean a fine of up to £10 for first offence. Also, Morant Baker Forceps are *not* on sale at the tobacconists, found in larger stations.

Sincerely,

Mrs Delia Palmers-Lane of Knightsbridge
Unwanted Hair Specialist

A Letter to Harry Nilsson

Harry Nilsson
Flat 12
9 Curzon Place
London W1

11 March 1977

Sweetest Harold,

Thank you for the tape 'Going Down'. Bernard (McKenna) and I like it alot. I am sending you a copy of the latest script of 'The Odd Job' ~~in the hope that you will want to put huge amounts of money into the production. Oh fuck, what a howling error.~~ If you can find the ~~fucking~~ time I'd be very pleased if you could read the script and tell me what you think of it as soon as ~~fucking~~ possible. Maybe you might like to write some more music for it?

Love from Graham to Harold, Una, and Beau.

Graham

LETTERS

Nilsson Replies (sort of)

Graham

That it's I don't think I was Thinking that your mind is another
Word . . . you know . . . something . . . yes? Let me put it this way
. . . (please . . .) Left to write or knought . . . etc . . . b.s. bla . . . bla
. . . bla . . . Well I must leave now . . . You know

it

is

six

o

clock

in

the

morning . . . AND IT IS TIME TO SAY THANK YOU AND
GOOOOOOOOOD
KNIGHT . . . YES?

LOVE

HARRY NILE SSOM

. . . LOVE

HARRY NILSSON

A Letter from Footlights

9 December '77

Dear Graham Chapman,

It is now five years since Falcon Yard was demolished and with it the old Footlights clubroom. I am very pleased to announce that this year a new clubroom has at last been found in the cellar of the Union Society in Round Church Street.

I am endeavouring to make the opening of the new roon, on Saturday February 25th, as memorable an occasion as possible, and to this end I hope that many old members as distinguished as yourself will come along. As the highlight to the evening, I plan to organize a short cabaret spot featuring performers from the most prominent past members of the club. Would you consider participating in the cabaret?

Best wishes,

Martin Bergman.

Graham Replies to Martin Bergman

12 December 1977

Dear Martin,

I would be delighted to attend the opening of the new roon. I've never been into a roon before. I hope it smells nice. Maybe some kind of spelling error has crept into one of our letters. It certainly has in mine.

There are two problems however. I shall be filming in February and although Saturday nights will probably not be

73

affected by this I can't think of a damn thing to do in a short cabaret spot.

Hopefully when my brain has recovered from the effects of a recent bout of tularemia I might have some thoughts for an extremely short cabaret spot.

I assume you will have written to John Cleese and Eric Idle – maybe we could do something together – unless, of course, they're ratting out on the very club that nurtured their talents.

Yours in a white wine sauce.

Graham Chapman

Graham Replies to Martin Bergman (later)

13 February 1978

Dear Martin,

I'm very sad to say that I shall not be able to be with you at the opening of your new 'room' on the 25th February.

To my own surprise I've managed to find enough money to make the film I hinted at in my last letter. Consequently every day for the next eight weeks will have to be totally devoted to this project – including eight-and-a-half hours in every twenty-four which I am determined to use for cleaning my teeth, sleep, going Number Ones and Twos and having a nice cold shower in an effort to keep Number Threes to a minimum.

As neither Eric Idle nor John Cleese are in my film they have no similar excuse.

I wish the new club room every success and a good barman.

Sorry.

Graham

Who Needs Charities Anyway?

1 April 1977

Dear *Nobody's Fool* Charity TV Concert Person,

I would like to explain why I am not appearing in this show tonight. The reason I have refused to turn up is that I think it's disgraceful that you can have people going on and on – just like this – and, frankly, boring the arse off the audience, just because they want to be seen to be appearing in public for the benefit of some charity.

Sometimes you help those less fortunate than yourself, but one has to draw the line somewhere. Take this evening and these so-called 'handicapped children'. I mean, if we start giving money to a lot of loonies we'll only encourage them. Same with spina bifida. We shouldn't be giving them financial incentives to stay abnormal, we should offer the carrot of cash grant to those of them who become normal. And what *about* normal people?! Who gives money to normal people; people who do not suffer from the advantage of being handicapped. We should be looking after ourselves, not pussy-footing around with a lot of spongers. Thank you and good night.

Sincerely,

Dr Graham 'April Fool' Chapman

Mark Ezra was later the co-writer of the 1987 British film *Love Potion #9* (aka *Shock Treatment*), which Graham had a hand in as Executive Producer. The film mentioned here (which had the working title of *The A–Z of Sex*) was never produced.

Mummy with a Dong

Mark Ezra
Ferrestone Films Ltd
44 Trinity Church Square
London SE1 4HY

8 August 1976

Dear Mr Chapman,

I am preparing to produce, in the very near future, an erotic anthology – or sex film, call it what you will – made up of various humorous episodes ranging from one to fifteen minutes in length, from one line fadeout jokes through to fully developed sketches.

Knowing of your experience in this field I felt you might wish to contribute either just an idea, or a storyline, or even a censored sketch that is gathering dust in your bottom drawer.

I am sorry my approach has had to be so blunt and direct, but time precludes a more delicate modus operandi.

Your sincerely,

Mark Ezra

Graham Replies

Dear Mark,

I can't say that I've received many letters like yours. It all sounds intriguing. A Sex film with laughs. I'll give it some thought. I hope it's not a problem if what I submit is more funny than filthy (although I'm certain it will also be quite filthy).

Yours,

Graham.

Ferrestone Films Replies

Dear Mr Chapman/Graham,

Not to worry if it's too funny. Just as long as there's plenty of filth. We hope to have more concrete details about the production within the next fortnight. And if we don't hear from you, you'll hear from us.

Yours sincerely,

Mark Ezra.

Graham Replies by Phone 27 September 1976

LETTERS

Ferrestone Films Replies

Ferrestone Films Ltd
44 Trinity Church Square
London SE1 4HY

29 September 1976

Dear Graham,

RE: 'MUMMY WITH A DONG SKETCH'

We would like to confirm the points discussed during your
telephone conversation with John Beech on Monday 27th
September. The idea you outlined would seem to fit in well with
the format of our proposed film.

Ideally, any sketch should be primarily visual, with voice-over
narration or effects covering the sound tracks. It should be set in
Victorian times, and should run no longer than five minutes.

Yours sincerely,

Mark Ezra

Graham Replies

Dear Mark,

Many thanks for your letter of 29.9.76. Yes, ideally it should be
set in Victorian times. I estimate the length to be no longer
than required. Of the sketch, that is.

Best regards,

Graham

PS Would it be all right if I played 'The Mummy' in a cameo
role?

New Gas Cooker

89 Southwood Lane
Highgate

9 July 1975

Dear Sir,

With reference to your recent threatening letter: I would like
to point out that the money asked for is inaccurate and that the
amount of £81.30 was paid on March 5th 1974, for which we
have a receipt (ref 10735677). Therefore your amount due
should be £56.75, for which I enclose a cheque, and for which
I would be grateful to have a receipt. The receipt which
reference number is noted above was for £101.13; this being
the receipt for the balance needed to pay off a hire-purchase
agreement on the purchase of two cookers: Parkinson 1500 and
a Stone's Crystal Cooker – the price of which was then £81.30,
which I have subtracted from the balance due to you. The
documents relating to this purchase are in my possession – I
trust that you have been efficient enough to retain copies
yourselves.

The New World 52 Mark I Gas Cooker was a replacement
needed because of the non-arrival of the Stone's Crystal
Cooker. I waited from the 5th March 1974 until the beginning
of December 1974, expecting delivery of this cooker only to be
told that this model was no longer available, and I decided
therefore on a more immediate delivery of a more expensive
cooker – the 'New World'. I would now like to point out that
the New World gas cooker is defective in that it was delivered
as a cooker with a flexible connection, but without the
necessary bracket and, therefore, leans constantly at an angle
of ten degrees to the horizontal. I would appreciate delivery of

this part immediately as saucepans tend to slide off. This famous cooker is also in urgent need of maintenance attention. The pilot lights do not work properly and also the electrically operated oven-timer appears not to work.

The Parkinson 1500 usually stands horizontally, unless you put a heavy saucepan on the front left-hand burner. This cooker's pilot light does not work, and we suffer the slight, but nevertheless noticeable, stench of gas. Perhaps you might consider the inconvenience caused to me as worth some recompense, rather than sending me any more offensive notes – written in red. Would you please do something to remedy this rather ridiculous situation? As a person who works in television I am sending a copy of this note to the *Nationwide* consumer unit whose Richard Stilgoe is a personal friend. I look forward to more pleasant correspondence in the future, and more active attention.

Yours, having had to waste what would otherwise have been a profitable writing-period composing, in the circumstances, a very pleasant letter,

Graham Chapman

PS I return to you your piece of paper with the red writing on it.

In July of 1976, Douglas Adams wrote Graham a letter (he had to write a letter as his phone had been disconnected). In the letter a frustrated Adams takes Graham to task for his seeming inability to commit to a regular writing schedule on *A Liar's Autobiography*, a project that Graham had brought Douglas in on, saying that he can only conclude the book is 'very low down your priority list' and that, consequentially, he has had to commit to a job guarding a royal Arab family. In concluding, Douglas explains how hard it is to concentrate on the launching of his own career when he has to deal with the constant frustration of 'endless cancelled or wasted days' and adds, 'hope the drying out goes all right'. The letter did not go over well with Graham, who was going through the horrors of the DTs at the time, and he dashed off a reply the next day.

Graham Replies to Douglas Adams

8 July 1976

Dear Douglas,

I have made my decision and that is that I do want to write this book, but I quite agree with you that it is a very good idea for you to go off and make your own way in the writing world for a bit. I think that working for the Arabs can only be a salutary experience and a valuable one. Who knows, you may be able to persuade the GPO to change their minds and have your phone reconnected.

I spent the entire day yesterday having a relatively mild form of *delirium tremens* and look forward to the day when you can afford to have the same problem.

Good luck with launching your own career. I trust you weren't considering Brighton Pier.

I thought your letter haughty and arrogant even for a person 6ft 5ins tall with a long nose.

I shall speak to Geoffrey Strachan* about rearranging the contract. You have already been paid more than a fair sum for the work contributed. However, I shall waive that matter if you come and collect your bleeding mo-ped which is cluttering up our garden.

Do you not think perhaps that your father has influenced your attitude to life just a little?

Your sincerely,

with qualified love,

Graham Chapman

PS Sorry that this is a copy but the original is being used in the book.†

---

* The publisher at Methuen Books who had commissioned *A Liar's Autobiography*. A bit of a visionary, Strachan was the first to see the literary potential of *Python* and published all of their now-classic books, as well as many of their solo efforts.

† *A Liar's Autobiography*. The letter exchange was eventually never used in that book, which is why it's included here.

Another Letter to God's Parents

Dear Mr and Mrs God,

God's behaviour this term has, I'm afraid, not been as exemplary as we would have wished. His/Her/Its attitude towards the staff, while always kind and considerate, shows a lack of discipline. He/She/It attempts to treat Masters as equals, and has no concern whatsoever about the school rules.

Coupled with the fact that He/She/It is with us at all times, everywhere, even inside our very beings, it is with reluctance that I write to you to tell you that we, for the sake of the other parents, no longer have room for Him/Her/It in this school.

Hoping that you will understand . . .

Yours,

J. H. Smallwood – Headmaster

ESSAYS

Before I begin my chat about
"what will the neighbours say" ~~what~~
~~what~~ could become a dissertation
on Peer pressure — to prevent
that — no, all of a sudden
to ~~little~~ tally on of I say people
~~empty~~ I need not necessarily
believe every thing I say

What should be what about 'What will
the neighbours say' could become a
dissertation, ~~a word~~ distinctable,
on 'Peer pressure' ~~anything~~
what is told flat and forgiven is an
to prevent the ~~instrument~~ a little
box in the ~~bottom~~ left of your screen
will ~~give~~ show the number of times
the ~~things~~ 'your password ~~was~~ used
(box appears with a 2 in it.)

Having ~~since~~ since I seem to have
become involved in a preface ~~forward~~
~~take it point out that~~ anyway

Introduction

Graham wrote for magazines, journals and occasionally newspapers. He was also approached by several small TV companies for his ideas on all sorts of topics. A selection of them are included here – in typical Graham fashion, they range from the funny to the shocking and astute.

Calcium Made Interesting

Calcium, an alkaline belonging to group 2A of the periodic table, has large breasts. Its metallic form is readily oxidized and releases hydrogen from water. It occurs naturally as the carbonate $CaCO_3$ in limestone, chalk, marble, and in brothels. This element makes up 3.4 per cent of the earth's crust and has wild parties 3.4 times a week round at its place. When Calcium Carbonate gets a bit heated it gives off CO_2, and when it drinks claret it gets so sloshed it forms Calcium Hydroxide a.k.a. $Ca(OH)_2$. The reaction of CaO and H_2O to form $Ca(OH)_2$ (a process which is called *slaking*, by the way) is very naughty indeed and can only be compared to sexual intercourse! At the climax of the reaction a white precipitate called Calcium Hydroxide appears and stains the sheets.

Calcium also occurs as the phosphate in Apatite and forms a large part of many silicate minerals which, if you're really stoned, is a great scene to get zonked on, man. How about $CaSO_4$ and $2H_2O$ as a mantra? Or more simply just repeat *'Gypsum'* to yourself – but take care because on a bad trip, if things get a bit hot, it turns into Plaster of Paris (where there are many prostitutes and a great gay scene – *see Ferrous Sulphate*). If Apatite, when finely ground and taken from between the thighs of a young school girl with blue knickers and white socks, is treated with Sulphuric Acid it produces super-phosphates which are used as fertilizers, if that's anybody's bag.

To sum up, Calcium is an aphrodisiac. In fact, just *reading* about it gives you both an orgasm and a high that you'll really phone home about! Try this excerpt on for size:

Meeting the hard calcereous rock he thought how Calcium is involved in almost every biological function. As his hand came

ever closer, up until it reached that place . . . Oh, the relief . . .
Oh! The ecstasy . . . He reflected upon how this amazing mineral
provides the electrical energy for the heart to beat and for all
muscle movement. Slowly, as his hand fell to his zip and he eased
his fingers, slowly inserting them into his flies and, groping, he
pondered upon how Calcium is responsible for feeding every cell.
To his surprise he was not embarrassed as he . . . and then he . . .

Wow! But if you want a real buzz, then get into other Calcium
compounds like Calcium Carbide (CaC_2) which is produced when it
is heated with 'coke'. It's something else, man, way out! It will not
only stimulate your erogenous zones but increase your vital statistics. (If you're interested it can be delivered to your home in a plain
brown wrapper. Details in the next chapter.)

What Will the Neighbours Say?

A chat about 'What will the neighbours say' *could* become a dissertation – a pompous word – on peer pressure, which is both glib *and* pompous. I'll try and watch this.

Now, since I seem to have become involved in a preface anyway, I'd like to use it to point out that I do not necessarily believe everything that I'm going to say. Sometimes I may exaggerate to emphasize a point, and at other times I shall lie quite deliberately – anything to make sure that you listen – though I shall try not to use italics unless I simply get bored myself. Falling off my seat is out. A cheap way to get attention.

Now that we've established these guidelines, I hope you'll all sit back and really enjoy this stunning chat. (Incidentally, towards the end there will be quite a lot of filthy talk, stories about sex, smutty revelations about big names and what they get up to between the sheets – yes, the low-down on the high-life of the high-flyers – rock superstars, film mega and giga stars – not just toward the end either, there may well be something quite lavatorial in a few minutes). There!

Well . . . What will the neighbours say? Now, as the son of a country copper, a parish PC – an urban district dickhead – I was made aware of this phrase at a very early age, for if any of my family were the subject of gossip, then that would put the mockers on Dad's promotional prospects. Perhaps it was being so aware of this that made me ignore it totally. I looked at my neighbours, and I didn't care *what* they thought; or even if they did. No, scandalizing and mocking nice decent ordinary folk became the mission of a lifetime.

Now one thing that neighbours say almost universally is that everyone should settle down, get married and have a family. What a load of donkey-doos. Why in Grantham should anyone commit themselves to a path of such mind-stunning mediocrity? It's not as if the one thing the world really needs is more children. There is nothing clever or difficult about the act of procreation. There are four and a half billion of us on this crowded little planet already, and this will rise to twelve billion by the year 2030 if people continue to settle down, get married and have families. Think of that: three times more people than there are now! Try and find a job then, you family-lovers!! Think of *that* during the rush hour, or while you're on a crowded beach in Ibiza . . . !!! . . . Now, I realize that my voice gets louder and rises in pitch as I warm to my theme, but I'll try and change that . . .

Of course, the population of Britain will not rise as quickly as that of the less-educated parts of the world but then, we're over-populated already you dumb-clucks. Oh, I'm sorry . . . Halve the population of Britain and there might be a hope of it being self-sufficient, with those who want to work in interesting jobs and those who don't, just reading books and playing snooker – recreating but not reproducing ourselves – while robots quite rightly do all the boring messy and dangerous jobs that we would have such fun creating for them to do. Like mucking out the anaconda. I mean, *swelp* me, two-thirds of the world is starving now! Our limited natural resources are rapidly being used up: oil, minerals, forestry, entire species of animals – all being wiped out by humanity's unthinking expansion. Think of this and then think how, in the name of God, if there is such an entity, can people adopt an attitude of 'high morality' when advising you to get married and have a family?

They are, of course, using an outdated morality. One of an age of primitive tribalism. This is perpetuated by many modern religious and political beliefs. In a tribal era, if you were going to survive primitive hand-to-hand combat with other tribes, then you needed more tribes-persons. Tribes-persons, through ignorance, were mal-nourished, ate lumps of dirt, swapped plagues with each other and were generally infected and infested, living short lives in verminous hutches. In those days, if they were going to survive at all then they had to reproduce like rabbits just to make up the deficit. It is precisely against such a background that many religions began. The trouble is, they haven't changed their act since. Silly people, silly Pope and, for those of you in Northern Ireland, silly Paisley.

Did you notice that I fell off my chair just then? Do you remember how I said I wouldn't do that? Of course you do, I commend your attention spans. For those of you who have short attention spans, and maybe are already staring blankly at the page or going back to your knitting or just chasing crabs – WAKE UP AND PAY ATTEN-TION! I do not intend to go over all this again. If you're that stupid, or have just opened this publication, I am talking about 'What will the neighbours say'. A little chat about peer pressure. The way the weak and feeble amongst us allow others to determine the course of our lives.

Now, where was I? You know, even before a child is born, parents begin to worry about what the neighbours will say about it. Do you want a boy or a girl? Now if it happens to be a boy there's often extra celebration, presumably because of the tender thought that a boy may well earn more money later on and not shame his family by getting married and/or getting pregnant. Also, it's thought that boys are more likely to become sports stars, pop singers, union leaders, airline pilots, Harley Street proctologists etcetera. But aren't they *also* more likely to become second-hand car salesmen, football hooligans and/or psychopathic mass murderers?

As soon as a new infant arrives in the world it is entered for a competition with the neighbours. Will she be called Sarah-Maude or Charlene-Cheryl? Will he be called Simon-Ben or Wayne or Daryl? How painful, or painless, was the delivery? How heavy was the baby? How long was it? Did it have hair and were all its bits and pieces there? Does it even remotely resemble its father? Was its name put down for a private school and, if so, how long before birth? Or is it so special that it should have no special privileges and be sent to one of the best local education authority schools that the parents could just happen to live near? Fortunately the neighbours have, at long last, admitted that they boobed over bottle-feeding and now sensibly recommend the breast.

★

The next neighbourly competition is called milestones. How much more quickly did your child learn to grin, crawl, walk, say 'Dada' and erupt teeth? All useful signs for the pediatrician looking for abnormalities, but even better for gossip. Neighbours love to count their blessings as they label others as weirdoes. Simply being left-handed once evoked prejudice. How many left-handed corkscrews or pianos have you seen? I mean left-handed pianos with the notes the other way round; as a left-handed person should have the right to expect? Not fair, is it?

Having decided the child's total gender/identity for it, the parents, motivated by fear of the neighbours, set about instilling in the creature how essentially all-male or all-female it must be. Little boys don't cry and little girls don't play with piston-engines. What mind-bogglingly pathetic and emotionally stunting little rules they make up. Dressed totally in pink, little girls are forced to play with cerebrum-shatteringly tedious dolls with little model houses, so that later on they'll not only merge in with their dull neighbours, but also play an important role in promoting conservatism without even knowing where they get their ideas from.

Similarly, little boys, kitted out in blue, are given tiny motor cars, cricket bats, toy hand-grenades and Exocets; and most importantly, even three- and four-year-old lads are given frequent coy propaganda about 'girlfriends' and plentiful reminders along the lines of 'when you've grown up and have children of your own you'll understand'. What! What! What! What are they so wound-up about? Because it would be a bad thing before one's neighbours if one's nice little girl turned into a bull-dyke or 'such a tough little boy became a raving queen'. Is homosexuality the common cause of parental death that parents imagine, or is it really fear of what the neighbours will say? If someone has the sense to do what they want and love someone of their own sex and not force replicas of themselves on the rest of this overcrowded world, good luck to them. They should be given medals, not demoted or importuned and locked up.

In this dreadful world of enforced sexual conformity, little girls are tutored to pure aspartame sweetness, and to raise their voices an octave – sounding more innocent and plaintive when asking for something in a shop, for instance. The cute little mite lisps 'Mummy, could I have thome of those nithe thweeties', when what she really needs is a smack in the teeth! Welcome to the real world. Little boys, on the other hand, are indulged to be conservatively naughty, cheeky and non-effeminately grimy. What they actually need for their education is one day a month compulsorily clad in a pink skirt. Would Boy George be as he is if he'd been forced to wear a pink skirt once a month from the age of six?

Er, you *are* paying attention, aren't you? I'm not saying all this for my own benefit, you know. I've gone to great lengths to research this so that the whole of mankind might benefit. It's inattention to education that causes war, you know. If the Germans had been wiser and had cared less about what the neighbours said, there would have been no World War II. But no, you don't want to know, and all peace protesters are weirdoes (so the neighbours say), and the Americans have got no history and therefore can't think; and the Russians are all very, very, very evil – though I'm not quite sure how, except that it somehow involves the KGB and red something or other. Oh you globeful of ninnies. Pull yourselves together, don't you realize that others think as you do?

At first a baby is a greedy, selfish creature. All it knows about are its own needs. If Monsieur Pasteur, Mister Lister, Herr Koch, Dr Fleming and Ms Nightingale had been this dim then most of us would have curled up our toes and died of infection long before reaching the ripe old age of twenty-seven. This is where education comes in. But there are two types. One is purely educational . . . in which society passes on its accumulated knowledge – artistic, historic and scientific; and is very, very, very, very, very good. The other is indoctrination, which poses as education but is excrementally treacherous, deceitful and prone to mythomania. Who in the world would stoop so low as to indoctrinate? All religious leaders and politicians. It's what their jobs are about.

They say, 'Here's a code of behaviour for you, now you won't have to do any of that difficult thinking. Put these blinkers on and follow us. Believe in God and all that we say He says, or believe in the Party and all we say, you say. Ooh say, can you see . . . Rule Britannia . . . We'll keep the red flag flying here . . . Our way is the Truth – I have seen the light!'

Yes, millions of people can be *very* wrong. They betray their ignorance by their intolerance of other moralities, and their insistence that theirs is the Only Way. I remember an ad for Volkswagen cars which said 'Twenty-five million Germans can't be wrong.' Oh really? Remember World War II? Need I say more? So think, don't blindly follow. Choose the best bits of all the philosophies so you can find and build your own. You don't have to be a Christian, a Muslim, a Buddhist, a Communist, a logical Positivist or a vegan to use your brain. In fact, to be committed to such a 'club' is to sentence millions of neurons to shameful inactivity.

Religion, nationalism and political fervour are the enemies of rational thought. At best, dearest reader, we should stroll a careful course, retaining our individualism and freedom of thought, while conforming only to social behaviour patterns which benefit and enlighten, rather than harm, others.

Of course, sometimes the neighbours can be right. Ultimately it is the corporate-consciousness of humanity against which our personal moralities are compared. Thankfully this corporate consciousness is not fixed. It is growing and developing as it absorbs and accepts new ideas – ideas pioneered by individuals who once it may have persecuted, and who eventually become the heroes of man's search for truth.

Well, that's the end of a very long, but well-intentioned and important, bit of chat. Now, some of you may have allowed your minds to wander – I know I did mine – so here's a summary: Do as you would be done by, and think for yourself.

So, back to peer pressure. During early childhood – I think I've just said 'peer pressure', oh dear – during early childhood, when selfishness predominates, fear of being 'the odd one out', of being ridiculed, jeered at or thumped, creates a dangerous need to belong to the gang, the club, the social set. Those excluded are punished by the exclusion itself – not being talked to, not being played with – through various types of psychological torment to actual physical abuse. Few of us leave this cruel early phase of our lives unbruised. 'Chapman's too thin'; 'Ooh, ooh skinny! Long streak of piss!'; 'Chapman's a poof'; etcetera. Gradually we unlearn these unwise ways and turn next to competition. We must compete against each other academically and in sport if we are not to be regarded as weird.

Competition can spur you on to greater efforts and seems to be essential to (mostly otherwise) lazy humans. But you must beware of placing too much importance on competition as it may lead to frustrations and feelings of failure, or, just as bad, false impressions of superiority. I remember Wilkinson, who was so brilliant in the sixth form, went straight on to get a first at Oxford, and then was never heard of again (although there was some talk of men in white coats). Now, of course, no one would tolerate a Brave New World mentality where people are conditioned to accept permanent labels of superiority, or inferiority, in graded classifications from alpha to epsilon. So isn't it surprising that that is exactly what we *do* accept?

The ignorant convince themselves by inverted snobbery that their superiors are, in fact, *inferior* because they can't see that lounging around and being a selfish lout is a lot less effort, and much more butch. Those who are educationally spoon-fed believe that it is only their own efforts that have brought about their superior status and that others simply didn't work hard enough, or are genetically inferior. Think for yourself and refuse to be categorized, or be influenced by category. Everyone should be encouraged to progress to the full extent of their potential, not be put in their places and forbidden further growth. Later in life the fear of 'not belonging' may even tempt us to be less true to our inner convictions, leading us to denounce them and even, paradoxically, actively campaign against them so convincingly that we hide our real thoughts. What a pathetic way to live. Whether you believe in an afterlife or not, I think it's wiser to assume that there is none and at least be true to yourself in life, as this is most likely your only shot at it.

*

So we pass through the selfishness of toddlerhood – the braggart cliqueishness of childhood – to come up against the obscenity of suddenly having a larger set of genitals clamped on to us. Some view this prospect with pride, and yet another valid area of competition (neah neah neah neah – hoo hoo hoo! Titter, titter, titter, whisper, whisper) because the *one* thing the neighbours can not openly talk to each other about is sex (even though, privately, it's their favourite topic of conversation). 'Didn't you know *that*?' one pubescent taunts another. The would-be grown-up is afraid to ask through ridicule. Parents should tell their children more about sex. *Parents* should be told more about sex. Teachers should teach more about sex, and friends and lavatory walls should be more sexually literate. There are fewer dark areas now, but it's not been long since neighbours thought that the female orgasm was unnecessary and rare; masturbation was thought to stunt growth and lead to madness; and marriage was the only cure. What blatherskitic bunk!

It's a common misconception of the sexually illiterate that sex consists of a male putting his penis into a vagina and pumping away until orgasm, and that is all; that there is another valid form of sex. This used to be regarded as the British missionary position – a form of sexual gratification indulged in by those wary of other, more entertaining, possibilities. I'm not just talking about a number of different sexual positions (which, despite the acrobatics, are still in essence penis-up-the-vagina), fun though they may be. Full sexual orgasm, as everyone should really know, can be achieved in mutual masturbation for instance – which is not only unwanted-pregnancy-free but minimizes the risk of venereal disease and teaches us a great deal about how to truly arouse our partner to heights of pleasure and gratification.

If there is one single area in which you can rely on your neighbours' ignorance and intolerance, it is sex. It may be a good way of meeting friends and forming deep relationships but, unfortunately, it can arouse very destructive feelings of guilt, envy and jealousy and it's for this reason that sensible discretion on sexual matters is still a necessity. I think you can expect people to object if you thrust sex under their nostrils.

*

Peer pressure . . . Fear of being themselves and what their immediate neighbours say pushes the young adult to conform by smoking carcinogenic cigarettes, drinking poisonous quantities of alcohol, sniffing glue, smoking dope, snorting coke, and shooting heroin in order to demonstrate their independence. 'Friends' won't easily let you say no. Sheeplike, you follow others into bizarre musical tastes – your attempt to dress differently, sadly, becomes a uniform as you desperately try to avoid the rut that you inevitably fall into. Pathetic, aren't we? Old age, our neighbours say, will make you less active, less attractive, more stupid and asexual – and it will, far sooner than it might if you make the mistake of believing stupid neighbours yet again.

Take care of your body – eat and drink sensibly – exercise your body and mind and old age will not be the trial that it is for many. Grow old gracefully, so say those bleeding neighbours – damn them. Well, don't give up without a huge struggle – yes – even with time. At last scientists are learning how to turn back some of our body clocks – good luck to them. It's theoretically possible for a human being to live to one hundred and fifty years of age. Let's push ourselves there and beyond. Limits are set to be broken. Let us begin to treat the ageing process as a group of diseases that can be treated, not as inevitable doom to be whispered about. People who think they have gracefully accepted the inevitable are fond of saying 'Oh, I wouldn't want to live for ever . . .' Oh yes they would if they thought they had a chance. The alternative is, after all, DEATH, which is a bit final.

Even if you think you're going to casually ooze off into some eternal nirvana, you've got the whole of eternity to do that in! Why be in such a rush to find out? It could be a dreadful disappointment, and there are no return tickets. I strongly suspect that death is the dullest state we could fall into, and it should never be looked upon favourably by the sane. It's nothing to be afraid of, just something to avoid.

Well, that's enough about death. Now, some smutty revelations about big names. Right! I happen to know that John Travolta, Neil Diamond, Marlon Brando and every commissioner of the

Metropolitan Police engage in XXXXXXXXXXXXXXXXXXXXX, except for one.

Now, Arabs. You may not want to know what an Arab thinks, but maybe you should. Arabs, it seems, do care about what we think. While the rulers in Iran were happy to bring back dismemberment as a fit punishment for certain crimes – because of education and perceived world opinion, those anachronistic leaders could not find enough unaware idiots to carry out the sentences. It seemed that nobody wanted to cut anyone's arms, or even hands, off. Now there's progress.

Fortunately, communications are breaking down political and national barriers, and we're able to see over, round and through them, to glimpse people everywhere as they really are, and not as leaders would like them to be seen. We don't have to be judged by our local neighbours anymore. There is a bigger, global neighbour who is more tolerant and understanding – and it is *you* – as you struggle to understand, tolerate or disapprove of the ways of others. Thank you. (And I think I only said 'peer pressure' six times.)

The Tits and Bingo Press

Searching for stability in a changing world? Looking for something to believe in; a path to follow? I hope that you are, but I
also hope that you're not being silly about it. Why is it that there
are so many alternatives in life? (I mean, there's All-Religion,
All-Medicine, All-Science, Diets, All-Journalism, All-'Societies' of all
kinds. Yes smartass, I know that grammatically there can only be
one alternative, but you can go boil your bum if you're going to
be *that* picky. Anyway, I'm speaking in parentheses.) It's a good
thing for people to question the way they've been living, and to
examine an alternative, but dissatisfaction with the norm can also
panic people into falling in love with the first philosophical piece
of tail that falls upon their inward eye. I think that there can
only be one alternative creed for a life sensibly lived and that the
proper alternative to all your alternatives is ... wait for it ...
SCIENCE!!!

Now I can see a lot of rather wet people who don't know the
first thing about science, and who probably look down on it as
being rather mundane and practical compared to people who ponce
around spouting about obscure composers – ballets to verbal noise
– people who won't have television in the house anymore and who
listen to Radio 3. This includes all lawyers, most accountants,
macramé pot-holder fiends, critics, *Time Out*, 51 per cent of historians, 90 per cent of all living trade unionists, a surprising 58 per
cent of the English medical profession, both far right and far left
politicians, all foreign-film buffs, fewer Anglican clergymen than
you'd have thought, one Minister of Science and Technology and
one female Prime Minister *and* her Minister for Education. All-in-all,
just about everyone who believes that life may have been better in

medieval England (unless they really would have liked to have died before the age of thirty).

The world is at 'that awkward age'. It's going through its adolescence and before we are grown-up enough to step out into the big wide universe we have to become a little more intelligent about ourselves and our objectives. Hence the restless probing for alternatives.

Not long ago, before the world began to grow hair under its armpits, we were all happy enough to belong to the gangs of our planet's childhood. It may be worthwhile to remind you here of some of them: The Christian Cliques, the Capitalist Cabals, the Marxist Mob, Muslims, Black Panthers, the Jew Boys, Buddhists, Taoists, Maoists, Pink Panthers, Adolph and the Aryans, Hindus, and Nationalists. Fascists all (including Adolph and the Aryans and the Macho Dago Mobs from Latinos in Europe to Latinos in North and South America). Most of these attracted members because they offered solutions to immediate problems, often with vague mystical (or so-called 'spiritual') advantages or benefits to give them a certain immunity to criticism and longevity.

People grew out of these confining, and often blatantly hypocritical, creeds and in the 1960s a search for *the* alternative began – just as it did in the early seventeenth century, following the resurgence of interest in exploration and science and thus producing an increase in trade, travel and communication and the emergence of leisure, e.g. the fruits of the Renaissance. (Just a little note to please the 49 per cent of historians who may have read as far as this.) But, sadly, the alternative of the sixties boiled down to Flower Power and Pop Music. There was a willingness to quest and to question – a feeling of Oneness – but no central drive; no ambition emerged, except that 'Everyone must love one another.' Laudable and simple in theory, but extremely difficult in practice what with so many immature and rather unpleasantly selfish gits still loitering in public offices and positions of power. And the sneering jibes of the emotionally stunted ordinary hypocrite in the street – who is forever ready to debunk a wonderful aspiration by projecting his own failings onto it – helped kill it stone dead don't you know, old horse.

But above all, what *really* died in the sixties was hope. The optimistic view that, given a problem, however large, if sufficient human beings put their minds to it, it could be solved. Alas, people couldn't be coerced into loving one another. The world didn't disarm. Wars carried on, as did famine, disease and ignorance. The Blue Meanies won the day, and the hypocrites in the media were the first to point out any hypocrisy in those who proclaimed a message of love. It happened to Bob Geldof when he got together Band Aid and Live Aid in order to help raise money for the starving people in Ethiopia. The British press labelled the whole thing as a publicity stunt for a man who hadn't had too many hit singles. Their eagerness to wish failure upon someone else could have doomed the project. Fortunately their voice wasn't loud enough to be heard by many. They could have been right about Bob Geldof, but their private feelings should have remained so, for there were bigger issues at stake.

It's typical Britain really. Ninety per cent of the UK appears to be made up of whining, whingeing pessimists. Come to the UK with a promising idea or business venture and the immediate reaction you can expect is the word 'no' followed by every conceivable reason as to why your venture will not succeed, backed up by government policies especially elaborated to make new ideas abort. Nowhere is this attitude more prevalent than in the press.

There is a kind of hollow, news-avoiding jollity about Britain's tits-and-bingo press. Rather than bother themselves with items of general news and information, they restrict themselves instead to popular themes such as the Royal family, TV soaps, football and racing. All harmless enough but, unfortunately, they are also not afraid to 'speak out' to the ignorant if they feel like stirring up prejudice, or if they reckon it will sell a few more newspapers. Which brings me back to ... science. (You thought I'd forgotten.)

When things don't look too bright in the UK (which is unfortunately rather often) the papers decide that it's time to scare the shit out of people. And nowhere is this whipping-up-of-a-pointless-scare more evident in the more popular tabloids than when they write in pseudoscientific terms about the disease AIDS.

Without bothering to give more accurate or complete information they've felt free to describe AIDS as a gay plague; to insinuate that it is sweeping uncontrolled throughout America and that the same will happen in Britain; that it is a dread and fatal disease and that all homosexuals are a reservoir of infection. Behind all of this is a kind of unspoken feeling that 'the gays have brought it on themselves by their evil ways'. The same kind of 'divine vengeance' thinking that belonged to the days when people ran around with Arks of the Covenant and blamed crop failure on menstruation.

Before we fully consider the attitude of the popular press – what is known about AIDS? AIDS is Acquired Immune Deficiency Syndrome. A virus known to American scientists as HTVL3, and to the French as LAV, has been implicated as the agent responsible for the disease, and it's believed the virus originated as a disease in the heterosexual communities of central Africa. Karposi's Sarcoma, a form of 'cancer' which may develop during the later phase of the illness in some AIDS patients, was previously only found in Africa. The virus causing immune deficiency and sarcoma in Uganda and Zambia could have mutated to produce the AIDS which we now hear so much about. The virus is passed from person to person via blood, or blood products. Drug addicts who inject themselves, or people who have transfusions of contaminated blood, or engage in anal epithelium, can also transmit the disease. So far there have been no cases where transmission of the virus by any other means, such as saliva, have been confirmed.

So *scientifically speaking*, AIDS is a disease which can only be caught in *extraordinary* circumstances – yet why have the popular press not been more specific about the way the disease is spread? If they have the high-minded 'duty to their readers' that they claim then their topmost priority should be just that – but instead they give the impression of a fatal disease getting rapidly out of control, in order to sell newspapers. And, other than medical ones that I've read, no newspapers have mentioned that AIDS most likely started as a *heterosexual* disease in Africa. (You would have thought that this might have been of interest to their heterosexual readers.)

Science may not be sexy, but it's a hell of a lot better than being needlessly scared to death, or entertained into mindless submission by endless exposés on the Royal family, TV soaps, football and racing. So I would suggest to the popular press that it should keep its mouth shut or inform its readers properly: that the only chance they have to contract this disease is for them to indulge in oral or anal intercourse of an abrasive nature with a carrier or victim, or to in some way accept contaminated blood (which, no doubt, are *everyday occurrences* for their readers).

This piece was originally earmarked for A Liar's Autobiography but was never used.

A Radical Alternative to Optimism

Anyone who sniggers at poofs and lesbians, or believes that homosexuality is a danger to society, should think about the real danger threatening the human race, and that is reproductive heterosexuality.

The population of the world is increasing rapidly. The natural resources of the world are decreasing rapidly. That is why everything is so bloody expensive. In the very near future, for example, there will be no oil even for Arabs. The rate of population growth in this country (Great Britain) is relatively slow, but each individual in it quite rightly expects at least an equal chance to live as well as his neighbour, as seen on TV. Sorry, each individual, you can't – there are too bloody many of you.

If the people of the world voluntarily decrease their numbers then, as a species, we shall survive. Failing this we have to rely on natural calamities: earthquakes, flood, drought, disease, famine, etc., or that faithful standby war, to do the job for us. All rather painful and messy, isn't it?

WHAT CAN I DO?

1. If you must have babies don't boast about it. It is far too common an occurrence for congratulations and needs no encouragement.

2. Form an action group calling for the phasing out of family allowances and the phasing in of higher taxation for those couples with more than two children of their own loins.

3. If you are a childless but child-loving couple of either or the same sex, then look after the excess children of those unable to cope with the new, sensible tax structure (see 2 above). Well-meaning single individuals who have to go to work may have a time problem with adoption, and larger groups could present difficulties . . . A child needs guidance to follow or to fight against, not a discussion programme.

4. Anyone who has the slightest inclination towards homosexuality should be encouraged, and the same for heterosexuality excepting where it leads to increasing our numbers.

5. Euthanasia and suicide should be given thumbs-up, but only if performed correctly and when a person really is useless.

6. Treat optimists as loonies. Anyone who says that the situation is not that bad and that with recycling of materials and the increased use of atomic power . . . and with the tremendous strides being made by our scientists in food technology, may, if they wish, eat their own shit and drink their own radioactive urine.

I do not intend to suggest that homosexuality is an answer to the problem of overpopulation, but does it make things worse?

Another praiseworthy sexual activity is masturbation. I am distressed that a word in common use meaning one, or those, who masturbate should be used as a term of abuse by simpletons. Idiots who, while if they admitted it, being in glasshouses themselves, lack the felicity of imagination necessary to raise this normal animal practice to the fine art it can become. The same idiots who would no doubt idolize one of their kind who went in for two-minute knee-tremblers with the local bicycle behind the bus shelter. The same yobs who cause trouble by corrupting youth, encouraging 'have it away' and 'give 'er one' type sexual intercourse; resulting in early unwanted children and marriages. Innocent youth so corrupted finds itself unable to fulfil its promise. Premature and unnecessary responsibility is a killer to ambition.

We have all seen these corrupters of youth encouraging naive sexual intercourse with feeble jokes about penises and vaginas, tits and arses, 'how many times so and so had someone or other'. Look at those big/small tits ... he's got a big/small one. These types often make a 'wahaying' sound while raising one forearm and thumping it with the other hand to accompany the 'joke'.

It is these people, mostly men, who have the primitive 'fear of the unknown' attitude towards the homosexual. They assume, even though they may be standing next to one, that any homosexual would want to do vile things to their vile bodies. The general public makes assumptions too: homosexuals should not be allowed to teach – interfering with my child, corruption, etc. Do they not realize that there are heterosexual school teachers as well who may well pervert innocent children into patterns of behaviour that are not natural to them?

Alone, most of us are incomplete people. We need the support of someone really close and special to us. The sex is immaterial, but there is no doubt that such close friendships lead to happier, less primitive and more productive lives.

I live with, and love, the same boy I met twelve years ago. I am not 'a homosexual'. I do not like 'science's' convenient labels for sexual behaviour and apologize for having used the word myself. I have always had splendidly mixed sexual experiences, but having had some medical education I am privileged enough to have had access to the closely guarded secrets of avoiding unwanted children and VD. If I am to be labelled anything then it is 'gay' and I sing because I'm glad to be.

A Plea for Understanding

The public lacks understanding and sympathy for one particular group of society outsiders. These people are often treated as subjects for smutty jokes merely because they are regarded as 'different' . . . 'abnormal' . . . 'not like us'. This, in turn, forces them more and more into their own cliques which, of course, merely makes their peculiarities more obvious – and may even become one of its strengths and lead to an almost aggressive behaviour in retaliation to society's callous attitude to their illness. Yes, these people must be regarded as ill. They have a disease, a type of mental disease which can often be successfully treated. I'm speaking of course about the UCT – or, as it is more commonly known, the Upper-Class Twit.

The UCT is typically found at regattas, in sports cars, at noisy parties, and at Hunt Balls. What causes this tendency towards Twitishness? Psychiatrists usually point to in-breeding and public schooling – and they are certainly to blame in many high-profile cases – but what causes an apparently normal person to suddenly lapse into Twitdom; to lounge about in public bars and be nasty in restaurants? And, more importantly, what can be done about it? Aversion therapy – whereby the Twit is repeatedly hit on the head with a wooden hammer, or kicked violently in the groin with a steel toecap whenever they insult a waiter or kick an old beggar – is one answer, and has had some (limited) success. However, there are some who have taken a sterner approach and demanded that the Twit be castrated or imprisoned. Harsh? Yes, and while I don't agree with this approach it is effective, for unfortunately, despite treatment, despite support organizations such as Twits Anonymous, in the end most Twits have to be locked away from society in castles, manor homes and palatial estates where they are forced to play roles as stockbrokers, Lords, barristers and members of Parliament.

What about the police? At the moment, Twits are tolerated by the police – however, attitudes *are* changing, especially in light of the recent All-Night Car Door Slamming incident in St John's Wood. In fact, Scotland Yard's new Flying Twit Squad have already seized many UCT-oriented publications, such as *Twitler*, and the *Evening Standard*, and conducted clandestine raids on several known UCT hangouts in the City and at Number 10, where they have removed 'certain substances' including cigars, waistcoats and black bowler hats. *What's next, raids on homosexuals?!* As preposterous as that may sound, intolerance breeds intolerance – which is why I am making a plea for a better understanding of the Twit (even though he is a nasty, despicable, vicious little bugger).

Intended for *A Liar's Autobiography*, this piece was not included in the final proof.

Some Very Personal Thoughts on a Seminar on Transexualism Given at the Royal Society of Medicine

Being medically qualified, and a poof, I went along to the Royal Society of Medicine's 'At Home' on homosexuality; an evening devoted largely to surgeons and urologists 'blowing their own trumpets' about recent male-to-female sex-change operations. A couple of psychiatrists gave their views too, so the evening wasn't totally devoted to physical butchery. My overall impression of the evening was that I was present at one of the conferences that some of Nazi Germany's so-called doctors must have had when they discussed the results of experiments carried out on the inmates of various prison camps.

Apart from a *very small* minority who genuinely *have* attributes of both sexes – part testicular/part ovarian (e.g. hidden testes in what appears outwardly to be an average female) – and who *can* be helped surgically to come down on one side of the fence or the other and made a 'normal' male or female in external appearance (which is probably a good thing), the majority of the evening was spent listening to arrogant surgeons explaining how they could convert what was obviously physically a male into an apparent female. I'd strongly advise any male who considers that he thinks in a feminine way (what is *called* psychologically a female), to think very carefully indeed before having 'the' operation. We were shown a film of a typical 'operation', the details outlined below.

Your balls having been previously removed in some other country (where it is legal), you present yourself with a 'psychiatrist's' recommendation to a urological surgeon. You will probably already have larger breasts because of the oestrogen therapy given to you – but there the femininity ends – and asexualization starts. The entire penis is removed, together with most of the erectile tissue at the base of the penis because this is likely to cause 'troublesome bleeding'. Sam Peckinpah has never *imagined* anything like this. And even if he had it *couldn't* have been shown. I sincerely hope very few of you have ever seen a penis being cut off by scissors.

The surgeon, having cleared the perineum of any sexual apparatus, then proceeds to fashion a vagina by placing skin grafts from the thigh (or wherever) around what amounts to a plastic penis – which is rather crudely thrust through the musculature of the perineum (the bit between your legs), in the hope that the skin will grow and form a 'vagina'. Everything is then sewn up and 'a woman' is born. A 'woman' that has no erectile tissue, and none of 'her' sexually excitable nervous tissue left, thus rendering 'her' incapable of orgasm. You may think, 'Well, at least this poor creature looks like a woman.' Looking at slides of the end results of this kind of surgery, the kind of vulva (outside bits of the vagina) that they managed to 'fashion' looked like an elderly arsehole with third-degree piles. In short, not altogether 'a woman'.

Even a rather fascist psychiatrist, who'd recommended several of these operations, admitted that the success rate wasn't too good. There had been several suicides, understandable divorces, etc. The meeting then seemed to get rather off the point in that the 'doctors' were more concerned about what kind of passport this newly created person should be given: male or female. Surgeons are so sweet to show such a human interest.

When I made a point at the end of the evening about their slight tendency to regard an operation of this kind as being distinctly preferable to life as a transvestite/homosexual and that I, as a doctor and homosexual, found that from experience this was not a 'condition-to-be-cured', they immediately assumed that I was a student troublemaker and made a move to eject me. It was only after I had assured them that I was here as an 'impartial' observer that their alarm abated and I was allowed to stay to hear the rest.

I hope this has given a few impressions of what it is like to have the 'operation'. I strongly urge any man who considers himself primarily a female to forget about it, keep his cock, and use his arse.

The Future Is in Your Hands

Unemployment, falling standards of living, dwindling natural resources, political refugees and unwanted children all give me the dry heaves. I am sick of feeling sick about these problems and call for action *now*.

There is one startlingly obvious answer to all these difficulties: reduce the size of the population. Yet to a Marxist, this would mean admitting the failure of the State to look after its own; to a capitalist, less cheap labour. Others would claim infringement of personal freedom and the right to have children. Why should any human beings imagine that they're so special that they deserve to perpetrate their progeny upon this earth? What conceit. Politicians, of course, never recommend population control – they're all too worried about votes. Actually, I admit there have been notable exceptions to this in India and China. In China, with the population reaching 1,000 million in 1980, the situation is so fucking bad that even politicians have had to admit it and act.

In the West, a few cling to the risible notion that people like the current crop of politicians might have the answers to unemployment by eventual economic recovery – provided they make no U-turns. I submit that the worst U-turns in history have been the fall of Sodom and Gomorrah and the collapse of depravity and sexual excess. Sex for sex's sake. Great. That should be the prime function of sex in the human. Fun. Not reproduction. Abstinence is too much to ask, so let us try to phase out the reproductive side of sex until each region of the world has a population that can enable it to become self-sufficient.

There are other answers to the problem of numbers, including famine, disease (that old panacea), war and, most unreliable of all, gigantic natural catastrophe. These are now hopelessly inadequate and are, in fact, taken into account when the United Nations population projections are estimated. They predict the global growth curve to level off by the year 2080 when the earth's population will have risen from the present 4,500 million persons to a horrendous, horripilant 11,000 million *or more*. If you think it's difficult to find a parking space now, hang on just a bit longer, buddy.

The nuclear holocaust might save us from all this, but it would be very messy ecologically, and extremely unfair when one considers that those administrators who have failed to act on over-population will, undoubtedly, all survive in their comfortable (but secret) bunkers. So . . . what is the answer?

A commendably thought-provoking piece of graffiti I've seen above several men's urinals (*'The future is in your hands'*) gives us a clue: let the population of the world literally take the problem in its own hands and masturbate; solitary or preferably the more energy-efficient mutual masturbation should be advocated in all ages and social groups. Homosexuality should be encouraged: anyone with the slightest tendency should, I say, *tend to it*. Masturbators and homosexuals should receive their long-awaited temporal and spiritual lionization.

There are some who believe that homosexuality in the male should be made compulsory until the age of thirty-one. I am not one of them because I believe that, properly dealt with, heterosexuality need not be the social scourge it is today. Higher taxation for each child born over a recommended 1.68 children per couple, increasing birth registration charges, lowering child welfare benefits and introducing death certificate bonuses would be an excess of bureaucracy. All that really needs to be achieved is a raising of consciousness about population; a rethink on education to change the social climate, so that children are not pressured into settling down, getting married and having 2.1 children or else being branded as abnormal, as they are at present blinkered, by outdated and antisocial parents, educational institutions and puritanically (or even worse) Vaticanally influenced media. I mean, come on, what is so great about getting married, having a couple of kids, a colour television set and a Volvo? Is that 'Life'? Forget all about that and leave yourself time to write a novel, become an athlete, or discover that wonder drug. Improve the lot of the extant.

Why should *your* children be so special anyway? Whoever heard of Mr and Mrs Einstein's eldest, 'Luigi' Galileo, or 'Julie' Newton? Even that nice young 'Mike' Shakespeare's name is met with cold indifference. But don't get the idea that I'm against children. If we had them in the right numbers they would be much better off. Neither am I suggesting non-reproductive promiscuity. There is the attendant danger of a bewildering variety of venereal diseases so, if you *must* be promiscuous and a penetrator (or penetratee), please spare a thought for regular check-ups and the protective sheath.

No, I'm all for love. Sexual love too. Pair-bonding can be most productive and life-enhancing, but need it be quite so *re*productive and life-degrading? Give animals and plants a chance. *Come off it, heteros!*

Originally written for a medical journal called *Pulse* in about 1979, this piece was never published.

Solving Tunisia

For a third-world country, Tunisia is well off and its Ministry of Tourism can afford to maintain its microtome thin 'Costa del Sol' veneer effectively enough to fool innocent tourists – however, the Tunisian, with an average per capita income of four hundred quid, is *not* well off. The haggling, the begging, the families living in one room with the sheep – or under a rug without a room near a sheep, and the sheepless troglodytes – are picturesquely and fascinatingly 'ethnic' and are really appalling. Nevertheless, the resilient Tunisians hate every minute of it.

While overtly afraid of an invasion by nearby, stinking-rich Libya, their main worry is that it will never happen. The Libyans are not notably keen on tourism, which discounts one of Tunisia's three assets, and so are unlikely to want to annex a country providing olives and dates in exchange for a larger, more vulnerable, border otherwise containing rocks and sand. I brooded over this problem while sitting on one of Tunisia's many heaps of rocks and sand, and came up with a solution which could give the Tunisians a chance to be at least as comfortably unhappy as the people of Sweden. This new wealth could be achieved without the intervention of nasty foreign do-gooders with their inevitable ulterior motives.

116

THE SOLUTION

1. An ancient recipe is found in the sands of the desert, carved on the under-surface of one of Tunisia's rocks (rather like the one I was sitting on earlier). On the rock the 'writing' should be unintelligible except for a hieroglyphic representation of what could be a date, appearing frequently in the baffling text. This recipe is put aside in a museum and used as ancient evidence later in glossy magazines.

2. At the same time, a box of dates should be sent for an extremely detailed chemical analysis at the world's most prestigious laboratory. The box should be accompanied by an innocent note explaining how the precise detailed knowledge of the chemistry of the date became the subject of an extremely valuable wager. We don't want any foreign pharmaceutical businessmen alerted at this stage. Think of the money they've already made out of a) polyunsaturates, b) vitamin C and vitamin E as 'natural health foods'. The general public has heard their cunningly introduced rumours and bought their carefully 'scientifically labelled' products to stop themselves having heart attacks, being ill at all, and to help them have greater sexual vigour and look younger while not taking 'synthetic' chemicals.

3. When the results of the chemical analysis of the dates are received, they should be studied carefully and a substance selected. It doesn't much matter what it is although preferably the dates should have more of it than, say, the orange or (more importantly) the apricot. NB The apricot was not particularly valuable, and did not travel well, but apricot oil sounded exotic and cheap to the pharmaceutical companies and we all know (tee-hee) that apricot oil contains mysterious ingredients which can halt, or reverse, the ageing process and has been used for centuries in obscure parts of the world, too vaguely conceived to be mentioned. 'It definitely makes you look younger or your money back! (If you can be bothered, which you can't.)' Even the poor date turns out to contain nothing interesting. It doesn't matter – it is the presence of one unimportant ingredient in

unique proportion to several other unimportant ingredients which gives it its importance.

4. You now turn to your recipe and find that it is an ancient, unique, soon-to-be-patented method of extracting something from dates. You are now in a position to produce huge quantities of extract-of-date capsules. Regular, Strong and Super-strength. No need to add anything like harmless quantities of iron or molybdenum or zinc – yet. Leave that a year or two later.

5. It is well known that . . . (here we mention the Kinsey Report in connection with someone else's report so that it sounds as though you *mean* the Kinsey Report, or any other credible sexual survey, oh and *The Perfumed Garden* . . . I've forgotten the page number, but you can look it up) . . . when the average size of the penis in humans is considered, that 'Mr Arab' does pretty well. 'The Arab looks Caucasian enough – why is he so well endowed?' Well, the answer is obvious. The Chinese are not noted date-takers, and most Europeans eat too few. The black African can be discounted as purely hereditary, with an astute reference to the Pygmies as a clincher as far as date-eating goes.

The advertising campaign about the date-extract need not stress the phallic implications, of course, or that extract-of-date cream gives you bigger tits (or your money back). These aspects should only be hinted at, while emphasizing other health-giving properties of the date. Any promises of eternal youth, increased religious fervour, appearance on television – nothing will match the 'long-lost, little-known secret' of the date, as discovered in the ancient desert. If anyone doubts the commercial possibilities of extract-of-date, think about ginseng, or nip over to California and find out why expensive zinc tablets should be part of every man's diet.

I shall pause there for an expensive serving of apricot juice (Vitamin A 45% of US recommended daily allowance, Vitamin C 40%, Niacin 2%, iron 2% and magnesium 2%). Active ingredient of date principal 0% (as yet). The above economic solution is my parting gift to Tunisia. After nine weeks there I returned to London and was confused at first by things like armchairs, carpets on the floors, conversation, food and newspapers.

While looking at the pictures in one newspaper, I accidentally happened to read a short column about a new method of childbirth. The standing-up position. Pregnant ladies are (apparently – being only experimental at the moment) allowed to stand up and go about their normal lives almost right up to the moment of birth. Good grief, that's getting dangerously close to natural childbirth, with no interference and without the unnecessary attentions of the usual labour ward. The natural position for labour is a squatting position, as it is for defecation. Would *you* like to lie on your side, or even flat on your back with your legs in the air, having your perineum peered at by a gaggle of midwives while straining at a particularly obstinate stool?

The ideal labour ward should be a clump of trees, or a thicket, into which the grand lady could discreetly withdraw to reappear moments later clutching the newborn, quite capable of picking up the thread of the conversation she had just momentarily abandoned. I exaggerate to make a point – I would settle for a world in which the ladies in the first stage of labour would excuse themselves all social engagements, have the 'presentation' checked, pick up a patient-to-midwife intercom and head for the foliage.

This recent rambling and disjointed dissertation says nothing about the week I've just spent in Amsterdam, or the fact that I'm over 6,000 miles away from there at the moment. I have been resting from the rigours of Tunisia, and am only now just rested from the rigours of my relaxing, and am exhausted. Perhaps what I need is some extract-of-date.

TELEPLAYS

Introduction

After the *Python* TV series ended, there was a big hole which Graham attempted to fill almost immediately for, despite his talents in film, radio, book, record and stage, sketches were what he knew best. They were what he'd cut his teeth on, and television was his medium. The following collection of teleplays ranges from the immediate post-*Python* mid-1970s through to the 1980s. The styles vary somewhat from script to script but they all share a commonality of approach, attitude and anarchy that is vintage Chapman.

Discounting his work on sitcoms such as *No That's Me Over Here, Now Look Here,* or *The Prince of Denmark,* the script for *Light Entertainment* from 1974 (page 126) is among the first (if not *the* first) attempt by Graham to create a cohesive, inter-linked, sketch-based, long-form script. It is the 'missing link' between his skit work on *Python* and what eventually metamorphosed into *Out of the Trees.* Created during the waning months of the *Monty Python* series, this half-hour script by Graham is a truly mad affair, written in a self-conscious and self-referential style that was completely different. He makes several in-jokes here about the *Doctor in the House* series (which he wrote for) and all of its many mutations (*Doctor at Sea, Doctor in Clover, Doctor at Large, Doctor in Love,* etc.). The script was never produced, nor is there any evidence that he attempted to have it produced.

Written in the mid-1970s, *The Sitcoms* (page 140) was inspired by (or, more accurately, written in response to) the many inane American sitcoms of the 1960s that featured ridiculous and manufactured situations affecting 'normal, everyday suburbanites' (the 'oh no, the big boss/client is coming to dinner' scenario being a common one). This short script takes on their form, their pat scenarios, and their stock characters and then turns them on their heads, creating an outlandish Kafkaesque situation full of gross stereotypes.

Out of the Trees (page 150) has a more haphazard history. According to David Sherlock it was Graham's concept, and one he initially began working on towards the end of the *Python* series with Douglas Adams, with whom he'd begun an on-and-off writing collaboration after John Cleese had finally made good his promise to cease working on *Python*. Graham had first seen Adams in the London production of the 1974 Footlights revue, *Chox*, they struck up a friendship and wrote a few items for the fourth series of *Python* (although most of it was subsequently rewritten, as was the wont of the team). When the *Trees* project came up, Graham naturally turned to Adams. They worked on the initial episode but it was not going well (a large degree of blame can be attributed to Graham's drinking). Following a letter from Adams (see page 81), Graham cooled on their relationship and brought in an old friend, writer Bernard McKenna, to help rework what they had done. 'Out of the Trees was really Graham and Douglas but they were getting nowhere,' recalls McKenna. 'I lived around the corner from Graham so I helped out and took over but not in time to fix it. I wanted to start again.' Later, Graham collaborated with writer David Yallop on episode two (included here), which was never produced. To help confuse matters even more, episode one (the one Graham started with Adams but later reworked with McKenna) was actually slated to be episode two, and episode two (the one written with Yallop and the one presented here) was to be episode one. If that's not flustering enough there is still yet another script, entitled *Than?* (unproduced), which encompasses much of the *Trees* material, and could even have been an early draft of *Out of the Trees* under a different title. If anything, all of this shows Graham's determination to get the series off the ground.

In retrospect, it's unfair that *Out of the Trees* (or *Than?* whichever you prefer) was rejected after just one episode by the powers that be at the BBC. While the one programme that was produced is uneven, it's not a failure by any stretch of the imagination. Given time and support, it could have been developed into a worthy successor to *Monty Python*. Televised on 10 January 1976 with little fanfare or advance promotion, at a time when most of its core audience would have been out for the evening (Saturday at 10 p.m.), it was little surprise that the viewing numbers were low and the reaction to the show was mixed. *Out of the Trees* was the first of several television programmes proposed by Graham over the years and, although he never successfully found another television outlet for his talents (unlike John Cleese with *Fawlty Towers*, Eric Idle with *The Rutles*, and the Palin/Jones team with *Ripping Yarns*), it serves as one of his better efforts and deserves another look – and a release on DVD. Whatever its title may be.

The Cough is an interesting piece. It draws heavily on Graham's medical experience, and yet it was not an extended sketch, nor was it the pilot episode for a proposed TV series. Written by Graham in 1981, he and Carol Cleveland performed it once at a sales convention in Paris for a healthcare company.

The last script included here, *Above Them, The Ground – The Dangerous Sports Club and Me*, was written in the mid-1980s as a proposed television special featuring the DSC – a group of ad hoc adrenaline junkies whose combination of 'sport' (if sliding down the sides of mountains on a grand piano on skis can be called sport) and absurd humour greatly appealed to Graham. This script takes the form of a quasi-documentary incorporating actual footage of some of their more outlandish stunts. It was never produced. While he never officially became a member of the club, he did participate in several DSC events and did a lot to publicize their activities. Graham also wrote a detailed draft for a Dangerous Sports Club feature film, and was keen to get it made, but his health problems prevented him from completing this.

Light Entertainment (L.E.)

SCENE: *An elaborate Light Entertainment studio set. Light bulbs, shapes, etc., 'da woiks'. Canned laughter and applause at various close-ups of set, cross-cuts with shots of bewildered* AUDIENCE *with exception of one* MAN *who is at first giggling and then laughing. Enter* HOST. *Wild laughter and applause.* HOST *sits on high stool. Hysterics.* HOST *loosens tie. Tears of joy, sobs of delight.* HOST *smiles at camera. Hoots of derision.*

HOST Hello, good evening, and of course to viewers at home, a special welcome . . .

Howls of laughter. The GIGGLING MAN *in audience is by now unable to control himself. He is helped, still convulsed, from his seat by a* UNIFORMED ATTENDANT. *The* AUDIENCE *are intrigued throughout.*

Cut to PEPPERPOTS *park scene: A dowdy little middle-aged lower-middle-class lady,* MRS SMOKER, *is sitting on a bench. As she unwraps a parcel she is calling to the birds . . .*

MRS SMOKER Birdies! Nice birdies! Coo-oo-tweet-tweet foodies . . .

She unwraps the parcel revealing a leg of lamb which she hurls at the gathering birds, killing one of them. She follows this with a couple of tins of pineapple and a huge jar of mayonnaise which she smashes messily. All the while she coos. MRS NON-SMOKER *arrives . . .*

MRS NON-SMOKER Good morning Mrs Smoker.

MRS SMOKER Oh, good morning Mrs Non-Smoker.

MRS NON-SMOKER Feeding the birds?

MRS SMOKER No.

MRS NON-SMOKER No!?

MRS SMOKER No, I'm sending them up rotten.

MRS NON-SMOKER Are you satirizing them?

MRS SMOKER Trenchantly!

MRS NON-SMOKER You mustn't do that!

MRS SMOKER Why not?

MRS NON-SMOKER Look . . .

She points to a notice which reads 'DO NOT SATIRIZE THE BIRDS'.

MRS SMOKER I'm not taking any notice of that.

MRS NON-SMOKER Why not?

MRS SMOKER Somebody's put that up since we started the sketch.

She produces a large revolver.

MRS SMOKER How's this for a quick lampoon then . . .

She blazes three shots in the direction of the birds. A POLICEMAN *appears
    from behind some suitable bush, statue, or from behind her.*

POLICEMAN Hallo hallo, what's going on here then?

MRS SMOKER Hallo copper.

POLICEMAN None of your lip. I been watching you.

MRS SMOKER Oh yes?

POLICEMAN You've been attempting to satirize them birds!

MRS SMOKER I was only decimating them.

POLICEMAN I shall have your name.

MRS SMOKER Mrs Franz Joseph Strauss.

POLICEMAN Blimey!

He leaps to attention and salutes.

MRS SMOKER Not really.

POLICEMAN In that case . . . *(He elbows her in the head)* Now watch
    it.

He walks off and MRS SMOKER *shoots him dead.* MRS NON-SMOKER *nudges*
    MRS SMOKER *and points at another notice: 'PLEASE DO NOT
    SHOOT THE POLICE'.*

MRS SMOKER Bloody red tape! Makes me sick!

She vomits into her handbag.

MRS NON-SMOKER Here, this has got a bit self-consciously bizarre, let's start again.

A SIX-FOOT GOOSE walks by.

MRS SMOKER Yes, all right.

A jump cut to exactly the same start except that MRS SMOKER is feeding the birds with crumbs. MRS NON-SMOKER approaches.

MRS NON-SMOKER Good morning Mrs Brown.

MRS SMOKER Who?

MRS NON-SMOKER Mrs Brown.

MRS SMOKER Ooh! We're changing names, are we? Sorry, start again.

A jump cut to the same start again.

MRS NON-SMOKER Good morning Mrs Brown.

MRS SMOKER Good morning Mrs Smith.

MRS NON-SMOKER suddenly rises two feet into the air and hovers there.

MRS SMOKER Where are you going?

MRS NON-SMOKER I haven't the slightest idea.

MRS SMOKER What are you doing Mrs Smith, going up into the air like that? It's forbidden!

MRS NON-SMOKER I didn't do it. It just happened.

MRS SMOKER Oh. Are you on a wire?

MRS NON-SMOKER *(Feels)* No . . . Am I on a box?

MRS SMOKER feels the space beneath MRS NON-SMOKER.

MRS SMOKER No.

A very long pause.

MRS NON-SMOKER Well, I must say I'm very much surprised that in a situation like this neither of us can think of a humorous remark.

MRS SMOKER Yes. You'd think it would be full of comic possibilities, wouldn't you?

MRS NON-SMOKER Think think. It may never happen again.

MRS SMOKER Oooh . . . Come in number nine, your time is up?
No . . .

MRS NON-SMOKER Just hanging around? No . . .

MRS SMOKER Er . . . ooohh . . . er . . .

*MRS NON-SMOKER comes slowly down again. MRS SMOKER suddenly realizes
MRS NON-SMOKER has landed.*

MRS SMOKER Oh bugger! Well, that's that then.

MRS NON-SMOKER Weren't we awful?

MRS SMOKER Terrible!

MRS NON-SMOKER Think of all the laughs Bob Hope would have
got.

MRS SMOKER He's a bit conventional though. He's not as 'way out'
as we are.

MRS NON-SMOKER True. I expect that will go down as one of the
great wasted opportunities in the history of comedy.

MRS SMOKER Ooh! I just thought of something. Tch! What a waste.

MRS NON-SMOKER Was it funny?

MRS SMOKER Ooh, very funny. Ho ho ho, ooooh!!

*She is rising up into the air and stops about the same height as MRS NON-
SMOKER was before.*

MRS NON-SMOKER Well say it then!

MRS SMOKER What?

MRS NON-SMOKER The funny thing you thought of – say it now!

MRS SMOKER No, it only works if it's me on the bench. OOH!

She kicks her legs.

MRS NON-SMOKER Oh this is disastrous!

POLICEMAN Hallo, you're sending up the birds again, aren't you?

MRS SMOKER What!?

POLICEMAN Hovering about, in that satirical fashion.

MRS NON-SMOKER We're doing a sketch.

POLICEMAN No sketches allowed.

He points at notice: 'SKETCHES FORBIDDEN'. He sees the camera.

POLICEMAN Good lord!

He walks towards the camera, covering up the lens with his hands.

POLICEMAN THAT'S IT! THAT'S THE LOT!

MRS SMOKER What an abortion that sketch was.

Cut to corridor scene.

SCENE: *A corridor, fairly butch. Each door is boldly sign painted
describing the function or position or rank each occupant holds. But
the occupants' names are hastily written on pieces of card and slotted
into suitable holders.*

First door (music is audible from within):

'EXECUTIVE PRODUCER' (LIGHT ENTERTAINMENT) *Air
Commodore Vivian Marwood-ffiskk. (Talbot).*

MAN (O.S.) . . . the other man's grass is always greener . . .

SECRETARY (O.S.) . . . and then Petula says, 'But it's no more greener
than DOWNTOWN!' . . .

MAN (O.S.) Oh I see, then she goes into 'Downtown'!

Second door (frenzied sawing and banging is heard):

'SENIOR EXECUTIVE PRODUCER OF EXECUTIVE PRODUCERS'
(LIGHT ENTERTAINMENT) *Lt. Col. Arthur Marion Brown
Q.U.R.S.T.V. (ABCDEFGHIJKLMNOP******WXYZ)*

Third door (someone is heard rehearsing lines):

'LAVATORY' (G.E.N.T.S.)

VOICE (O.S.) Hello, good evening and woolcome. Bo, er . . . Hello,
good evening and wilcome. No, er . . . Hello, good evening . . .

Fourth door:

'SENIOR EXECUTIVE'
'EXECUTIVE EXECUTIVE'
'PRODUCER PRODUCER'
'LIGHT ENTERTAINMENT (L.E.)' *Rear Admiral Tuppin Bowie R.N.*

Ret. A.C. D.C. & Bar,
(A.N.D.B.Y.G.O.D.H.E.C.A.N.S.I.N.K.A.F.E.W.)

HIM (O.S.) They *are* large, aren't they! Damned large! Vast, great things . . . Oh, sorry. Carry on, where was I?

SECRETARY (O.S.) Toronto, sir?

HIM (O.S.) No no, not last week – in the letter.

SECRETARY (O.S.) Oh, sorry sir. Ah yes. *(Reading back)* 'Whereas albeit, comma, the idea was, quote, "quite appealing", unquote, and would make compulsive enormous oooh let me have a look erm viewing oh go on just a little peep' . . .

HIM Oh no no no. That won't do. Start a new page. Where was I?

SECRETARY Toronto, sir?

HIM Oh Leslie, why pretend?

We hear a struggle and shrieks.

Fifth door (the big one):

'EXECUTIVE EXECUTIVE EXECUTIVE'
'PRODUCERS CONFERENCE ROOM OF EXECUTIVE PRODUCERS
    CONFERENCES' (LIGHT ENTERTAINMENT) ONLY. (O.N.L.Y.)
(KEY WITH SENIOR SENIOR EXECUTIVE PRODUCER)
(FOR LIGHT ENTERTAINMENT)
(W.H.O.I.S.U.N.A.V.A.I.L.A.B.L.E.F.O.R.C.O.M.M.E.N.T.)
(AND EXECUTIVE HEAD OF BRACKETS)
(ASS. TO HEAD OF BRACKETS)
(P.A.R.E.N.T.H.E.S.I.S.)
(BRACKETS)
(PLEASE KNOCK)

Eventually cut to interior of above conference room. Plenty of drink, bits of zebra, and the head (literally) of Light Entertainment in suitably labelled drawer of filing cabinet.

SENIOR EXECUTIVE . . . that's all very well, but I have to remind you that we are, after all, only one slice of the cake. We simply can't get a bigger budget.

ASSISTANT Budgie?

SENIOR EXECUTIVE No, he left I think.

CONTROLLER Wouldn't mind a bit of cake. Umm, chocolate cake. Delicious.

ASSISTANT My auntie had a budgie, amusing little chap. Used to stick his head in a bell. Unusual name . . . What did she call him . . . Mr Tweet? Joey? Xerxes?

SENIOR EXECUTIVE Well anyway, we just haven't got any more money.

EXECUTIVE We could repeat the repeats.

ASSISTANT What, repeat the repeats of the repeats?

EXECUTIVE Yes. And then repeat them.

SENIOR EXECUTIVE *(Looking at watch)* Good lord, the bar's open!

All scramble madly to their feet.

SENIOR EXECUTIVE Oh, sorry, I was looking at the little hand that goes around very fast.

ALL Damn. Blast.

They sit down reluctantly.

EXECUTIVE I'VE GOT IT!

CONTROLLER What, the cake?

EXECUTIVE No no, not the cake. Why don't we retitle the repeats?

ASSISTANT What, give them different names?

SENIOR EXECUTIVE Wouldn't that mean re-shooting the titles?

CONTROLLER Well, it's cheap enough.

ASSISTANT Bloody good idea!

SENIOR EXECUTIVE Brilliant! Old Joe Public hasn't a clue what he's watching anyway.

ASSISTANT Quite!

CONTROLLER Exactly!

SENIOR EXECUTIVE We need names then. Any suggestions?

ASSISTANT How about 'And Mother Makes One More'?

SENIOR EXECUTIVE Quite like that.

CONTROLLER 'Dad's Navy'?

SENIOR EXECUTIVE Nearly nearly . . .

EXECUTIVE 'Doctor At Bee'!

ALL What!?

There is a knock at the door.

CONTROLLER Someone's knocking at the door.

SENIOR EXECUTIVE Not bad. A bit long though.

ASSISTANT Yes, too long . . .

EXECUTIVE 'I Married Lucy'!

SENIOR EXECUTIVE Hasn't that been done?

EXECUTIVE Yes, but a long time ago.

ASSISTANT 'Doctor At Tree'!

Another more persistent knock at the door.

CONTROLLER Listen, someone is actually knocking at the door.

SENIOR EXECUTIVE No no, that's even longer!

ASSISTANT 'I Married A Tree'?

SENIOR EXECUTIVE 'And Mother Makes Tree' . . . No no . . .

EXECUTIVE 'Doctor At Cake'!

Continuous knocking at door.

CONTROLLER Look! I'm trying to impress upon you the fact that someone is actually knocking on the door!!

SENIOR EXECUTIVE That's ridiculous. Half the programme gone, stop lengthening it.

EXECUTIVE *(Desperate)* 'I Married A Cake'!!!

ASSISTANT *(Over-excited)* 'I Married Three Rabbit Jelly Moulds'!!!

SENIOR EXECUTIVE Prefer cake. Especially chocky cake . . .

CONTROLLER Christ! Look, you stupid perverts, don't you bleedin' realize there is someone or something outside this sodding door trying to attract your attention??!!

SENIOR EXECUTIVE *(Shaking head)* Never get that past the censor . . .

The door breaks in. Enter a Neo-Fascist-looking SECURITY MAN *in a wheelchair with an Oriental sword through his head.*

SENIOR EXECUTIVE You're supposed to knock!

SECURITY MAN Sorry sir, but there's trouble at Studio Five.

ASSISTANT You're security aren't you?

SECURITY MAN Yes sir.

ASSISTANT Well, *you're* not allowed to suggest programme titles!

CONTROLLER I AM! I've been working in Light Entertainment, brackets, L.E., for the past 25 cakes – years – and I'm fed up with chocolate – pompous asses like you who don't doughnut, mmmm, doughnut, jam in the middle . . . Sugary fingers . . . chocky . . . chocky . . . chocky . . . chocky . . .

SECURITY MAN There *is* trouble at Studio Five, sir.

SENIOR EXECUTIVE *(Unable to conceal his contempt for the* SECURITY MAN*)* Never did like cripples. Too disturbing.

CONTROLLER: . . . chocky fudge . . . chocky fudge, chocky fudge . . .

ASSISTANT Had an aunt with a parrot . . . What was its name? Polly? Ramses? Crippin? No – Cripple! That's it! Cripple. Only had one wing, half a beak, no feathers. Died of course. She trod on it. Awful noise. It went SQUARRGGHHHHHHHH!

EXECUTIVE What?

ASSISTANT: No, it went SQUARRRRGGGGHHHHHH!!

EXECUTIVE: Blind people are worse. Tapping you on the leg with their sticks . . . Haven't a clue . . .

SENIOR EXECUTIVE No no, cripples are worse, damned wheelchairs, they only do it to attract attention. Hang dog expressions. Eugh!

EXECUTIVE I dunno . . . I should know, the wife's in an iron lung.

ASSISTANT 'I Married An Iron Lung'!

EXECUTIVE No, *I* married an iron lung . . .

SENIOR EXECUTIVE 'And Mother Makes Iron Lung'? No . . .

CONTROLLER 'Doctor In Iron Lung'! Chocky fudge, chocky fudge . . .

SECURITY MAN Where's the comedy in that?

Slight pause. Then all set about him violently.

Cut to Studio Five. The original Light Entertainment set seen on the monitoring screens in the Production Suite. There is a DIRECTOR, PRODUCER, P.A. (with big ones). Large quantities of drink and a VISION MIXER on a drip-feed who has one horn out of the side of his head. We hear laughter and applause and pan into one of the monitors. We see a large Les Dawson-shaped COMEDIAN nearing the end of his act.

COMEDIAN *(Out of applause)* Thank you . . . thank you . . . But seriously though, I know lots of comedians make jokes about their mothers-in-law, but mine . . . mine . . . She's like a million dollars. All green and crinkly and – thank you . . . thank you . . .

Cut to Production Suite.

DIRECTOR Cue laughter and applause . . .

'Applause' button is pressed.

DIRECTOR . . . up on 3 . . . *(Holding out empty glass)* Make it a big one this time please.

Cut back to studio. The COMEDIAN takes a bow and goes off. On comes the HOST, grinning and applauding, gesturing towards the COMEDIAN. He then waves his hands to settle the 'audience'.

Cut to Production Studio.

DIRECTOR Fade applause . . . No ice . . .

The P.A. is stuffing herself with peanuts at a terrific rate. Without looking, she drops two ice cubes into the DIRECTOR's glass.

Cut to studio.

HOST You know, one of the nicest things about working in Show Business is that you get the chance to meet people who really are like a million dollars and . . . er . . . and er . . . and . . . er . . .

Cut to TWO MEN holding enormous cue cards. One of them gestures to the other, suggesting that the HOST now read the card next to his.

HOST ... Oh! My next guests are no exception ...

DIRECTOR (O.S.) Stand by applause ...

HOST ... Roger Green and Lance Crinkley!

Enter GREEN *and* CRINKLEY, *both have bright green Afro wigs on. An Everly Brothers-type duo. They go into song. As the song plays we intercut Production Suite scenes.*

PRODUCER There's something wrong with that link.

DIRECTOR Cut to 4 ...

P.A. *(Through mouth full of nuts)* Soda?

DIRECTOR Just a dash ... Up on 3 ...

P.A. *gives* DIRECTOR *a dash of soda and places the siphon on the 'Applause' button. An immediate burst of laughter and applause interrupts but does not stop the song.*

DIRECTOR Back to 2 ... *(Tastes drink)* Just a dash more in there I think ... Zoom 3 ...

P.A. *takes soda siphon off button, fills* DIRECTOR'S *glass to overflowing and returns to her nuts.*

DIRECTOR Up on 4 ... *(Drains glass)* Make it a large one this time ...

PRODUCER *(To unseen assistant)* Another crate ...

P.A. Are there any more nuts?

PRODUCER *(Pointing)* Over there ...

P.A. *reaches for the nuts with some effort and in doing so, one of her large boobs makes contact with 'Applause' button. Laughter and applause until she manages to get the nuts. Meanwhile, the singers are trying not to look too worried. We see some of the* AUDIENCE *leaving.*

DIRECTOR Cut to 7 ...

VISION MIXER We haven't got a 7!

DIRECTOR 5?

VISION MIXER *nods.*

DIRECTOR Cut to 5 ... Up on 2 ... Down on 3 ... Refill ...

Enter the CONTROLLER, *the 'cake loony', complete with sun helmet.*

CONTROLLER Nobody move! Not a muscle . . . Don't panic . . .
There's nothing to worry about . . .

PRODUCER *(To* P.A.*)* I can't catch his drift . . .

DIRECTOR Up on 3 . . . Down on 2 . . .

CONTROLLER There's a snake in the box!

P.A. A snake?!

*She gives a little squeal and scrambles on to the control console, frequently
treading on and off the 'Applause' button. This goes on for the rest of
the scene, as do shots of the* SINGERS *and more and more* AUDIENCE
leaving.

CONTROLLER Yes . . . Black Mamba . . . A Black Mamba! *(Aside)*
That's not a bad title . . .

PRODUCER Black Mamba?

CONTROLLER Hold still everybody . . . *(Calling)* Get the forked stick!
Get the forked stick!

PRODUCER The forked stick?

DIRECTOR Cue forked stick . . .

VISION MIXER There isn't one.

CONTROLLER Should be! Every control suite should have one.
Ordered 'em myself. When I was in Malaysia every room had a
forked stick . . . Jab 'em back of the neck . . . Flap flap flap flap
flap . . . Stamp on their heads. No problem.

PRODUCER But there isn't a snake!

CONTROLLER *(Slight pause)* This is Five, isn't it?

PRODUCER Yes, but there is *no* snake.

CONTROLLER Where? Chocolate, is it?

PRODUCER What?

CONTROLLER The cake.

PRODUCER Snake, not cake!

CONTROLLER *(Smacking his lips)* Chocolate, is it?

DIRECTOR What's he on about?

PRODUCER Sssh! Yes, quite right, there is a cake. Yes, cake's the word. Cake by name, cake by nature. Ha ha! Nothing like a good cake . . .

CONTROLLER Good . . . good. Right, carry on. Yes . . . well done.

DIRECTOR What bloody cake?

CONTROLLER *(To Director)* Cake's fine, cut out bloody. Can't have 'bloody' after the news. Right then . . . good . . . good . . . Tip top. Keep it up. *(To P.A.)* Don't forget the cake. Good lord! They *are* large, aren't they? Carry on.

The SINGERS *bravely finish their song to no* AUDIENCE *at all. Cut to* PEPPERPOTS *at home watching TV. One is knitting a bodice with some difficulty round a dead lobster. The other holds a sub-machine gun.*

MRS SMOKER Rubbish! Absolute rubbish!

MRS NON-SMOKER Yes, same old stuff. I don't know why we watch it.

MRS SMOKER We don't.

MRS NON-SMOKER We do, we just have been.

MRS SMOKER I wasn't watching it.

MRS NON-SMOKER Yes you were!

MRS SMOKER I wasn't.

MRS NON-SMOKER You were!

MRS SMOKER I wasn't. I was watching you watching it.

MRS NON-SMOKER *(Pause)* I wasn't watching it, I was merely staring blankly into space, trying to achieve Alpha-Rhythms.

MRS SMOKER Alpha what?

MRS NON-SMOKER Alpha-Rhythms. Brain waves. Like that nice Mr Einstein used to have. He used to stare at nothing at all for hours and hours on end. Hours and hours on end. Stare stare stare. Hours and hours and hours on end.

MRS SMOKER What good did that do?

MRS NON-SMOKER What *good* did that do? He only invented *air*!

MRS SMOKER Air????

MRS NON-SMOKER Yes, the air you breathe.

MRS SMOKER No he didn't.

MRS NON-SMOKER: *(After a pause)* Ooh! No, sorry, he invented Africa.

MRS SMOKER You can't invent *Africa*! Nobody can. It's just *there*!

*A NEGRO'S HEAD in tribal gear pops up from behind sideboard or
    something suitable.*

NEGRO'S HEAD Good evening ladies . . .

MRS NON-SMOKER Urgh! Get off!

*She lets go a rapid burst of machine gun fire in the general direction of
    the African, who ducks. A moment's pause until she's sure he won't
    pop up again.*

MRS NON-SMOKER Anyway, he was a clever man.

MRS SMOKER Who was?

MRS NON-SMOKER EINSTEIN!

MRS SMOKER Well, if he was so bleedin' clever, why didn't he
    invent a Theory of Relativity?

MRS NON-SMOKER There's no future in it.

MRS SMOKER I suppose not. Let's try the other side.

MRS NON-SMOKER *(Vaguely)* No . . .

She gets up and switches the channel on the TV set.

The Sitcoms

A Negro gardener, COLCHESTER, is hosing the lawn in front of a neat all-American suburban house. Patriotic/wah-wah doorbell is rung by a MAN in a neat suit. The door is opened by LUCY SITCOM, a kooky blonde with 'convincing' corkscrew nose. The gardener jumps to attention and salutes the doorbell.

MAN Hello . . . Mrs Lucy Sitcom?

She embraces him eagerly.

LUCY Hello darling, you're home early. I didn't expect you so soon. There's absolutely nothing suspicious going on!!!

MAN I'm not your husband.

LUCY Oh no, that's odd. I *felt* guilty . . . Well, what do you want?

MAN I'm collecting for the Church of . . . Christ Almighty—

LUCY What's the matter?

MAN —You're standing on my foot!

LUCY No I'm not.

MAN No no, the Church of Christ Almighty You're Standing On My Foot. That's the name of our worldwide organization. It's a kind of Anabaptist thought-combining orthodoxy blinkered by the chapel of the money of Our Lord The Impossible. But it's mainly fascist.

LUCY Well, it certainly sounds like a good cause to me. Do you take credit cards?

MAN Of course.

LUCY Just a moment then . . .

She goes into house and returns with a suitcase full of credit cards and tosses it to him.

LUCY Here you are.

MAN Why, thank you ma'am, you're more than stupid.

LUCY My pleasure. *(As he leaves)* What a nice man . . .

She wriggles her corkscrew nose and the MAN *becomes a Nazi/Easy Rider complete with impressive motorbike.*

MAN Wow! Far out! This is outtasite! Too much! This is really keen, what I always wanted. Hello yellow brick road!

He roars off down the garden path. As he goes so we see COLCHESTER *who is 'whited-up', all except for around his mouth. He drops his salute only to find that his trousers are bulging full of water.*

LUCY Oh Colchester!

COLCHESTER Yessum?

LUCY I'm going back inside.

COLCHESTER Yessum. *(Eyes trousers)* Water . . . N . . . muhpants! Catfish a-jumpin'! Eyeballs-a-rollin'! Mmm, yessum . . . *(She goes in)* White trash.

Cut to: INTERIOR *of modern kitchen/dining lounge, an enormous room full of coffee percolators, all shapes and sizes, all on the boil.*

LUCY Now let me see . . . What was I doing? Oh yes! I must call Lucy Spinoff who lives next door and who also does all kinds of kooky scenes loosely based on misunderstandings that eventually turn out okay for everyone concerned.

She picks up the phone.

LUCY Hello, Lucy? Hi, this is Lucy. I'm fine. Listen, I was just making some coffee and I wondered if you'd care to come round and do a bit of kooky dialogue . . . Fine. Ah, tootle toot!

She hangs up the phone and wriggles her nose. LUCY SPINOFF *appears instantly.*

LUCY SPINOFF Hi Lucy! *(To camera)* Hi based on misunderstandings which eventually turn out okay for everyone concerned – but it's slightly less fascist. *(To Lucy)* Say Lucy, I—

LUCY Yes, Lucy?

LUCY SPINOFF Do you have a cup of coffee? I'm fresh out.

LUCY Sure Lucy, I've got one right here.

LUCY SPINOFF Could you fix it for me? Boy, am I pooped.

LUCY Sure, I'll fix it right now.

LUCY SPINOFF I sure fixed a beautiful bar-b-que on the patio last night.

LUCY Oh Lucy, what did you fix?

LUCY SPINOFF I fixed lobster tail and T-bone steak, Southern-style meatloaf with thousand island dressing.

LUCY A la mode?

LUCY SPINOFF A la mode! Already, she's asking me?

SFX: Canned laughter/doorbell

JOHN SITCOM enters, Lucy's all-American USAF uniform-wearing husband.

JOHN Hello darling – I'm home!

He comes in and falls over. More canned laughter. We see a laughter machine, rather like a computer with tapes.

JOHN Oh hi Lucy, hi Lucy . . . (To machines) Hi Lucy.

The machine responds with a twitch of its tape reels.

JOHN Hi everybody, I'm John Sitcom, the white Anglo-Saxon Protestant in this series, and only slightly fascist. Where's Junior?

LUCY Oh he's out mugging with his wino buddies.

JOHN How about that boy!

SFX: Canned laughter

LUCY By the way darling, Mr Ulcer phoned.

JOHN Mr Ulcer? What did he say?

LUCY He said he can't come to dinner tonight.

LUCY SPINOFF So who's Mr Ulcer?

LUCY He's John's boss and also president of the WASP Club.

JOHN And now he's not coming! *(Pause)* So how are we going to get into any tight spots tonight?

LUCY SPINOFF Oh-oh, I heard all this before, I'm going.

She exits to canned laughter.

JOHN He was supposed to be bringing Mr Milkdiet, our biggest client, the one whose account we can't afford to lose. All kinds of things could have gone wrong. Oh why'd this have to happen? Just when we were all set for an evening of hilarity . . .

LUCY Don't worry darling, I've invited Doctor Atbee and some of his friends. I thought if we couldn't have the president of the WASP Club and your most important client, Doctor Atbee was the obvious second choice.

JOHN *(Double-takes)* You invited Doctor Atbee? Oh no – he's much too bizarre for our network audience!

SFX: Doorbell

LUCY Oh no, that must be him now! What'll I do? I look such a mess, my hair . . . My face . . . This dress . . . What'll I do?

JOHN Use your nose!

LUCY Of course!

She twitches her nose. JOHN is suddenly wearing her dress while she has turned into a fridge wearing USAF uniform.

JOHN Oh no, not that icebox routine again . . .

LUCY *(As fridge)* That's better!

SFX: Canned laughter/doorbell

DOCTOR ATBEE enters. He is half Doctor/white coat stethoscope etc and half bee/large bee abdomen.

ATBEE Hi, the door was open so I just came right in.

He falls over. Canned laughter.

ATBEE Oops, sorry! Fell over a bedpan!

SFX: Enormous laugh and we see tapes on laughter machine go round very fast indeed.

JOHN No you didn't!

ATBEE Well, it got a laugh. BEDPAN!

SFX: More laughter

JOHN What, just by saying 'bedpan'?

SFX: Enormous laughter. Smoke comes out of the machine.

ATBEE Yes – bedpan!

SFX: Laughter

ATBEE See? Never fails. Bedpan!

SFX: Laughter

ATBEE BEDPAN!!!

SFX: Laughter. More and more smoke comes out of the machine, filling the room. The fridge starts singing 'Green Fields of Summer'.

ATBEE Go on, you try it.

JOHN Bedpan.

SFX: Enormous cackle from the machine.

JOHN It works! Bedpan! Bedpan! Bedpan!

The machine explodes.

LUCY *(Still as the fridge)* Oh gosh – the machine exploded! Oh Jesus! No – I said gosh! Oh gosh, I said Jesus! We'll be taken off the air!

An ENGLISH BUS CONDUCTOR enters.

CONDUCTOR Have you been saying bedpan? We usually just say 'po' and laugh like this all the time – (Goes into raucous laughter)

ATBEE is face-to-face with wreck of the machine, repeating 'bedpan' at it. It smokes and does nothing.

LUCY *(As fridge)* What'll we do?

JOHN Might as well watch television.

He switches on the TV and all sit around it. On the TV a Cliff Richard-type, CHRISTIAN PENGUIN, is finishing a song: 'Rampage'. His best friend, PIGGY, is with him as is a GIRL, and his manager, BRAINS.

PIGGY Wow, that was a great song, Christian.

GIRL Yeah, like really great.

CHRISTIAN Aw shucks, c'mon.

BRAINS No, no it works. It'll be just fine for the old people's charity hop we've organized for the old people tonight.

PIGGY The what?

BRAINS You know, Piggy, the party we're throwing to collect money for old people.

PIGGY Oh yeah, check. Will there be any food?

ALL HAHAHAHAHAHA!

CHRISTIAN C'mon, Piggy, don't you think of anything but food? Don't you want to help other people, especially the old folks?

PIGGY Sure, but how'm I supposed to do that on an empty stomach?

SFX: *Canned laughter*

BRAINS Say, that sounds like a great title for a song!

CHRISTIAN Yeah . . . wait a minute. *(Starts to hum)* Yeah, I think I've got it . . . Two, three *(Sings)* 'How can a guy do that on an empty stomach . . .'

BRAINS No, that's awful.

CHRISTIAN Gee, then I don't think I can go through with the show.

GIRL But Christian, you've got to! You can't let down the old folks!

CHRISTIAN No, if I go out there tonight I can't help feeling the name of Christian Penguin will become the laughing stock of Benidorm. If tonight is a failure Mr Nastyperson, the club owner, will tear up our contract and that would mean the end of our working holiday.

Cut back to LUCY *and* JOHN *and* ATBEE.

JOHN That's the way to do it . . .

LUCY Yes, his show is so much better than ours.

Back to CHRISTIAN.

BRAINS You know what you need?

CHRISTIAN What?

BRAINS A steady girl.

CHRISTIAN Oh. No, I'm strictly a 'bachelor boy'.

BRAINS Now *that's* a great idea for a song!

CHRISTIAN Listen Brains, I want the girl that I marry to be, well, be more like a feller. No! Whatever made me say that? I mean more like a . . . No, I want the girl that I marry to be more like a . . . Well, a kind of a sort of a . . . With a bit of a . . . Yeah, a feller.

SFX: *Canned laughter*

The GIRL *runs out of the room in tears.*

BRAINS This is terrible! If this gets out . . . Why, who'd buy your records? You'd be finished! Your career in ruins! Damn you Christian Penguin!

Back to LUCY *and* JOHN *and* ATBEE. *They whistle and applaud.*

LUCY Wow! What a complication!

JOHN Makes our show look like a pile of donkey doos!

Back to CHRISTIAN.

CHRISTIAN Okay, you win. Piggy, go out and find me a steady girl. Preferably upper-class, unintelligent, and not too demanding – and not a word to Manuel.

SFX: *Canned laughter*

PIGGY Aw, why me, Chris?

CHRISTIAN Because that's what I pay you for. Now get!

PIGGY Consider it done!

PIGGY *exits.*

BRAINS Okay, but what about the show tonight? You still haven't rehearsed your big hit, 'Get 'Em Off Baby Give It To Me Now'.

CHRISTIAN You're right, Brains. Two, three, four . . . *(Sings)*
Get 'em off baby . . .
Give it to me now . . .
I'm throbbin' like a whippoorwill

Come on you stupid cow.
Love is a piston engine
You're a field I'm gonna plough
Get 'em off baby . . .
Give it to me now!'

Cut to A NEWSREADER on TV.

NEWSREADER Here is a news flash. The Spanish holiday resort of
Benidorm has been the scene of a number of mystery deaths.
All of the victims appeared to have suffered from animal bites.
Although the possibility of rabies has been vehemently denied
by the Spanish authorities, the Home Office advises travellers
and holidaymakers to avoid the area as the present outbreak of
cholera, strongly denied by the Spanish authorities, has officially
been declared by the WHO as an uncontrolled epidemic.

Cut to LUCY, JOHN and ATBEE who are still watching TV.

LUCY That was a downer.

ATBEE Yes, that wasn't a very good link.

JOHN No, rotten. Not as good as that nice Petula Clark.

ATBEE Well, she has it all written down for her.

JOHN No she doesn't, that's Cilla Black.

ATBEE Oh yes . . .

LUCY You don't get Sonny and Cher or Tom Jones coming out
with 'and now, "Downtown"' just like that, just off the cuff.
It's all written down on huge boards. *(Points)* Like that.

JOHN What does it say?

LUCY What you just said.

ATBEE What a strange means of communication.

LUCY That's written down too. It's all a fantasy world.

JOHN What is?

LUCY Television. They don't answer when you talk to them.

ATBEE Who doesn't?

LUCY *(Points to TV)* Them. The people on television.

JOHN I know, they're so wrapped up in themselves . . .

ATBEE I know. The other day I was watching TV and I asked that nice Dinah Shore if she'd like a cup of coffee. No response at all. Not so much as a 'Not just now, thank you.'

LUCY They've got no time for the general public.

JOHN I agree. When I offered Johnny Carson a macaroon the other night he just carried on speaking to Ann-Margret as though I wasn't even there!

LUCY Well, you weren't there, dear.

JOHN That's not the point. *He* was there!

ATBEE People on television treat the public like idiots.

LUCY Well, we *are* idiots.

JOHN No we're not!

LUCY I am.

JOHN How do you know you're an idiot?

LUCY I can prove it.

Go into a SHORT FILM. *She comes out of a door in a tree and runs head first into a wall several times. She pulls someone out of a taxi while at a traffic light. Takes a slice of bread from her handbag and throws it some distance down the road telling the driver to 'follow that toast!' then gets out and throws it a bit further. Sequence is repeated several times, speeded up. She makes occasional funny faces in strange costumes in various locations. Different parts of her body explode. She throws a passing cyclist into a canal. Goes into a bank to cash a cheque. 'How would you like it, Madame?' 'Inner tubes, please.' She stuffs large quantities of inner tubes into her handbag. Cut back to living room.*

LUCY There, are you convinced?

JOHN That was all worked out beforehand and filmed!

LUCY Just because it was on film doesn't mean it wasn't zany or madcap, or that I'm not an idiot.

ATBEE Yes it does. Simply because of the physical time it takes to set up a whacky situation in front of the camera. The laws governing the whole medium means that the action has to be predetermined. You have merely offered a conscious attempt at representing lunacy which can not be regarded as proof of being an idiot. In fact, just the opposite.

COLCHESTER *enters, his trousers still bulging full of water.*

COLCHESTER Step-N-fetch-it! Lordy-lordy-lordy! Laws-a-mercy, I done *gots* to let dis here water outtamuhdadblamedpants!

He unzips and sprays them all with water. A pause. They laugh.

JOHN Colchester – you silly Negro!

SFX: *End theme music/applause*

LUCY, JOHN, COLCHESTER *and* ATBEE *walk arm-in-arm, theatrical style, towards the unseen audience and bow. Run credits.*

Out of the Trees

Episode Two

Teleplay by Graham Chapman with David Yallop

Opens. Screen shows view through binocular viewer. We are supposedly looking at a penny peep show at the seaside. The scene is that of a lonely idyllic beach setting. A COUPLE meet and kiss and embrace. The scene gets very torrid very quickly and as blatantly sexual as possible.

KEMP (V.O.) Cor, look at that . . . phew, you should see this . . .

The couple start to undress and it gets very wicked and licentious, but just as they are about to reveal all and be extremely naughty there is a sudden CLUNK! and the screen goes dark.

KEMP (V.O.) Oh damn – quick, have you got another ten pence? Just as we were getting to the good bit.

MICHAEL EDWARDS *(Noises of him fumbling for change)* Er, no. I've got a fifty and a five and a couple of twos – no that's all.

KEMP (V.O.) Oh damn, just as I was getting all worked up. Oh well.

Camera pulls back from viewer as KEMP stands up. We see that the scene he was watching through the viewer is in fact happening right in front of them. They are on the beach and the couple are now completely undressed but sufficiently entwined to hide the very naughty bits. KEMP and EDWARDS ignore them completely and walk away. The couple are rather disappointed not to be noticed.

KEMP Time, you see, is an interesting phenomenon . . .

EDWARDS Really?

Graham in the late 1940s. Even at this age you could tell he was going to be trouble.

Graham (centre) looking bored and David Sherlock (second from left) at a party at their flat in Belsize Park, 1968. Taken just hours before the 'Severance of a Peony Incident'.

Graham in an early publicity photo, circa 1966–7.

Graham, John Cleese, Marty Feldman and Tim Brooke-Taylor demonstrate why ballroom dancing is a lost art. From *At Last the 1948 Show*, 1967–8.

A gathering of writers and performers circa 1967–8 including, from left, John Cleese, Tim Brooke-Taylor, Jo Kendall (in tweed suit), Dick Vosburgh (in beard), Barry Cryer (leaning over desk), Graham and Marty Feldman.

On the set of
Monty Python's Flying Circus
in the early 1970s.

Right. David Jason and Graham
on the set of *The Odd Job* in the
mid-1970s. The movie would prove
to be both a critical and artistic
disappointment as well as a
financial hardship for Graham.

Top. From left: Terry Jones, Graham and Michael Palin during a *Python* visit to New York City in the mid-1970s.

Middle. Graham (centre) with some friends: Robert DeNiro (left) and Harry Nilsson (second from right) in Los Angeles, early 1980s.

Bottom. From left: Harry Nilsson, Graham, Ringo Starr and Graham's manager Major Sloane in London in the mid-70s.

Top. David Sherlock and one of their beloved beagles enjoy a little puppy/master time in London in the late 1970s.

Middle. John Tomiczek, Graham and David's adopted son, taken sometime during the early 1980s.

Bottom. Graham poses by an aeroplane-on-skis in St Moritz during the Dangerous Sports Club's Winter Sports in 1985.

Graham captured live
in Atlanta during a tour of
US college campuses in 1988.
This was one of his last
public performances.

KEMP Yes, as my mother always used to say . . . Oh yes, I remember she used to put me on her knee in the evening and bounce me up and down and say 'Oootchicoo Kempypoo, who's got a little icky icky tum tum then?' And then she'd say 'Time is a limited stretch or space of continued existencipoo.' And then went on to say 'Or, the period through which an action, condition, or state continues yeauhhh.'

EDWARDS Yeauhhh?

KEMP Wet nappy, you see.

EDWARDS How very human.

Cut to what we later discover to be a sea wall. The opening credit for Out of the Trees is painted on it. Camera pulls back to see them walking along the sea wall.

EDWARDS What did your father do?

KEMP He used to go . . . *(Does a strange gesture and squawks very loudly)*

EDWARDS Was that his job?

KEMP Well, he thought so – he used to do it from nine to five. Out of his tree, he was. Look, I've got this recording of him which will show you.

KEMP turns on a tape recorder for a few seconds. There is dead silence.

EDWARDS But that was just silence.

KEMP Yes, I had it recorded posthumously – but it does show that he was completely mad.

EDWARDS Does it?

KEMP Oh yes.

EDWARDS Play it again.

KEMP Alright.

He plays the silent bit again.

EDWARDS Oh yes, I see what you mean.

Meanwhile, the tape keeps running and we hear a bit of PARTY NOISE.

VOICE 1 (V.O.) I thought that was a really super demonstration.

VOICE 2 (V.O.) Oh yes, quite the best of the season.

KEMP *turns the tape off.*

EDWARDS Oh, what was that?

KEMP Just a recording I made at a party. I often do that. It's amazing what people say when they haven't got anything to say.

EDWARDS Play a bit more.

KEMP Alright.

KEMP *rewinds the tape and plays it again.*

VOICE 1 (V.O.) I thought that was a really super demonstration.

VOICE 2 (V.O.) Oh yes, quite the best of the season.

At this point we cut to the actual party. There are lots (or at least a few) obviously rich TRENDY PEOPLE standing around drinking cocktails in a trendy apartment furnished with lots of glass, stainless steel and leather. Above a table covered with expensive-looking bottles of spirits, is a silk screen print of Lenin in a stainless steel frame. Ditto elsewhere, prints of Chairman Mao, Ho Chi Minh, Vanessa Redgrave (and one of Margaret Thatcher crossed out). Conversation continues . . .

VOICE 1 Not so much style as the abortion rally, but such a super solidarity.

VOICE 3 Do you always come to these do's afterwards?

VOICE 2 Oh yes, I never miss out on the Après March.

VOICE 1 Yes, the nice thing about having a social conscience is it gives you such a warm glow when you get pissed afterwards.

VOICE 3 *(Pointing to someone smoking a pipe)* Who's that?

VOICE 1 I don't know, but he's not saying anything so he must be intelligent.

VOICE 3 Anyway, yes, social conscience, one mustn't forget the starving Williams.

VOICE 1 Williams? Is he starving?

VOICE 3 Oh yes, apparently. I heard something about it on the radio – at least I think that's what I heard.

VOICE 2 Did you hear that Patrick has sent a crate of Château Latour to Bangladesh?

VOICE 1 Oh he's awfully human . . .

Cut back to KEMP *and* EDWARDS.

EDWARDS Good God! Have you got any other party tapes?

KEMP Oh yes, this is one of my favourites – there's this appalling woman . . .

Cut to a very middle-class cocktail party. A HENPECKED HUSBAND *and his rather awful* WIFE *approach a* MAN *who is standing on his own.*

WIFE Good Lord, haven't you grown!

MAN No.

WIFE But you're putting on a bit of weight.

MAN No.

WIFE Hair's a bit longer?

MAN No.

WIFE Shorter?

MAN No.

WIFE Oh . . .

MAN *(Helpfully)* I've had my left breast off.

Camera pulls back to reveal this is true.

WIFE I thought you'd changed!

Satisfied, she wanders off dragging her husband with her.

HUSBAND I preferred him as a woman.

WIFE Nice amputation though.

They go up to a man who as it happens is a SOLICITOR.

WIFE Hello! How *are* you?

The SOLICITOR *is baffled because he has obviously never met her before.*

SOLICITOR I'm sorry, I don't think I er . . .

WIFE *(Brightly)* Don't apologize to us!

SOLICITOR I'm sorry I don't follow . . .

WIFE Oh, bet you do, what with all these lovely girls around!

SOLICITOR I beg your pardon, I don't think I've had the pleasure . . .

WIFE *(Yowling with laughter at her own* double entendres*)* Oh, I'm sure you haven't! A grown man like you . . .

The SOLICITOR, *in a sudden fury, hits her to the ground.*

HUSBAND Sorry about that.

SOLICITOR Oh, not at all.

HUSBAND She had it coming.

WIFE *(Rolling on the floor with hysterical laughter)* Yes! Twice in the car!

They both kick her.

WIFE Oh! Bang bang!

The SOLICITOR *takes out a gun and shoots her.*

HUSBAND Oh, that's very brave of you. Won't there be terrible legal problems?

SOLICITOR No, I'm a solicitor actually.

HUSBAND That must be terribly tricky what with all those exams and things.

SOLICITOR No, you see I'm actually fairly intelligent – look, I am terribly sorry about your wife.

HUSBAND Oh, not at all.

SOLICITOR No, really I am, it's just that I can't stand that terrible feeble-minded sort of joke – all those fat comedians on television making smutty little jokes about tits and bums – I mean, if they actually had anything to *say* about sex I'd be prepared to listen. I can't stand it. I am going on a bit. Sorry.

Look, your wife and everything . . . must have seemed awfully rude.

HUSBAND Oh, don't give it a mensh, have that one on me.

SOLICITOR Careful!

HUSBAND Anyway, solicitor eh? That's very interesting actually, perhaps I shouldn't bore you with it here, off-duty and all that, but it's our garden fence, we've got a bit of a problem you see . . .

The SOLICITOR registers instant boredom.

SOLICITOR Really . . . ?

HUSBAND Yes. You see, the neighbour on our right refuses to mend the fence, and it's not our fence it's his fence . . . Only you see, the dog keeps on getting through and he—

SOLICITOR And the other thing I can't stand is people who expect me to dole out free legal advice.

HUSBAND What's that you say, squire? Come again?

The SOLICITOR shoots him. Cut to a different group at the same party. A MOUSEY MAN and his WIFE are talking to a SCRIPTWRITER.

MAN Oh, so you're a scriptwriter are you? That must be interesting – what, sort of plays and things?

WRITER No, comedy mostly.

MAN Oh, jokes and that? Where do you get all your ideas from? Do you think of them yourself?

WRITER No, the dog does most of it. It's specially trained to think up jokes.

MAN Really?

WRITER Yes, it came from a funny kennel.

MAN Well tell us one then . . .

WRITER Woof.

The MAN titters rather stupidly then whispers aside to his WIFE.

MAN I didn't think that was very funny.

WIFE No.

MAN *(To Scriptwriter)* Well, thank you very much, look forward to seeing your name on the box then, bye.

The SOLICITOR *comes up to the* SCRIPTWRITER.

SOLICITOR Excuse me, did I hear you say you were a scriptwriter?

WRITER Yes.

SOLICITOR Ahm, how do you do? I'm Buscombe, solicitor.

WRITER At last, someone intelligent to talk to.

SOLICITOR My thoughts exactly. Comedy I think I heard?

WRITER That's right.

SOLICITOR Have you heard this one?

WRITER I don't like jokes.

SOLICITOR What's black and yellow—

WRITER Please don't.

SOLICITOR No listen, what's black and yellow and dangerous?

WRITER Shark-infested custard.

SOLICITOR Shark-infested custard! Rather amusing don't you think? You can have that one if you like.

WRITER No thank you.

SOLICITOR What's green and hairy and—

WRITER I'm afraid you haven't got much more to say.

SOLICITOR What do you mean?

WRITER Well you see, I wrote this.

SOLICITOR Did you?

WRITER Yes.

SOLICITOR And this?

WRITER Yes.

SOLICITOR Oh .... You left me a long pause there.

WRITER Quite. Then the scriptwriter character, i.e. me, says he
feels it's getting a bit long – which it is, don't you think?

The SOLICITOR *doesn't reply.*

WRITER Oh yes, sorry, no more lines. Then there's this dentist
character who gets so fed-up with people talking to him
professionally at parties he actually brings along his chair and
starts taking out their teeth . . .

*As he says this, a dentist's chair is wheeled across the scene in front of
them.* A DENTIST *is extracting the tooth of a* PARTY GUEST *who still has
a glass of Champagne in one hand and a plate of canapés in the
other, They are followed by a* MAORI WARRIOR *wearing a space helmet
and carrying a pink cricket bat.*

WRITER . . . And that's where I start doodling a bit. Then I get
bored with dialogue and decide to go for something visually
stunning.

Cut immediately to Alpine scene. We see a BODY *falling down the
mountainside. It lands at the bottom and the picture freezes with the
body still there. Camera pulls away to see that the picture is a framed
photograph hanging on the wall of a pub.*

*The pub is mock Olde English type, and is decorated in a misguided
attempt to make it look Chaucerian. It has plastic wooden beams,
plastic straw bales, stuffed sheep for people to sit on. There is a
hatchway with a naked bottom sticking through it as a permanent
exhibit.*

The SERVING WENCHES *would to a trained-eye look mock Tudor, which is
simply ignorance on the part of the brewery. During the scene, which
takes place in the pub, we pick up various different scenes dotted
about the place like 'Nonne's Priest's Lounge', 'Epilogue to the
Merchant's Tale Lounge'. The signs on the lavatory doors are
respectively 'Wives of Bath' and 'Husbands of Bath'. There is a
'shove half a groat' board, a sign advertising 'Collins Cocktail 50p',
and another sign saying 'You don't have to be a manciple to work
here, but if you are it helps.'*

Towards the end we see another sign which says 'The Nothing To Do

With Chaucer At All Bar, twenty-five miles'. There is also a stuffed donkey with a sign saying 'Chaucer's donkey' on it. KEMP and EDWARDS are at the bar being served by the BARMAN.

BARMAN Here you are, two gin and tonics and a pint of keg bitter.

KEMP Thanks.

He tips the beer into the sink behind the bar.

BARMAN What did you do that for?

KEMP I don't like the stuff.

BARMAN Well, why did you order it?

KEMP Just to make the point.

EDWARDS Those beams are made of plastic!

BARMAN Oh, there's real ones underneath.

KEMP and EDWARDS exchange appalled looks. Cut to a coach arriving outside. On the side it has the slogan 'Canterbury Coaches Climited' with each of the C's printed large in a different colour.

Pan up to see pub sign, which has a picture of Geoffrey Chaucer with the caption 'The Chaucer Chinn' underneath. Beneath this is another sign in Gothic script saying 'Parkynge At Reare'. Cut back to KEMP and EDWARDS.

EDWARDS Look at this . . .

He picks up a menu and reads off it.

EDWARDS 'Cream of Miller's Tale Soup, Pardoner's Pâté, Prologue Prawns . . .'

KEMP Yes, 'Vindaloo ala Wife of Bath' and 'He was a verray parfitt gentil knight's Hamburger with Canterbury Croutons and Thousand Island Dressing'.

During the last couple of exchanges the coach tour arrives. The GUIDE has a peaked cap with 'Canterbury Coaches Climited' written on it. He is followed by CLIFFORD ALDISS, TWO LADIES, an AMERICAN COUPLE who are very impressed by the plastic, a YOUNG LADY with very large tits, a YOUNG COUPLE very much in love. The busty lady passes a table where FOUR YOBBOS are sitting.

YOBBO 1 Cor, look at that!

YOBBO 2 Areolae like table mats!

YOBBO 3 Yeah, and the Astley Cooper ligaments – like steel hawsers, they are!

YOBBO 4 Bloody hell, I wouldn't mind getting my hands round those race horse-like vestibula glands!

YOBBO 1 And cop a load of those circuli venosi! Like tinned spaghetti!

YOBBO 2 Yeah, and she's got lactiferous ducts like beer taps!

YOBBO 3 I reckon she's got a mullerian tubicle like the Post Office Tower!

YOBBO 1 And fimbria like . . . like . . . like gardening gloves!

KEMP *(To the 4 Yobbos)* Here, have you seen that girl with the big knockers?

ALL No – where?

KEMP and EDWARDS exchange glances. Cut to the TWO LADIES who have overheard the preceding conversation.

MRS 1 My knockers were bigger than that when I was fourteen.

MRS 2 When I was only ten I had to have mine strapped down to stop them incommoding passers-by.

MRS 1 When I was not quite six and a half I had to have a team of pall-bearers to carry my breasts to infant school.

MRS 2 Before I was even nought my tits were so large that my mother had to spend her entire confinement in the Albert Hall.

MRS 1 Listen . . . When I was just an embryo one single nipple of mine was so huge I couldn't even be born.

MRS 2 Even the twinkle in my father's eyes were such enormous nipples that he had to wear a bra round his eyes – so he missed my mother completely and I was never even conceived.

Cut to KEMP and EDWARDS.

KEMP *(Holding his shirt open)* See, bet my chest is hairier than yours.

EDWARDS *(Holding his shirt open)* Oh, yes, so it is. End of argument.

KEMP Quite.

They return to the bar next to the YOUNG COUPLE.

YOUNG MAN Would you like a drink, darling?

GIRL Oh thank you.

An ADMAN is standing next to them. He is dripping wet.

ADMAN Let *me* get them.

YOUNG MAN You're soaking wet.

ADMAN Oh, you noticed – it's all part of our campaign to launch our new product.

YOUNG MAN What are you talking about?

ADMAN *(Very theatrically)* 'The drinks are on me!' I'm covered in it. Get it? You see, because I'm covered in the product, 'The Drinks Are On Me!' Ha ha ha.

People around exchange glances.

ADMAN So . . . pints of Adam's Ale all around!

People flock round as the bar staff rapidly produce pints of water. They look surprised, then taste it and register disappointment.

GIRL It's water.

ADMAN *(Gleefully)* Yes it is!

ALL Oh . . .

ADMAN It contains nothing but health-giving halogens and some water-flavouring additives.

YOUNG MAN So it's just tap water?

ADMAN That's the whole point. Look, it's not as fizzy as keg beer, it doesn't contain all those nasty artificial hop additives – it's a bit more expensive than keg beer . . .

YOUNG MAN But there's no alcohol in it.

ADMAN No, but if you drink enough of it you still fall over and throw-up as you do on ordinary beer.

GIRL But will people want it?

ADMAN They will when you tell them they do. I can see it now, millions of people chanting 'What we want is water!'

GIRL I can't see people going for it.

ADMAN Ah, but they will – for a start, anyone over the age of nought can drink it. It's death-preventing—

GIRL Eh?

ADMAN Well you can't live without water. It doubles the libido.

YOUNG MAN Eh?

ADMAN Well, anything does if you think it does. It doesn't stain carpets, and given the right conditions you can ski on it.

YOUNG MAN Thank you, I think *I'll* get the next round.

CLIFFORD ALDISS *approaches the bar, dressed boringly with a Scout badge in his lapel and a small rucksack on his back.*

ALDISS A glass of clear fresh sparkling lemonade please.

KEMP Oh God, it's him again.

KEMP *and* EDWARDS *turn away.* ALDISS *joins the* YOUNG COUPLE.

ALDISS Yes, some boys ask why beer, wine and spirits exist if they are not meant by God for man's use. But man makes them himself, out of things when they're going bad. You don't eat putrid meat and say that it is meant for man's use. Grapes and barley are meant generally to be used before they ferment. So I want you boys just to take up what I've said with both hands *(This is addressed to Kemp and Michael Edwards)* and stuff it into your coconuts. Hello, my name's E.W. Clifford Aldiss, but you can call me 'W' . . .

KEMP I think it's time to leave.

EDWARDS I think you're right.

Cut to roadside. KEMP *and* EDWARDS *are trying to hitch a lift. A car stops. It is a very well-kept cheap old car. Probably a Ford Popular or similar. The* DRIVER, *who is dressed as a rather shabby but clean school teacher, is in fact another Clifford Aldiss, but they don't notice immediately.*

DRIVER *(Also-Clifford-Aldiss)* Where do you want to go?

KEMP *(Quizzically to Edwards)* Istanbul?

EDWARDS Why not?

DRIVER Oh yes, I'm going there, hop in.

KEMP Oh, thank you very much.

They get in.

EDWARDS Are we really going to Istanbul?

KEMP Why not?

DRIVER Allow me to introduce myself gentlemen, my name's Also-Clifford-Aldiss.

EDWARDS What?

DRIVER E.W. Also-Clifford-Aldiss. My brother was E.W. Clifford Aldiss and my mother called me E.W. Also-Clifford-Aldiss because she didn't have much imagination.

KEMP Oh God.

DRIVER I tell all my boys that there is little benefit to one's body in the internal combustion engine – you see, you two boys remind me of my pack of lads – and I tell them that there is nothing that pistons and camshafts and spark plugs can do that their own lithe young muscles can't do better, with more benefit to themselves. The boy Jesus would never have said 'I want a fast twelve-cylinder sports car with a chrome petrol cap so that I can pull all the birds.' He wouldn't have said to his sister 'See you later you tart, for I have a faster donkey than you.' He would have said 'Have my donkey, let me give thee a leg-up and I will ride with thee,' for it did the young Messiah more good than all the Formula One racing cars that you've ever wished you had.

KEMP Er, which part of Istanbul did you say you were going to?

DRIVER I'm going to the youth hostel at Sultanahmet to spread the word.

KEMP Ah, well, we were rather hoping to get to the Sirkeci part.

DRIVER Well, that's only two minutes walk from Sultanahmet and the exercise would—

KEMP Well yes, we were rather hoping to get straight there . . .

EDWARDS nudges KEMP and points out a large Rolls-Royce driving along next to the car.

DRIVER Well lads . . .

KEMP Thank you, it's not quite what we wanted.

KEMP and EDWARDS climb out of the window and into the open back of the Rolls, which is being driven by a HIGH COURT JUDGE. In the passenger seat is a BARRISTER.

BARRISTER Who the hell are you?

KEMP We're just the people sitting in the back of the car.

BARRISTER Is that legal?

KEMP Oh yes.

The BARRISTER thumbs through a law book.

BARRISTER There's no case law on it.

KEMP Well that's all right then, where are you going?

JUDGE Just going to work.

EDWARDS That's where we're going. *(To Kemp)* Who do you think they are?

KEMP I don't know, but they're obviously very rich.

Cut to a waiting room for a set of rich consultants' offices. A MAN knocks on the door of the first office. A CONSULTANT opens it.

CONSULTANT That'll be £25.

MAN What for?

CONSULTANT Fee for professional services.

MAN But you haven't done anything yet.

CONSULTANT I opened the door for you.

MAN £25 for opening a door? That's a bit steep.

CONSULTANT I'm sick and tired of people who think they can get professional services for free.

MAN There's nothing particularly professional about opening a door.

CONSULTANT Well . . . it depends who opens it. I mean, by the time you've spent six years being beaten up by the local kids because you go to an expensive public school, three years at University studying law with everyone laughing at you and, on top of that, two years being articulated to the sort of person I've now become . . . I mean, you really get kicked around as an articulated clerk. Just watch this . . .

A CLERK has entered and is fiddling with things on the desk. The CONSULTANT hits him, kicks him, slaps him in the face, pours ink over him and then pulls a lever which opens a trap door, through which the CLERK falls.

CLERK *(As he disappears through floor)* Thank you sir!

CONSULTANT You see it's senseless, isn't it?

MAN Then why do you do it?

CONSULTANT It's all tied in with making people unhappy. And I think I ought to advise you at this stage that you now owe me £148.

MAN How much?!

CONSULTANT £152.

MAN Why suddenly the extra £4?

CONSULTANT Well, you don't think I'm going to tell you how much you owe me for free, do you? I mean, for professional services I think this is pretty cheap, especially considering I've waived the £3 surcharge for looking at you through these glasses – and they cost a bomb, I can tell you!

MAN I'm going.

CONSULTANT I'll open the door for you.

MAN No you won't.

The MAN *exits.*

CONSULTANT You're just like all the others, you don't love me at all.

Cut to corridor. The MAN *enters another office door. Cut to interior of second office. Inside is* CONSULTANT 2.

CONSULTANT 2 Good morning.

MAN That's not good enough.

CONSULTANT 2 Alright. *(Ridiculously deliberate pronunciation)* Gooo-o-o-ooood Mo-o-o-o-orni-i-ingggg.

MAN Alright, I'll pay for that one.

CONSULTANT 2 That'll be £58.90p.

MAN What? That's ridiculous, I'm off!

Exits to corridor.

CONSULTANT 2 *(Shouts after him)* Yoo-hoo! Can't afford my services! So, who's from the lower income bracket then? Run along and cry to some second-rate failed barrister which is all you'll get on legal aid – legal ay-eed! I bet your father hasn't got electric wind-up windows in *his* car. I bet your father spends less on tax than mine does on ankle hygiene!

Cut to interior of rear of Rolls-Royce (Studio). KEMP *and* EDWARDS *are enjoying the luxury of it and have helped themselves to drinks from the cabinet.*

The JUDGE *and* BARRISTER *obviously find their sheer bravado a little hard to cope with and keep turning round to say something, but can never think of anything to say.* KEMP *and* EDWARDS *play with the buttons in the arm rests, causing the windows to go up and down, the drinks cabinet to open and close, the reading lights to go on and off.*

One of them opens a door which reveals a fridge containing canapés, to which they help themselves. The other leans forward and opens another small door, which reveals a small television. They turn it on.

We see a horse race with an incredibly fast and utterly incomprehensible commentary.

They exchange looks and switch channels. We see the BBC-2 test card and hear a typical annoying whine. The camera zooms in . . .

EDWARDS That's better.

The card now fills the whole screen. The noise ends abruptly, the BBC-2 logo appears, then the Open University logo and music. We see an ANNOUNCER and the caption saying 'English History Part 443'. A second caption says 'March 1602–April 1602'.

ANNOUNCER Yesterday we had Professor Whinnet Keats discussing the first week of April 1602, this morning Dr Towser Tomiczek covered the Friday morning of the 2nd of March, 1602, and, in a few moments we are very privileged to have with us the world's leading expert on the two seconds immediately preceding 12.25 p.m. on the eleventh of March, 1602: Dr Bennett Kenelm.

Cut to BENNETT KENELM in his own fairly ramshackle study/museum.

KENELM It is not generally known that it is during these two seconds that William Shakespeare wrote the famous words 'To be or not to' and during which Queen Elizabeth I started the movement which eventually resulted in her stubbing her toe – and the same two seconds during which René Descartes, the famous French philosopher, at the time only six, went 'ehe'.

He manipulates a model of Descartes as a boy which makes this rather strange noise.

KENELM It was during this period also that a piece of phlegm from the mouth of Galileo flew three-quarters of the way across a room . . .

There is a small model of Galileo at one side of the room, and a few feet away a thin pole standing upright on the floor with a piece of phlegm mounted on the end.

KENELM . . . and this marked the point the phlegm had reached by the end of the period. Historians of later periods argue that it continued its trajectory and landed in a portion of what is believed to be an early form of macaroni.

We see this on the other side of the room.

KENELM What a fascinating and vital period, so formative in the structure of later world history. Bare factual information about these two seconds and all the legends built up around them fade into insignificance when we confront the sheer exuberance of this, maybe brief but significant, epoch. See how much of the vigour and confidence of the age is expressed in that single gobbing movement. It is amazing how little you can learn from so much.

He is beginning to get very excited and Patrick Moore-like. He gets progressively faster and faster in his delivery.

KENELM Here I have collected together over the years, many of the more centrally important relics and documentary records of the period. Here for instance is the original manuscript of Shakespeare's 'To be or not to', one of the most fascinating pieces of literature of this age: five seemingly inexplicable words, though those of you who have read my book *Shakespeare's 'Ends Romans and Countr* period will be familiar with the methods of study.

The manuscript consists of a large sheet of black paper with the appropriate line, obviously cut out of the original manuscript. By this stage he is now talking incredibly quickly.

KENELM Most experts agree that these two seconds can be divided into five short, but distinct, eras of development. In the first sub-period, during which Shakespeare wrote the word 'To', Sir Francis Bacon was beginning to fall out of a window.

We now see five large glass cages, each with a model of Sir Francis Bacon in them. The models each show him upside-down and obviously falling. Each one being slightly lower than the previous one.

KENELM As we can see, a very characteristic falling pose for the period. In the second sub-period, as we can see, the fall continued and he became considerably closer to the ground.

Also during this second stage, Shakespeare's 'Be' period, the House of Commons was thought to have done nothing. This is carried on through the third or 'Or' sub-period. Bacon, as you can see, was beginning to look nervous. In the fourth sub-period, during which Shakespeare achieved the full artistic maturity of 'Not', George Weymouth, one of the earliest polar explorers, as you can see from this filmed simulation, took this—

Film insert of half-a-second of EXPLORER *taking a step.*

KENELM —half-step. To help to reach an understanding of the full significance of this half-step, let's see it again in slow motion.

This we see.

KENELM We see here the typical late-Elizabethan habit of beginning to put one foot in front of the other. Note the antagonistic use of the gluteous maximus set against the quadriceps, resulting in the inception of a perambulatory movement . . .

He gasps and suddenly expires. The STAGE MANAGER *comes on and prods him a bit, then goes off and comes back with another* STAGE MANAGER *and a stretcher. They carry him out. The picture cuts back to the* ANNOUNCER.

ANNOUNCER In a programme later tonight, we'll be looking at the question of the pornography of hyacinths, and we'll examine the way that these filthy little flowers, some of which are *pink*, keep pollinating each other and budding-off asexually, and sprouting out of the ground in lewd postures . . .

Pull back into Rolls. KEMP *and* EDWARDS *turn off the TV. The Rolls is now stationary outside the law courts. The* JUDGE *and* BARRISTER *have gone.*

EDWARDS Pornography? What is pornography?

KEMP No idea, let's look it up.

He presses a button, a cupboard opens revealing the two-volume edition of the Shorter Oxford Dictionary. KEMP *takes out volume two and flips though the pages.*

KEMP P . . . P . . . P . . . porcupine, porkwood . . .

They get out of the car and walk towards the law courts.

KEMP Ah . . . pornography. *(Reads)* Description of the life, manners etc. of prostitutes and their patrons, hence the expression or suggestion of obscene or unchaste subjects in literature or art.

They enter the building (Cut to studio). They walk down the corridor we saw earlier.

EDWARDS What do they mean by obscene?

KEMP flips through the dictionary again.

KEMP Obituary . . . oblong . . . ah, obscene. *(Reads)* Offensive to modesty or decency.

EDWARDS *(Frustrated)* Yes, but what do they mean by modesty?

KEMP I've only got N to Z.

A WOMAN enters wearing a dowdy twin-set and pearls. She's carrying small parcels of socks and underpants, half a chicken, a cake and some bottles of home-made wine. She drags along with her a slightly SHABBY MAN with a three-piece suit, turn-ups and a small moustache.

WOMAN Peter? Peter? Ah, there you are Petey-wetey, ooh you'll catch your death. Hair's a bit long dear, I don't know why I bother to send you those woolly vests – anyway I've brought you some more.

KEMP I beg your pardon?

WOMAN . . . and some underpants, nice sensible ones, all warm and snug, you don't want to go to hospital in those things.

KEMP What hospital?

WOMAN Don't be silly dear, you know it's good for you, and I've brought you a cake. I specially cooked the sort you like.

KEMP I don't like them.

WOMAN Don't be silly dear, you know you like these, I've always told you you like them.

KEMP They're horrible.

WOMAN And I've brought your father, you know, the one you like.

MAN I'm not his father.

WOMAN Don't be silly dear – and your father's brought you some home-made wine.

MAN I didn't make that.

WOMAN Don't be silly dear, that's condensed milk wine – you can't buy that in the shops. Anyway Peter, your father and I . . .

MAN I'm not his father.

WOMAN Don't be silly Norman.

MAN I'm not Norman, I'm John.

WOMAN Don't be silly John, make yourself useful, give him that chicken. I've cooked it the way you like it.

KEMP I don't like chicken.

WOMAN You'll like it the way I've cooked it, you know you will, I've told you that before.

MAN She just picked me off the street.

WOMAN Don't be silly Jurgen.

MAN My name's John!

WOMAN Be quiet Norman. I've brought you some nice sensible books and some nice sensible suppositories and a nice sensible hypodermic and a nice sensible piece of guttering. Anyway, it's past your bedtime.

She slaps KEMP round the face.

WOMAN I've turned down the sheets – don't forget to take the bottle out – I've put a glass of Ribena and a night light by your bed and keep your hands above the sheets and Mummy will bring you a nice cup of weak tea in the morning. Now I think that's all, and I shall now ascend into heaven.

She ascends in a radiant glow with a Mormon chorus singing in the background.

EDWARDS Was that your mother?

KEMP No, never seen her before in my life.

During the last two lines their attention is distracted by the MAN we saw earlier with the consultants. He knocks on a third door. Cut to interior of BARRISTER's office.

BARRISTER Come in.

MAN *(Putting his head round the door)* How much?

BARRISTER What?

MAN How much do you charge for listening to me saying 'How much'?

BARRISTER Well nothing. Curious question.

MAN You don't insult people who don't have enormous sums of money?

BARRISTER Good Lord no. Ah, you must have visited my two colleagues up the corridor – that explains it. I'm sorry you had to go through all that.

MAN Oh, doesn't worry me.

BARRISTER Oh that's good. I was just worried because you might be feeling a little self-conscious wearing such appalling clothes.

MAN What?

BARRISTER Well, I mean the Prince of Wales check jacket, pinstripe trousers, brown shoes – and as for that tie . . .

He makes a horrible grimace.

MAN I'm not here to be insulted!

BARRISTER It wasn't meant as an insult. I'm sorry, it's a bit of a fault of mine, I just can't help being completely open and honest. Would you like to sit down?

The MAN goes to sit in a chair.

BARRISTER Oh, I wouldn't sit on that one if I were you, I've sawn through one of the legs.

MAN What?

BARRISTER It was going to be a little joke of mine. Client sits on

chair, chair collapses tee hee hee. But I've spoilt it by telling
you – happens to a lot of my jokes. And before you sit down
on that chair, I'd unplug it from the mains. Oh dear, I've done
it again.

*The MAN unplugs the chair and sits. The BARRISTER takes out a custard
pie.*

MAN What are you going to do with that?

BARRISTER Well I *was* going to push it in your face, but I've lost the
element of surprise now. Never mind. Oh, that really is an
appalling jacket. Oh dear, this business of being honest the
whole time is such a nuisance.

MAN But surely it's a very good thing, isn't it?

BARRISTER You mean you really wouldn't mind if I told you what I
think of you so far?

MAN Well, er no, not if you're really being honest.

BARRISTER No, I don't think you do think that.

MAN Of course I do. There isn't enough honesty in this world!
I think people should speak what's on their minds – it would
save so much pointless heartache.

BARRISTER You're perfectly sure about that?

MAN Of course I am.

BARRISTER Well, I think you're an uninspiring, insensitive,
ineffectual, ill-bred, provincial, tasteless, philistine . . . Who said
'Religion is the opium of the people'?

MAN I don't know.

BARRISTER . . . ignorant, uncultured, plebeian excrescence of a wet.

MAN Well. I think you've probably raised some very interesting
points there.

BARRISTER And you're spineless.

MAN Well, er, perhaps.

BARRISTER Not perhaps, you are.

MAN Er, yes.

BARRISTER Well? Come on then, why don't you tell me what you think of me then?

MAN Well, I think you're a . . . barrister?

BARRISTER Good, yes, that's a start, bit of a dig there, ouch. What about my nose?

MAN Ah. Well I think it's er . . .

BARRISTER Long?

MAN Ah, well, yes, I suppose it is. A bit. But it's in proportion with your face.

BARRISTER Ah, so I've got a long face have I?

MAN Now I didn't say that.

BARRISTER Oh come on, I must have.

MAN Well, not so much long as . . . as . . . lengthy perhaps?

BARRISTER That's a bit pathetic. Isn't there anything else?

MAN Well, not really, I think you're very nice.

BARRISTER Oh dear. Well I haven't washed my feet for three weeks for a start – the smell's appalling! I'm wearing the most dreadfully obvious toupee, it should be quite apparent that I'm more than a little pissed – in fact, for the record, I'm a total alcoholic. And also my second wife left me because she found me in bed with a married man.

MAN You do lead an interesting life, don't you?

BARRISTER Look, shut up and let's get this case into court.

MAN But I haven't told you what it is yet.

BARRISTER Doesn't matter, it's all the same to me – few silly clothes *(Puts on gown and wig)*, a few long words, humiliate the judge by quoting some case he's never heard of because I made it up myself, then run rings round the police intellectually which isn't too difficult as they've usually only got three 'O' levels and one of those is usually geography, and perhaps an 'E' in maths. Dead pushover being a barrister, really.

During the above speech the BARRISTER *and the* MAN *leave and walk down the corridor, passing* KEMP *and* EDWARDS. *The* MAN *and the* BARRISTER *sit on the bench outside the courtroom as* KEMP *and* EDWARDS *go and look inside the courtroom. The* JUDGE *is summing up a case.*

JUDGE And so the accused is found guilty as charged, to whit that he did on the 21st day of April in the year of our Lord, nineteen hundred and seventy-six cause, or did cause to be caused, by means of leaden projectiles ejected by means of explosive force from the aforementioned automatic firearm and/or firearms, the deaths, expiration or cessation of life of two hundred and thirty-eight people present at that time in the location known as the High Street Brentwood, in the County of Essex, for no apparent reason. But in consideration of the plea of extreme provocation offered by the learned counsel for the defense, viz. and to whit, and I quote a 'pansy' unquote, by a member of the public, I am prepared to be lenient and sentence you to a suspended sentence of two seconds. You may now leave the dock a free man. Clerk of the Court, may we please move on to the next case.

CLERK Call Mr Scapegoat – er sorry, Mr Dawson.

The MAN *from the previous sketch enters and sits in the box. The* BARRISTER *also enters and takes up his appropriate position.*

CLERK Mr Dawson, you are hereby charged that on the ninth day of—

JUDGE *(Looks at watch)* Look, get on with it will you? It's four o'clock already.

The JUDGE *tries out the whip of a fishing rod.*

JUDGE You *(Addressing a* POLICE SUPERINTENDENT*)* Just tell me what he did.

SUPER What? Oh, I'm on! Ah . . .

He flips hurriedly through his notebook.

SUPER The accused is charged that on the ninth day of—

JUDGE *(Putting on a sou'wester)* Look – what did he *do*?

SUPER He . . . (*Desperately*) He . . . er, he raped several members of the Royal family.

JUDGE What? Really? That sounds quite interesting . . .

He takes off his fishing gear.

SUPER Sorry m'lud, I turned over two pages . . . No, it's a tax-evasion case. No, it isn't either. It's er, hang on a mo . . .

JUDGE Look, just skip all that.

SUPER Really, I'll find it in a tick. I had it this morning . . .

JUDGE Can we please just move straight on to the summing-up for the defence?

The BARRISTER stands up. He looks surprised as he'd been busy falling asleep.

BARRISTER What? What's that m'lud?

The JUDGE is standing and slipping on his wellington boots. He has a catch net, bait box and a couple of expensive-looking suitcases.

JUDGE Look, just get on with it, will you?

BARRISTER Ah, well m'lud . . . (*Shuffles through notes*) My client was about to plead not guilty, which puts me in rather an awkward position as I know that sure as hell he is guilty. I mean, I know I'm supposed to stand up here and say that he didn't do whatever it was, and be terribly clever, and get him off the hook, but as I can't seem to find my notes, I really can't be bothered.

JUDGE (*Astounded*) Well, that's the best summing-up I've ever heard! Look, I don't believe in long prison sentences – hang him.

CLERK We're not allowed to do that anymore.

JUDGE Well, nearest thing then.

A LIVERIED PAGE brings in some fishing flies on a velvet cushion. At the same time we see KEMP and EDWARDS leave the court room and close the door behind them.

JUDGE (*To Barrister*) Do you fancy a spot of fishing at the weekend?

They exit.

BARRISTER My, haven't you got a spotty face . . .

Cut to car park. The JUDGE *and* BARRISTER *get into the Rolls-Royce.* KEMP *and* EDWARDS *are already sitting in it. The Judge has his Sou'wester on over wig, red robes tucked into his oilskins, and waders with an Order of the Garter insignia.*

JUDGE Glad we put him away, bloody foreigner.

BARRISTER He was English, actually.

JUDGE Good Lord, was he? I thought he was a darky – dear oh dear, should we go and get him out then?

BARRISTER Is it worth it?

JUDGE Quite right, yes. Yes, we've got to get up to Scotland. Must see the optician though.

EDWARDS Oh, we're going to Scotland then are we?

KEMP *nods. The* JUDGE *and* BARRISTER *give them both curious looks then drive away. The coach passes the Rolls, causing it to swerve. Cut to inside of the coach, focusing on the* TWO LADIES.

MRS 1 Oooh. Nearly an accident, that was bad driving.

MRS 2 Call that bad driving? I've seen worse driving than that in our garage.

MRS 1 Garage? We had a five car pile-up in our front room.

MRS 2 Front room! We had two petrol tankers collide in our kitchen.

MRS 1 We had a fully laden car transporter crash into a fully passengered Boeing 747 in our linen cupboard, and I was so badly injured I had to be bandaged all over.

MRS 2 In my accident they couldn't bandage me all over because my head was cut off.

MRS 1 Oh. My whole body was cut off.

MRS 2 Well, my accident was so bad they wouldn't even show it on the telly news.

MRS 1 My accident was so bad the censor wouldn't even give it an 'X' certificate.

MRS 2 My accident was so bad it made Sam Peckinpah throw up!

MRS 1 My accident was so bad that I'm dead.

MRS 1 *looks gloatingly at* MRS 2, *expecting a reply.* MRS 2 *hurriedly tries to change the subject.*

MRS 2 Oh look, isn't that Eton College down there?

Cut to Rolls-Royce, focus on KEMP *and* EDWARDS.

KEMP Oh look, Eton College.

EDWARDS We must be going the wrong way for Scotland.

KEMP Does it matter?

EDWARDS No.

KEMP *(Adopting a lecturing tone)* If a complete history of the English public schools is ever written, it will in reality be a history of England . . .

EDWARDS If you're going to say that then I'm going to have a drink.

He gets a drink out of the automatic drinks cabinet.

KEMP Eton College . . .

Mix through to scenic shots of Windsor countryside, gradually picking out the school. We see odd bits that indicate people arriving at the beginning of a new term. Over this we hear:

KEMP (V.O.) . . . nestling between Etna Volcano and Etruria, almost exactly seven pages before exacerbate, it lolls in an almost pauntly fashion against the sun-poked banks of the River Thames, gazing impossibly at the plump bitter walls of Windsor Castle, peeping defiantly at the pink airportliness of Mighty Heathrow – its qualities as an ancient seat of learning can only be described in a sentence more sensible than this one is. Founded in 1440 by Henry VI, it has over the years been a bastion of the upper-classes, a place of education for the sons of gentlemen and peers of the realm.

He coughs. Cut back to the Rolls.

EDWARDS Here, have a drink.

KEMP Thanks.

Cut back to Eton scenes.

KEMP (V.O.) But now its exclusivity has had to be tempered in response to the querulous demands of an increasingly egalitarian society, and it has been obliged to throw open its doors to the less privileged . . . Yes, this is the story of 'A Haddock at Eton' . . .

We see cars arriving outside Eton, BOYS getting out, trunks being unloaded. There are one or two SHEIKS in evidence. The camera tightens on one particular Rolls and we see a small fish tank on the back seat. It has a HADDOCK in it, wearing an Eton collar. In the background we see a HOUSEMASTER welcoming the Boys.

There is a REPORTER with a stick mic. standing by the Housemaster as he talks to one NEW BOY with several others queuing up behind.

HOUSEMASTER Ah, new boy aren't you? You must be Pickering minor. Just like your brother – understand you're very good at art – well you won't be doing *that* here – push along! Give that boy back his toupee, Jenkins!

He turns back to the REPORTER.

HOUSEMASTER No, a boy from any walk of life who is intelligent enough to pass the entrance exams and a simple interview, can gain a place at Eton.

REPORTER You interviewed the Haddock?

HOUSEMASTER Oh yes, a mere formality in his case – his guardian was so rich.

REPORTER I see, a rich guardian. So, the fact that you've admitted a haddock to your school isn't actually a step towards equality of opportunity.

HOUSEMASTER I think that it is – you name me a so-called comprehensive school that's admitted any fish, let alone a haddock. You boy – give me that!

He turns to a couple of BOYS *who are punching each other. He grabs the Boy's fist and pulls it off his arm then puts the fist in his pocket.*

HOUSEMASTER You can collect it after prep – and no fighting with the stump or else I'll have that too!

REPORTER And what special arrangements have you made for the haddock's life here?

HOUSEMASTER None at all, we'll be treating him like any other boy, he'll have to go through the normal starvation, bullying, torture, sleeping with the head boy, this sort of thing.

A couple of BOYS *carry* HADDOCK'S *tank to the* HOUSEMASTER. *It has a label on it which reads 'N. St.Q. Haddock'.*

HOUSEMASTER Ah. Another new boy. Name? *(Looks down list)* Ah yes, you must be Haddock. Now, I've read the letter from your guardian, but I'm afraid you can't be excused games. You'll just have to learn to muck-in with all the other boys. Bullard! Take Haddock off to see Matron. You boy! What are you doing with all those bruises over you? Oh, it's you Bradfield.

He picks up a cricket bat and begins to lay about BRADFIELD.

KEMP (V.O.) And so Haddock was duly treated like any other boy, and at the time of the Feast of the Conversion of St Paul, was dragged out of his dormitory and carried up the hill, ad montem, where the Freshmen of the Year were initiated . . .

We see this happen in a very military fashion. The fish tank is dragged along the ground and up the hill. We see the PREVIOUS INITIATE *being dragged off in a bloody blanket and into a Red Cross ambulance, whilst other* BOYS *pelt him with tomatoes and eggs.*

The fish tank gets put on a blanket and is tossed, after which some BOYS *pour ink in the tank, whilst others poke* HADDOCK *with sprigs of holly.*

Cut to classroom. A Latin lesson is in progress. Towards the end of the scene we see the fish tank on top of the desk, HADDOCK *is now quite obviously dead and lying white-side up. The tank now has a blue ink tinge to it, plus a few sprigs of holly floating in it. The outside is spattered with congealed lumps of tomato and egg.*

FORM MASTER *De Bello Gallico* Book 1, starts at the top of page ten. Keep your hands above the desk, Cornwall. Now. *Omnia Gallia in tres partes divisa est.* Translate, Cornwall, come on Cornwall, you're slacking boy!

He hits CORNWALL *with a cricket stump.*

CORNWALL Um . . . ah . . . er . . . um . . . ugghhh . . . er . . . um . . . ah . . .

FORM MASTER *(A word to a stroke)* All Gaul is divided into three parts! Now, Haddock! All Gaul is divided into – how many parts?

He stoops and peers into the murky tank, stirring the water with the cricket stump.

FORM MASTER Come on Haddock!

WORCESTERSHIRE *Three* parts, sir! Three parts, three parts!

FORM MASTER Shut up, Worcestershire! Well Haddock? You haven't been listening at all have you?

He hits the tank with the stump.

FORM MASTER Right. Cornwall, take Haddock off to see the Housemaster.

WORCESTERSHIRE Three parts sir . . . !

FORM MASTER All right, Worcestershire, all *what* is divided into three parts?

WORCESTERSHIRE Er . . . umm . . . er . . . ah . . .

The FORM MASTER *lays about him with the cricket stump. Cut to the* HOUSEMASTER's *study. There is a* BOY *with him.*

HOUSEMASTER Now West Riding, I understand that you have to be punished – do you remember with what it was in connection?

WEST RIDING No sir.

HOUSEMASTER No, neither do I.

WEST RIDING Actually sir, I don't think I had to be punished at all.

HOUSEMASTER No, perhaps not. But perhaps I'd better punish you just to be on the safe side. Bend over.

WEST RIDING Yes sir, thank you sir.

He bends over the desk.

HOUSEMASTER Now this is going to hurt you.

WEST RIDING Yes sir.

Cut to low-angle close-up on WEST RIDING's face. We hear swishing noises and yelps from the boy. Pull back to reveal that the HOUSEMASTER is throwing knives into the BOY's bottom.

HOUSEMASTER OK, that's enough.

WEST RIDING *(Standing)* Thank you very much indeed sir.

He exits with the knives sticking in his bottom. He looks back in.

WEST RIDING Cornwall and Haddock are outside sir.

HOUSEMASTER Send them in.

CORNWALL enters with the fish tank.

HOUSEMASTER Yes, what is it boy?

CORNWALL It's Haddock sir, he's . . .

HOUSEMASTER Let Haddock speak for himself boy.

Pause. Dead silence.

HOUSEMASTER Yes, well perhaps you'd better tell me.

CORNWALL Well sir, he hasn't been attending class.

HOUSEMASTER I see. Well Haddock, I've had a number of complaints – you don't seem to be making much of an effort to fit in with the other boys. Now there's one thing we *are* very keen on in this school, but I'm not going to do it to you now. So, from now on I'm going to put you on extra fagging duties. You'll have to be pretty sharp about it because you're due on corps parade in half an hour, and I wouldn't like to be in your . . . er . . . shoes, if your rifle isn't spotlessly clean. Now piss off.

They exit.

HOUSEMASTER I think I put him at his ease. Now, oh yes, phone.

He picks up the telephone, which is lying off the hook.

HOUSEMASTER *(To phone)* Sorry to have kept you, got a bit held up being cruel to people. Now, what was it? Oh yes, now I'm afraid I can't put your son into the tax-evasion tutorials, no, he breaks down far too easily under interrogation – but look, we'll put him down for a couple of terms in the nanny-battering stream . . .

Cut to corridor outside studies. A study door opens. Cry of 'Fag!' and out comes a SIXTH-FORM BOY in an outrageously Etonian costume. Behind him is another FAG who has a GIRL under one arm and a BOY under the other, both of whom are scantily dressed.

SIXTH FORMER Fag! Fag! Where the hell is Haddock? I want my boots cleaning boy. Fag! Haddock! Ah, there you are . . .

He practically trips over the tank. He dumps his boots into it.

SIXTH FORMER Clean my boots boy! And *don't* get them wet you semi-moribund pescatorial imbecile!

He turns to the other FAG.

SIXTH FORMER Now, eeny meeny miny mo . . . Oh, I can't be bothered, it's your turn Doncaster.

He takes the FAG back into the study, then turns to the tank.

SIXTH FORMER Shouldn't you be in corps, Haddock?

Cut to corps parade. We hear shooting. The camera follows a line of BOYS in corps uniform who are shooting at targets. The camera passes the fish tank, which has a rifle sticking out of it. They are shooting at cut-out targets of soldiers, each one of which is hit. One of the targets is a cut-out of an armed fish. It hasn't been hit at all.

KEMP (V.O.) And next week we'll be bringing you a Sergeant Major at Billingsgate.

Cut to see a SERGEANT MAJOR shouting orders at a stall full of fish.

KEMP (V.O.) And later in the series we'll be having a three-toed sloth at West Point; an enormous breast at Frencham Heights; a non-pearl-bearing oyster at Oxford; a bit of snot at St John's College Cambridge, sort of studying social and political sciences; a

prostatic utricle at the Inns of Court (probably Lincoln's); a turd
in the Cabinet . . .

Whilst KEMP *speaks, we see the captions rolled over a shot of* KEMP *and*
EDWARDS *getting out of the Rolls, parked on the sea front.* KEMP
interrupts himself to say 'Sorry' to the JUDGE, *and throws a huge cod
in through the window of the car. They walk down the beach, past a
pile of naked, writhing bodies.*

EDWARDS By the way, you didn't seem to react to that nude couple
we saw earlier on the beach.

KEMP It's funny you should say that – I thought you hadn't noticed
them.

EDWARDS Oh I noticed. You don't miss things like that.

*They are now well past the pile, which is shouting in chorus 'Hey, what
about us then?'*

EDWARDS I thought she was a bit of all right.

KEMP He wasn't too bad either.

They fade into the distance.

THE END

The Cough

by Graham Chapman

GRAHAM *dressed as a Harley Street consultant physician, three-piece suit, half-moon spectacles, stethoscope round neck.*

GRAHAM The cough . . . As in most therapeutic areas, the most rational counter-prescribing of remedies demands a sound working knowledge of the mechanisms behind the condition. If we are going to offer treatment for a cough it is useful to remind ourselves first of all of the cough reflex itself.

JANET, *in limbo, wearing a white lab coat over a magician's assistant's spangly leotard and fishnet tights, blows a puff of smoke at a man from a small bespangled set of bellows. No response from the man. Janet, thinking 'quickly', finally gives a little 'cough' herself. She does magician's assistant's 'How about that' gestures and bows to a musical 'sting' followed by canned applause.*

GRAHAM Thank you nurse. The internal lining of the larynx—

JANET *rushes in with a pointer and indicates larynx on diagram or model. She has added an ostrich-plumed headband to her ensemble.*

GRAHAM —trachea and bronchi—

She points.

GRAHAM —contains many, tiny, sensory receptors.

During the following, JANET, *without lab coat, mimes 'tiny'. Something touching something 'tiny' and then gives a little squeal.*

GRAHAM These sensory receptors, stimulated by any small—

She mimes 'small'.

GRAHAM —particles inhaled, send messages via nerve fibres—

She gives a small shiver.

GRAHAM —to the base of the brain.

JANET *mimes as though she had just been thumped on the back of the neck and goes 'Ooh, the medulla!'*

GRAHAM The medulla of the brain.

JANET *points to diagram.*

GRAHAM If for any reason these receptors are stimulated—

JANET *blows smoke at the model/diagram from the bellows.*

GRAHAM —the result is a short inspiration—

Close up of JANET's *breasts rising.*

GRAHAM —followed immediately by closure of the glottis.

She holds up a small flashing sign reading 'glottis'.

GRAHAM The glottis: the entrance of the larynx!!

She points to it on model/diagram.

GRAHAM Contraction of the expiratory muscles then follows, which creates a high pressure within the lower respiratory tract.

JANET, *keeping her glottis closed, attempts a forced expiration pointing at the muscles of her lower chest and abdomen.*

GRAHAM The glottis then opens, suddenly allowing the air to escape in a blast and this is what we hear as . . . 'The cough'!!

JANET *gives polite cough 'Ahem'.*

GRAHAM This involuntary action is 'the cough reflex' itself.

GRAHAM, *becoming more showbiz.*

GRAHAM Ladies and gentlemen, we bring you . . . the cough reflex!!

Shot of man, in limbo, standing around looking bored. Janet now wearing tiny spangled, be-feathered bra and panties enters. She tries with small set of bellows and then enters again with a huge set of bellows. Puffs a cloud of smoke at him. No reaction. She skips off and returns with a bucket of flour which she hurls over him. No reaction from the man, but JANET *begins to cough involuntarily, so much so that she is hard-pressed to get in her gestures and bow, with a musical 'sting' and applause.*

GRAHAM Thank you, nurse. But – what starts this complex sequence of events?

JANET, wearing her bra and pants, and leather thigh boots and carrying a whip, stands, smiling sweetly, beside 'doctor's' desk.

GRAHAM Under what circumstances are the sensory receptors—

Still smiling, she flexes whip.

GRAHAM —stimulated? We have now come to realize that at least two factors are important in causing a cough: First, inflammation and irritation of the lining—

Shot of man, in limbo, still standing looking bored. Enter JANET with stuffed fish which she plunges down his throat. He begins to cough in earnest. Janet does 'as-if-by-magic' gestures. Acknowledges 'applause' on behalf of herself and the fish as the man lies spluttering on the floor, convulsed, behind her.

GRAHAM —er, first, inflammation and irritation in the lining and, secondly, the presence of excessive amounts of mucus and foreign material in the respiratory tract.

Shot of man still writhing on floor.

GRAHAM Discrimination between the two types of triggering factors is crucial if the various types of cough remedies are to be used to their full potential.

Gesticulating with script.

GRAHAM How about that for a dull paragraph? I mean, we're splitting a gut here trying to make this thing interesting and what do I get to say? 'Discrimination between the two types of triggering factors is crucial if . . .' I mean, what are they on about? Why couldn't they just say you cough because the lining of the breathing tubes gets irritated by bugs – or bits of dust – or, if you didn't completely cough out the bits of dust in the first place then that causes huge lumps of phlegm to hang about, which also makes you cough?

    Of course you bloody well ought to know which type of bleedin' cough it is if you're going to treat the bleedin' thing properly! Oh. I'm sorry . . . I'm sorry . . . *(Back into character)*

The first type, an inflamed and irritated respiratory tract lining, is often associated with acute upper respiratory tract infections, leading to nasopharyngitis, laryngitis and tracheitis—

Forgetting himself again.

GRAHAM You see what I mean? I mean, why use words like that? By 'upper respiratory tract' they bloody mean the bigger bits nearer the outside air!

He points on diagram/model.

GRAHAM —as opposed to the lower respiratory tract, the smaller bits – which aren't – the nasopharynx is the bit behind the nose and mouth.

He points.

GRAHAM Below that is the voice-box or larynx. Lower down still is the big tube called the trachea, and it is something which some clever doctors put after any big word they can think up, meaning it's inflamed.

Reading from notes.

GRAHAM In these circumstances the mere passage of . . . ooh . . .

Throws down notes.

GRAHAM Look, when the lining of the bigger bits is inflamed the cough receptors are so tensed up that the ordinary air you breathe over them can trigger off the cough reflex, thus giving you a dry, irritating cough.

JANET *emits a couple of polite coughs.*

JANET Ahuh. Ahuh . . .

GRAHAM The other thing which can trigger off—

JANET Ahem ahem . . .

GRAHAM —the cough—

JANET Ahem ahem!

GRAHAM —reflex is, as you'll remember—

'Ahems' adlibbed by JANET.

GRAHAM —the presence of excess amounts of mucus and foreign

material . . . phlegm in the air passages – *(To Janet)* will you stop that!?! . . . Now that gives you a tight, congested, chesty cough.

JANET, *with a great deal of noise and kerfuffle, gives a very bad impression of a congested, chesty cough.*

GRAHAM What on earth are you doing?

JANET I'm sorry but I'm just not very good at tight, congested chesty coughs.

SFX: *Congested chesty coughing effects begins.*

GRAHAM *(During it)* You don't need to be, we're going to listen to a tape of one.

JANET They've just played it.

GRAHAM Have they?

JANET I was supposed to mime to the tape but you changed the script so they couldn't cue the cough. You messed it all up.

GRAHAM I'm sorry . . . I'm sorry . . .

JANET That was my big moment, the mime.

GRAHAM Look, I'm sorry about changing the words only – it's not much fun for me you know. This isn't what I was trained for. No scope at all for acting with this kind of 'gup' . . .

He picks up notes.

GRAHAM *(To Janet)* You go and change. *(Looking at script)* Where were we? 'Chesty cough'. . . Oh yes . . . *(Back into character)* To understand why this situation might arise, we must first remind ourselves how the body prevents airborne particles – dust or micro-organisms – from damaging the delicate respiratory machinery.

He points.

GRAHAM Inertial deposition of solid particles takes place in the nares, the nose and nasopharynx, where the air is forced to change rapidly. These inertial passages are rippled to give a large surface area, and are heavily supplied with blood vessels to maintain a warm, moist surface. irritation and infection –

even minor – can lead to a marked inflammatory response, resulting in narrowing of the airways. Foreign matter small enough to pass these obstacles is collected by deposition on the walls of the lower respiratory tract – that is, the bronchi and bronchioles.

The lining, or epithelium, of the trachea and bronchial tree is made of cells which have tiny hair-like projections called cilia, which can move about, and it secretes mucus. The fine particles of dust in the turbulent air stream are trapped by the mucus, and are swept away from the lungs by the action of the cilia. This continuous movement of mucus towards the oesophagus is called the ciliary-mucus escalator. Finally—

There is loud square-dance music and JANET *enters wearing a new bizarre costume doing a new bizarre dance. After a few bars it stops suddenly. She bows.*

GRAHAM What the hell was that?

JANET That was my ciliary-mucus-escalator dance.

GRAHAM Oh. I rather liked that.

He joins in a reprise of the dance which is stopped by a floor manager wearing headphones who drags him to one side of the set. A heated discussion takes place. We overhear GRAHAM *say:*

GRAHAM Look, we were only trying to make it more interesting. Right, but I still think I should have done it as a character part.

Still mumbling, the STUDIO MANAGER *walks off.* GRAHAM *returns to desk and begins lecture again but this time in an Australian accent.*

GRAHAM Finally, any minute, foreign particles penetrating as far as the alveoli—

STUDIO MANAGER (V.O.) Just do your doctor. It's good.

GRAHAM Well I – do you really think so?

STUDIO MANAGER (V.O.) Yes, your doctor is fantastic.

GRAHAM Oh, thank you. The accent – good though, wasn't it?

STUDIO MANAGER (V.O.) Yes, yes but your doctor is a classic.

GRAHAM Oh. Well, pr'aps you're right. Yes. (*Back in character*)

Finally, any minute, foreign particles penetrating as far as the alveoli – little air sacs at the end of the bronchioles *(He's now really getting into the part)* are swallowed up by large cells called *phagocytes* which move on up the tract by *ameboid* movement until they reach a ciliated section and are *swept away* in the mucus!! Other phagocytic cells then enter the lymphatic circulation and are carried to the lymph nodes at the *roots of the lungs*!!!!

These nodes can become quite black when air laden with carbon particles is inhaled; this often occurs with coal miners, but is also evident in city-dwellers ... *(To o.s.)* I'm really rather enjoying this bit ... *(Back in character)* So, under normal circumstances, the delicate exchange surfaces of the lungs are well protected from the damaging effects of airborne particles by a combination of inertial deposition in the nose, mouth, pharynx and larynx, and by entrapment in mucous secretions in the lower respiratory tract. However, during various illnesses, the number of micro-organisms in the respiratory tract is increased enormously!!! *(To o.s.)* This really *is* quite interesting ...

For example, the common cold is due to infection of the upper respiratory tract with *rhinovirus*. These virus particles replicate extensively in the epithelial cells lining the nasopharynx. This firstly leads to the production of an excess of thin, watery mucus – the runny nose. Then the contents of many dead cells are released. An excess of highly viscous mucus is thus generated, and the sufferer feels that his cold has 'gone onto his chest'. If the infection is particularly severe, there comes a point when so much debris is produced that the ciliary-mucus escalator *cannot cope*.

SFX: *Silly music begins again and* JANET *starts to enter.*

GRAHAM Janet please, this is serious. As a result, the air passages of the bronchial tree tend to become blocked, thus increasing the resistance to airflow. Under such circumstances, the body *must* clear the respiratory airways or *die*!!!! And it does this, of course, by ... coughing. The build-up of mucus being detected

by the sensory receptors. In other words, this type of cough –
the productive cough – should be thought of as a normal
reaction to partial respiratory tract blockage.

The problem is that, whilst under normal circumstances the
occasional cough is hardly noticed, during illness – when the air
passages are full of debris and thick mucus – coughing is often
painful and difficult, and causes considerable distress.

Because such coughing is performing, or at least trying to
perform, a useful function, suppressing the symptoms with a
cough suppressant or antihistamine is by no means ideal, since
it would do nothing to help the underlying problem of excess
tenacious mucus. Indeed, if anything, they tend to dry up and
thicken the bronchial secretions even further.

Putting on Australian bush hat and 'cracking' a tube.

GRAHAM *(To o.s.)* I still liked the bit with the accent. *(Back into
character)* So to sum up: 'Coughing is a useful mechanism for
clearing air passages of foreign materials and excess mucus, and
clearly the complete abolition of coughing would not be
desirable.' We must indeed keep that old ciliary-mucus escalator
going! Got that, snot-face? Right. Now . . . take it away Bruce!

Square-dance music enters. GRAHAM *and* JANET *both cavort wildly to a
reprise of the Ciliary-Mucus-Escalator dance.*

v.o. That was 'The Cough' explained by Doctor Graham
Chapman. Next week, Graham will explain sneezing – with
music and lyrics by Burt Bacharach and Carol Bayer-Sager, and
with special guests: The full West End cast of 'The Fantasticks'.
Good night.

THE END

Above Them, the Ground
The Dangerous Sports Club and Me

Teleplay by Graham Chapman

A comedic, but true, documentary in which GRAHAM CHAPMAN *finds himself joining the Dangerous Sports Club.*

VIDEO: *Exaggerated pop video treatment for a montage of exciting DSC archive footage. People on elastic ropes leap off bridges over terrifying chasms, are catapulted on hang-gliders in San Francisco, and ski down mountainsides on an odd assortment of objects (such as: a tandem, a grand piano, an inflatable elephant and a stuffed hunting horse); they are catapulted from cranes and hang-glide over volcanoes.*

Exaggeratedly dramatic, and appallingly trendy pop music is played over this obviously clever piece of editing. All the usual clichés are there, including freeze frame, slow motion, fast forward, fast back, artistic but awful zooms in and out, and stuttering instant repetitions. A slow motion version of a short section of the sequence in which DAVID KIRKE, *wearing a top hat and tuxedo, and holding his pipe and brandy glass, falls from bridge into chasm, is repeated and intercut with great significance. The shots used in this montage will serve as an excellent teaser for the rest of the show.*

The title 'Above Them, the Ground' is superimposed over the first shot of DAVID *falling. This is closely followed by the caption: 'The Dangerous Sports Club'.*

Shots of GRAHAM, *sitting relatively motionless at a desk in an office, intrude in this frenetic montage. In the first few interruptions he sits pensively at the desk. Later, signs of impatience begin to become gradually more obvious.*

The rest of the opening credit captions are seen over, and throughout the above.

EXT. *for* INT. *Day.* GRAHAM, *looking straight to camera, sits behind a desk in the corner of an office, potted plant behind him.*

GRAHAM *(Under his breath and still trying to look pensive)* Come on, come on! Surely they've got enough of this by now? How much of me sitting at a desk looking pensive can an audience take? *(Pause)* Ooh strewth! Find out what they're up to, Dave.

DAVE *(o.s. and speaking into a hand transmitter)* Hello, Mike, what's happening? Graham's getting a bit pissed off, over.

GRAHAM *(Under his breath and still trying to look pensive)* I don't see how this will ever cut with the opening credits.

DAVE (O.S.) Mike says 'No problem. Looks great' . . . and all that sort of rubbish. Oh, and 'Cue coming up. Cue Graham.'

GRAHAM *(From looking pensively into the distance he sits up and looks straight into camera, as though interrupted while at work)* A couple of years ago, I was writing at this desk, when I was interrupted by a telephone call from . . .

DAVE (O.S.) You forgot the telephone.

GRAHAM . . . from a newspaper who wanted to know . . . *(He grinds to a halt and looks camera right, towards DAVE)* We cut the telephone didn't we? I thought we had. I mean it's so artificial. Look, tell him that we are not doing a dramatic reconstruction. We are going to be showing actual footage of real people putting their lives at risk. That sort of thing in a fictional setting, with rigged phone calls and people staring pensively into cameras for hours, just trivializes everything.

DAVE KIRKE *wearing a headset, comes into shot and gives* GRAHAM *the hand transmitter.*

GRAHAM *(Into transmitter)* Look, Mike! *(Presses button)* Mike?

MIKE (O.S.) OK. OK. Kill the phone. I agree, forget the script – great! These guys are really unbelievable. We'll go for realism. We'll even keep this.

GRAHAM We'll see about that.

MIKE (O.S.) Let's go for it!

GRAHAM Meanwhile I can just get on and tell the story in my own way?

MIKE (O.S.) Absolutely. That's what we want. And . . . cue Graham.

GRAHAM *swiftly gives the transmitter back to* DAVE, *who rapidly exits frame with it.*

GRAHAM *(Breaking from his hurriedly resumed thoughtful pose)* A couple of years ago I was sitting here trying to write, when I had a phone call from a British newspaper who wanted to know what I would do if I were to win their Million Pound Bingo Competition. Well, I was a bit irritated by the interruption and told them that I would give it to John Cleese so that he could take an afternoon off. They thought that this was quite funny, but a bit cruel. They also added that I was interested in going to the Andes. I had mentioned this. I do like mountains. The same day this story appeared, I had a phone call from someone who said he was the chairman of the Dangerous Sports Club, Mr David Kirke.

DAVE (O.S.) Yes? *(He half appears in shot)* . . . Ooh, sorry. *(He exits)*

GRAHAM *(Picking it up)* . . . The same day I had a call from the Chairman of the Dangerous Sports Club, who wondered if I would like to hang-glide over active volcanoes in Ecuador. Well, I said no to the hang-gliding. I didn't think it would be an ideal place to learn; but I was interested in a free trip to Ecuador, provided that I didn't have to do anything particularly dangerous. I was also curious to find out why anyone would want to do such things. *(He stops and looks pleased with himself after the long take.)*

DAVE *(Wearing headset, walks into shot and puts his brandy bottle on the desk)* Fair enough, but we'll be cutting away to film during all that won't we?

GRAHAM *(Irritated)* I don't think so. There's plenty of action coming up.

DAVE All right, Gov. I'm not the expert but it just seems a bit of a flat couple of minutes to open up an all-action show.

GRAHAM There's all that action in the opening credits just before this . . . and anyway, people are interested to know why people do things . . . that's what this is all about. It's a social document. It's . . . *(Realizing)* They're not still rolling this are they?

DAVE Looks like it.

GRAHAM That 'social document' stuff sounded a bit pompous. Still we can edit that out.

DAVE They all love it up there. Camera's still rolling.

GRAHAM I'll soon stop that. *(He stands and turns. In head and shoulder shot we can not see all, but it is obvious that he has mooned the crew.)*

DAVE They're falling about now.

GRAHAM *(Grabs transmitter from DAVE)* OK, OK. We've all had a bit of a laugh. Just give me a cue and we'll start again, remembering that we've got eight more minutes to do today.

MIKE *(o.s. with the sound of laughter from crew in background)* OK! Ready for the next segment. And . . . cue Graham.

GRAHAM I'm not ready for the next segment. We've got to do the opening again, haven't we?

MIKE (O.S.) If we've got time at the end of the day, but it looks great on playback. You'll love it. It's natural. The real you. We fell about at the mooning. Warn us next time you're going to do anything like that though, over.

PRODUCER (O.S.) Fantastic, Graham! Over.

GRAHAM They loved it! Surely we must do it agai—

MIKE (O.S.) . . . and cue Graham!

GRAHAM *(Quickly regaining poise)* The Dangerous Sports Club began . . . *(Notices brandy bottle and swiftly hides it behind desk)* The Dangerous Sports Club began at Oxford University. A group of friends became bored with conventional danger sports such as the Cresta Run bob-sleighing and decided to invent their own fun.

He finishes and waits, looking straight into camera for a second or two. DAVE *walks into shot and stoops to pick up the bottle.*

DAVE *(Wearily)* Well, that was OK, and the next bit's all voice-over.

An old photograph album labelled 'The Dangerous Sports Club' opens and from old stills we go into a sequence, already filmed, showing the early days of the club at Oxford University. GRAHAM's *and* DAVID's *voices are heard over this, explaining the sequence.*

The montage includes establishing shots of Oxford, in which we see that undergraduates are certainly not afraid to be different. Tea party footage showing sedan chair tennis, peculiar roller skates etc. Then clips of the early days of bungee-jumping. We see the first bungee-jump as the CLUB MEMBER *is thrown from a bridge over a river while seated in a wheelchair. The Member and the wheelchair bounce successfully beneath the bridge on the bungee cord.*

This is followed by a bungee-jump made by HENRY ROBINSON *from the upper storey of a building into a busy Oxford High Street. He times his fall so that he narrowly misses a double-deck bus, just to make it more exciting. Other clips include* MARTIN LYSTER *making a base-jump out of a bucket suspended from a crane only 120 or so feet above the ground, and one or two examples of horrifyingly uncontrolled descents of dangerous Swiss ski slopes,* DAVID KIRKE *in voice-over describes the development of travel in the huge inflatable plastic bubble, and the club's attempt to ski on blocks of ice.*

A MAN IN A GORILLA SUIT *flies a motorized hang-glider around the Houses of Parliament, and beneath Clifton suspension bridge. We catch sight of someone dropping (on a bungee) from the bridge behind him.*

DAVID (V.O.) . . . There were some interesting developments.

Compilation of variety of bungee-jumps. From buckets on cranes (including one or two touch-downs). Clifton Suspension Bridge and the police arrest. The Golden Gate Bridge jump, including news on radio and the avoidance of arrest. The incredible shots of the Arizona gorge jump.

EXT. *Scottish mountainside. Day.*

DAVID *and* GRAHAM, *wearing climbing gear, sit on a rock. There is a suitably impressive vista behind them. They chat, oblivious to the camera:*

DAVE *(Looking at map)* . . . It's only eight miles away.

GRAHAM What is?

DAVE The bridge the lads have found. The drop's only a couple of hundred feet, if that. Fancy a jump?

GRAHAM Well, we are a bit busy.

DAVE We can go, straight after this.

GRAHAM *(Feeling cornered)* Is the bridge over water?

DAVE There's a stream.

GRAHAM No, I definitely want my first jump to be over water. Deep water.

DAVE Fair enough. How long is this going to take?

GRAHAM We should have finished by now. *(Looks around)* Doesn't look much like Ecuador does it? It'll never match.

DAVE Sod Ecuador. Hardly one of our better jobs. After the jump we thought we might have a bit of Aberdeen sleaze.

GRAHAM Count me out. *(Realizing)* I think they're running on us. *(Looks straight into camera)* They have been – and are – filming us.

DAVE Fair enough. *(Assumes 'about to be interviewed' pose)* Fire away.

GRAHAM I wish they wouldn't do that. Most unsettling. OK, now, David . . . Oh, this is David Kirke by the way, a founder member of the Dangerous Sports Club. David, hang-gliding over active volcanoes in Ecuador – now that sounds tricky.

DAVID Well, we'd already flown from the top of Kilimanjaro . . . that's 19,000 feet and extinct . . . so we knew that two big problems were going to be acclimatization to the altitude, and humping the hang-gliders through the jungle and up there.

GRAHAM You've got some footage of the Kilimanjaro jump haven't you? *(After a pause staring straight at the nodding* DAVID. *He snaps out of his 'interviewer mode', but the camera still rolls)* Didn't like that. Sounded scripted.

Cut to scenes (already filmed) of the Kilimanjaro ascent.

GRAHAM (V.O.) None of them were acclimatized to the altitude, so they all had terrible headaches, and had to fight against falling asleep and freezing to death.

We see some of them struggle up.

GRAHAM (V.O.) There were one or two unsuccessful attempts to glide from the summit. *(We see one)* Now this was only the fifth time you'd ever been hang-gliding, and the conditions were not good and . . .

EXT. *Summit of Kilimanjaro. Day (already filmed).*

DAVE *(Talking to the exhausted* HANG-GLIDERS*)* . . . What do you think about the conditions?

The response is unenthusiastic.

DAVE . . . Well, I simply can't be bothered to walk back down.

GRAHAM (V.O.) And neither could Alan Weston, who launched himself off the mountain in a horrendously precarious take-off. *(We see this)* Only to land somewhere out in the endless jungle. Or somewhere . . .

We see the end of ALAN'S *flight as he crashes into the rocky mountainside.*

GRAHAM (V.O.) . . . rather badly.

Alan lands dreadfully.

INT. *Sleazy South American bathroom.*

GRAHAM *stands, unaware that he is on film, rubbing some lotion into his balding pate.*

GRAHAM *(Singing)* 'Always look on the bright side of life. Always look on the bright side of life. Oh, life's a piece of sh— *(Sees camera)* No. No, oh no. Not again.

MIKE (V.O.) Very informal. It'll work. Carry on.

GRAHAM *tries to improve his appearance.*

GRAHAM I don't know about this . . . (*Runs through a few 'TV Person poses'*) Well, I agreed to go to Ecuador, but I did say 'No' to hang-gliding over active volcanoes. I didn't think it was the ideal place to learn.

EXT. *The DSC in Ecuadorian countryside (already filmed).*

Establishing panoramic shots of Ecuador and Quito, GRAHAM *introduces Quito and some of the group at the foot of the enormous statue of the Madonna. Travelling shots of Ecuadorian landscape. More club members are introduced. Mount Sangay is pointed out in v.o. by Graham.*

GRAHAM (V.O.) Sangay is an active volcano. You get to it by hacking through the jungle for a week with a machete. This 18,000-foot peak erupts every ten minutes or so, sending red-hot rocks bouncing down its slopes to discourage visitors.

Graham explains the following, where necessary, by v.o.

Hang-gliding practice from the hills above Quito and the DSC travelling to Cotapaxi, a 20,000-foot volcano that hasn't erupted for about seventeen years. On the way the members take time off to do comic bungee-jumping from a bridge. They explore an extinct volcano crater and hang-glide from it. Two club members do a base-jump, taking off by running headlong down into the crater until their parachutes open and they glide down to the lake-filled centre of the volcano.

Shots of llamas and the climb to the mountain hut. Shots of the non-mountaineer DSC members practising falling on a snow slope with their ice axes. GRAHAM *in v.o. emphasizes that while they may take risks, they are calculated risks.*

GRAHAM (V.O.) Because Cotapaxi is on the equator we had to climb it at night. If you're on the mountain after about eight in the morning, the sun heats up the snow and ice above, and lumps of ice are apt to fall on you. On this occasion we were within about 1,000 feet of the summit, taking six incredibly deep breaths every step, all with thumping headaches, when we lost our way because of fresh snow falls. One of the party got altitude sickness. We decided to go back down.

GRAHAM *interviews* DAVID KIRKE *as they both sit on a glacier on Cotapaxi in an appalling hail storm.* DAVE *is asked why people do things like this (already on film), over shots of DSC carrying hang-gliders up the 21,000-foot Chimborazo.*

GRAHAM (V.O.) The Ecuadorian army, who had promised help lifting the hang-gliders on Cotapaxi, didn't turn up. Probably all had hair appointments . . . And so the DSC decided to have a go on their own, to see if they could carry hang-gliders up the 21,000-foot peak, Chimborazo. They managed it, only to find that they couldn't take off from the summit, because the snow was over waist deep.

Shots of DAVID KIRKE *doing silly mime on the summit.*

GRAHAM (V.O.) They stayed up there long enough to get frostbite, and agreed that they would fly from the summit of Sangay next time.

Dramatic shots of Sangay.

INT. *Bedroom. Day.*

CLOSE ON GRAHAM, *who is asleep. He's prodded with a pole from someone behind camera. He wakes up in a bad mood.*

GRAHAM Strewth! Look, you're supposed to be filming a story about how I came to join the Dangerous Sports Club, not a story about how a film crew irritated someone to the point of blind rage.

GRAHAM *advances threateningly on the camera. He blocks out the screen. Cut to a shot from another camera.* GRAHAM *notices some of the crew glancing behind him. He turns, sees the other camera.*

GRAHAM Oh, I see. *(To Camera 2/folks at home)* Evening all. Sorry about this.

He hurls a bedside glass of water straight at the lens. The picture becomes a watery wobble as indicating passage of time. We fade to:

EXT. *Tower Bridge, London. Day.*

GRAHAM *stands on the upper level observation walkway. Moody vista of London spreads out behind.* DAVE *and other DSCs are seen furtively fixing bungee elastic to the structure.*

GRAHAM Aren't directors wonderful? What a link. How do they think up these things? Oh *(Insincerely)* sorry about the cameras rolling . . . Anyway, after only a week in Ecuador, I left. I'd deliberately invented lots of important meetings that I had to go to so that there was less chance of me having to do anything too dangerous. But – I had become a sort of honorary member of the Dangerous Sports Club – I felt a bit of a fraud. I hadn't done anything dangerous. See, you're supposed to do three different events before you can become a member. I decided that, in a sensibly timed sort of a way, I would become a legitimate member. Maybe the Winter Sports. Falling in snow wouldn't be too bad. Or perhaps a bungee-jump from a low bridge over deep water . . .

In the background DSC members take turns leaping off the bridge. As each member drops, the camera leaves GRAHAM's *close-up to follow the fall. In fact,* GRAHAM *is hardly in shot at all.*

GRAHAM During that week in Ecuador, I did get to know the DSC a bit and found they were a very varied group of people; varying from stylish, if slightly demented close relations of royalty, to the average out-of-work English delinquent. A varied group, but they all had one thing in common, they liked to do things which scared them. They got a buzz out of being adrenaline junkies. *(Ends speech. Turns to off camera)* I'm a bit worried about that, Mike. Do you need another?

MIKE (V.O.) Hmmm, that was great for us.

DAVE *enters shot.*

DAVE Jumps are all right!

GRAHAM Oh, that's good. I hope I didn't mess things up by getting in shot too much.

DAVE *looks to off camera.*

DAVE You did get the jumps?

MIKE (V.O.) We covered it all.

GRAHAM Not that it's vital, but do you think anyone will listen to what I'm saying which, incidentally, I thought we all liked, if maniacs in tuxedos are leaping off bridges behind my left ear lobe?

MIKE (V.O.) I think you'll be pleased with it. Honestly.

GRAHAM Oh. OK. Good. I'm happy. *(Mumbling)* We'll see. I've short-changed myself too much in the past. I don't mind if it's all voice-over. You could get someone else . . .

DAVE OK guv?

GRAHAM Yes, fine.

DAVE It's nice deep water. Want a go?

GRAHAM Well yes, I could. Great. But I've got a few things I must sort out with Mike. Anyway, it's better for the film . . . dramatically . . . if I don't jump 'til the end.

DAVE Fair enough.

Without any more ado, DAVID KIRKE *hurls himself off the bridge. We carry on filming during the subsequent police action and arrests, should they occur (as usual). As members of the DSC are hauled up to the catwalk,* GRAHAM *continues his v.o.*

GRAHAM . . . So I decided that I would go with the club to their annual Winter Sports to be held that year in St Moritz, Switzerland. I would go. Whether I would take part or not, I would decide later.

EXT. *Establishing shot of St Moritz (already filmed).*

The DSC prepare their various contraptions on which they intend to hurtle out of control down the snow slopes.

GRAHAM (V.O.) The only rule for this winter event is that you should make an uncontrolled descent of a snow slope. There has to be some object between yourself and the skis, making control impossible. Extra points are awarded for imagination in choice of this object. It could be anything from a wheelchair to a grand piano. The only method of braking is 'the crash'. I had firmly made up my mind that I was going to be very adult about my decision whether to take part or not. I was going to look at the slope and the machine chosen for me; coolly and critically assess my chances of injury and be adult and sensible enough to say 'no'. Peer pressure would not influence me. *(To off camera)* You see, Mike, I think it is going to be better if we just tell the story and don't fart around so much.

MIKE (V.O.) You could be right.

GRAHAM (V.O.) . . . and no putting this in, right?

MIKE (V.O.) You're the boss.

GRAHAM (V.O.) Just checking. Now, where was I . . . Ah! Pick-up from 'influence me' . . . Take 1 . . . From 'influence me'. Take 1.

EXT. *Ski slopes of St Moritz.*

Assembly of DSC archive film/video plays to match the continued v.o. as much as possible.

GRAHAM (V.O.) Dee dum, dee dum 'influence me.' *(Pause)* Well, I arrived on the mountain to find the DSC grumbling to the organizers that they'd been given too gentle a slope. It looked fine to me. But they won their argument, and we were given the end of a black ski run. Now, this was steeper, bumpier, and had no run-off area at the bottom . . . just a drop with a few trees poking up. Even so, ten members set off down the slope in wheelchairs on skis.

EXT. *St Moritz. Day (already filmed).*

Compilation of footage from past Winter Sports, described when necessary by v.o. Ten people set off down slope in wheelchairs on skis.

GRAHAM (V.O.) Only one of them reached the bottom, and he was lucky enough to hit a tree.

A cruise missile (full-scale replica) and a bath-tub, both on skis, make their descent.

GRAHAM (V.O.) Hubie Gibbs made an error when he decided he would be better off not being strapped into his vehicle.

HUBIE GIBBS *makes his descent in his race car.*

GRAHAM (V.O) The paramedics arrived quickly, but Hubie was concussed and had a gash where a section of the steering wheel had pierced his leg. He also suffered loss of memory for five days.

Shots of more preparation at the top.

GRAHAM (V.O.) Something urged me to go home at this point, but although the others must have been similarly affected, they didn't show it. I wasn't brave enough to chicken out. To cheer everyone up, David Kirke decided he would be the next person down the mountain. He sat in a C5, a small electric car. Not a commercial success, but on skis it was very aerodynamic. David sped down the slope.

DAVID *and car hurtle down hill, coming to an abrupt halt at some projection. He is slow to move.*

GRAHAM (V.O.) When he eventually staggered out of the car, there was a trickle of blood coming from his right temple and it was my turn next. I looked around for the slowest vehicle at the top of the slope.

EXT. *Mountainside. Day. Close-up.*

GRAHAM (V.O.) Which happened to be a wooden Venetian gondola, borrowed from some Italian restaurant. It looked slow and relatively safe. No nasty metal bits to stick into you. I sat in the back of this tumbrel, next to Lord Xan Rufus Isaacs and in the front of the gondola was Eric. Now Eric is the Dangerous Sports Club mascot. He is in the shape of a man, totally bandaged from head to foot. He has eyes that swivel, always smokes a cigarette and, for some reason, wears a pair of boxer shorts beneath which is what can only be described as an erection . . . A rather mobile erection at that. They use Eric to annoy people in restaurants, at which he is singularly successful.

EXT. *Dorchester Hotel. Day. (already filmed).*

Eric arrives for lunch in a car driven by DAVID KIRKE. *We see the commissionaire acknowledge him.*

EXT. *St Moritz. Ski Slope. Day (already filmed).*

Various vehicles are prepared.

EXT. *Scottish mountainside. Day.*

GRAHAM (V.O.) So Xan Rufus Isaacs, myself and Eric waited to be pushed off at the top of the slope, wondering how we would crash. Xan cheered me up by remarking that 'It looks like a bit of a brown trouser job this afternoon.' . . . and we were pushed off.

The descent of the gondola (already filmed).

GRAHAM (V.O.) By the second bump we were airborne. The thought 'broken leg' passed through my mind as I found myself flying through the air, over Xan Rufus Isaacs' head. Then I noticed him flying over my head as we both fell down the slope pursued by the wretched wooden gondola.

It crashes.

EXT. *Scottish mountainside. Day.*

GRAHAM (V.O.) We both finished up badly winded – but alive! I felt great, I'd done it and survived. I felt good for two weeks after that. The whole world was put into proper perspective for me. Unpaid bills and the Bank Manager were no longer important. Was I beginning to get hooked? No way! Well, certainly not enough to try my luck again that afternoon. But others did.

Compilation (suitably stirring music over) of amazing DSC archive footage of past ski events, including: dinner for two, COSMO's startling exercise bike ride, the two-man sofa, the tandem, the duet at a grand piano, Second World War biplanes, the rowing eight, the huge inflatable elephant, etc. All ending with COSMO on the hunting horse. This sequence will be some four minutes long and needs no explanatory V.O.

INT. *St Moritz Hotel. Night (already filmed).*

Shots of boisterous party after day's events. Includes the sight of COSMO resting, plus minor explosions etc.

GRAHAM (V.O.) The Dangerous Sports Club certainly believe in a good party, and not in prudish professionalism. For them, fanatical devotion to training would take the edge off the danger. Like Edwardian gentlemen amateurs, they would rather enjoy themselves – not win.

INT. *Hotel St Moritz. Night.*

More party shots. FITZ *executes his jump over the table and into a barrel.*

INT. *Another bar posing as opposite number in St Moritz.*

MARK CHAMBERLIN The thing about Graham Snotface, is that he's very polite.

DAVID Actually, what we really liked about Graham was that he was a shy and thoughtful intellectual.

NINA The sort of chap you could bring home to your parents.

Cut. Quick reprise of GRAHAM *advancing angrily on camera.*

Cut.

INT. *Scottish inn. Day.*

Mountainside still visible behind GRAHAM *as a black and white photograph on bar wall. The 'inn' is a hotel in a touristically scenic area. Layers of plastic authentically almost hide the genuine article. The residents and customers are nice people, who like to be nice.*

GRAHAM *(In close-up, conspiratorially)* Style is important. The style with which you do something enhances the experience. How about this for style.

Shot of DAVID KIRKE *flying in the pouch of an inflatable kangaroo.*

GRAHAM (V.O.) The exhilaration of the experience is enough for them. They don't want an audience. But they need money for their schemes, and so they need sponsorship.

Shot of Foster's Lager logo on kangaroo. (NB: Approach Foster's for money for this exposure??) GRAHAM, *in close-up, turns his head. He has just been recording himself using a small video camera. At first he thinks of trying to hide this as* DAVID KIRKE *comes in to have a shit and joins him at his table.* COSMO *follows and sits. Oblivious to* GRAHAM *and his camera, he contemplates the universe over a pint of heavy and a malt whisky chaser.*

DAVID Was that another long speech to camera?

GRAHAM No. Just voice-over and links.

DAVID . . . I mean we've got a lot of action.

GRAHAM Look, before Mike starts rolling over there *(Reaches towards camera to turn it, taking in* MIKE *at the bar)* . . . why don't we knock off a bit of an interview ourselves. *(The camera turns again to take in Graham and David Kirke)* It's much more relaxed and natural.

DAVID Interview?

GRAHAM Well, introductions to action shots.

DAVID Fire away.

He sits as GRAHAM *positions his camera.*

GRAHAM Bureaucracy. The club . . . Dave, do you think the bottle should be in the shot? May give the wrong impression.

DAVID We are in a bar. Relaxed and natural.

GRAHAM You're right. *(Lights up a cigarillo, gets comfortable)* Dave, the club has a tradition of problems with bureaucracy?

DAVID Inevitably. You can't do anything these days without giving employment to the suit and tie brigade. Bureaucracy stifles adventure and confines individuality.

GRAHAM That was a bit glib, but you're right I suppose. Like, when you flew across the English Channel from England to France in the pouch of the thirty-foot-high inflatable kangaroo . . .

Shots of DAVID's *kangaroo take-off and flight.*

INT. *Scottish inn. Day.*

DAVID Yes, I was spotted by a civil airliner at 10,000 feet. The pilot was probably disappointed it wasn't a flying saucer and reported it to the Civil Aviation Authority and they indicted me for flying without a licence. Of course, if I'd asked for a licence to fly the kangaroo in the first place, they wouldn't have given me one.

GRAHAM Quite right. It would have increased the risk.

DAVID We had a few problems with a church steeple and electricity lines, but it developed a new type of gas ballooning; which could lead to good things . . .

Shots of flying horse model, followed by the actual flying horse . . . A seventy-foot wingspan helium balloon. Pegasus with passenger on his back.

INT. *Scottish inn. Day.*

GRAHAM ... and Martin Lyster, back there, you had some problems with a base-jump from an electricity pylon.

DAVID Martin! *(Looks over shoulder)* Mark!

He pulls MARTIN LYSTER *into shot.*

MARTIN Well fortunately we got away just before the police arrived.

Scenes of pylon jump.

MARTIN (V.O.) ... You can see Mark and me climbing the pylon, very early in the day. But there was a problem. Mark's chute wouldn't open properly.

We see this dramatic jump and their speedy escape ahead of the law. A discussion develops (ad lib) with GRAHAM *about the high adrenaline factor in base-jumping. Shots of* HENRY ROBINSON *in gorilla suit making his parachute jump from a microlite.*

INT. *Scottish inn. Day.*

From Mike's camera's viewpoint at the other end of the bar, we see Graham, David Kirke, Cosmo, MARK *and Martin in front of Graham's camera.*

MIKE (V.O.) OK, quiet everyone. And cue Graham.

GRAHAM *squares up to face camera as it zooms in to him through the bar.*

GRAHAM We've already done this bit on my camera. It'll look great. Sure you'll like it.

MIKE (V.O.) Great! If you've got it, we'll use it. I hated the zoom.

His sarcasm wasted, GRAHAM *looks disappointed.* MARK *spots something at the side of the room and exits frame.*

GRAHAM *(To David)* All of us sitting round a table like this, being interviewed ... I've got déjà vu.

Cut.

Shots from Australian TV interview leading up to the point where DAVID

KIRKE *picks up* TOMMY LEIGH-PEMBERTON *and slams him down onto the Cafe Royale dining table, shattering their Waterford crystal and scattering the TV crew.*

INT. *Scottish inn. Day.*

Scene as before. They sit at the table and reminisce in silence.

MIKE (V.O.) Still rolling.

GRAHAM Well I'd finished.

DAVID . . . There's the intro to catapulting.

GRAHAM *(Aside to David)* I thought I'd do that quietly in the toilet.

MIKE (V.O.) OK, catapulting . . . and cue!

GRAHAM Catapulting, catapulting. Er . . . *(Coughs)* So I'd taken part in the winter sports, but I still had two more events to go before I could become a member of the Dangerous . . .

A WAITRESS *arrives at their table and puts a huge plateful of steak and kidney pie and a magnum of claret in front of a now animated* COSMO. GRAHAM *continues:*

GRAHAM . . . two more events. I didn't feel ready for a bungee-jump yet, but when David rang suggesting that I could be catapulted from a crane, I thought I would go along and check it out at least. Now this was for a charity event in . . .

There is a loud crash. Drinks and tableware take to the air as MARK CHAMBERLAIN *plummets down into the middle of their table (having dropped almost vertically from a step-ladder; we see this in frame as* MIKE *widens the shot a little). Debris flies everywhere and crew scatter.* GRAHAM *carries on over the chaos.*

GRAHAM We'll just see it as it happened.

EXT. *Grassy area. Day.*

A 150-foot crane stands in the middle. Two or three people huddle round where the 'rope' from the crane stretches down to the ground. 'ERIC', who is being used as a test dummy, suddenly rockets up into the air courtesy of the stretched elastic from the crane. He hits the ground and suffers considerable damage. The elastic rope is detached from his remains.

EXT. *At the foot of the rope.*

GRAHAM, *with a clip-on microphone and a couple of mini-cameras taped to him, is just being fitted into a climbing harness by* DAVID. HUGO SPOWERS *hangs on to the end of the 'rope', which in fact is heavy-duty aircraft-carrier elastic.*

GRAHAM So, you've shortened the rope then?

DAVID Yes, yes, no worries.

GRAHAM *(To Hugo)* Now, you tie this climbing harness to the ground behind me . . . ?

HUGO *(Ties onto concrete block)* Yes, and then this . . . *(Clips elastic rope onto front of climbing harness)* . . . clips on here. The crane starts up . . . *(He signals as it does so, stretching the rope)* . . . and then when the rope's really stretched, I cut the rope behind you with this knife.

GRAHAM Yes I see. Any particular advice?

HUGO You must hold your hands behind your neck like this *(Demonstrates)* otherwise you'll get whiplash . . .

GRAHAM *(Does so)* Will. Not *might*?

DAVID You'll be experiencing a force of some 6Gs . . . We're being kind to you. Hugo's been through eleven and a half . . .

Shot of crane getting higher and 'rope' tautening. A BUTLER, *with a lavish cream tea, joins the group.*

HUGO *(While selecting cake)* . . . then when you get to the top of your flight, you'll see lots of coils of rope floating about. Don't get tangled in them, otherwise you could strangle yourself on the way down.

GRAHAM You wait till now to tell me this?

The crane is close to its full height and the 'rope' is now taut with ominous power.

DAVID . . . and when you reach the bottom of your flight, be sure to hold your arms up like this *(Demonstrates)* or the rope could smash you in the nose or eye, and slightly modify the profile.

GRAHAM I think I'll remember that.

HUGO We're all ready. Count to five.

GRAHAM If I don't get to five could you *(Holding up his knife, Hugo nods)* One, two, three, four, strange thi—

In an instant, GRAHAM zooms vertically up 150 feet or so. The use of various cameras here will give the audience at home a real feeling for the event. Different angles, slo-mo, etc. Before long GRAHAM is bouncing up and down safely at the end of the elastic. We get an impression of his relief and elation as he unharnesses.

Then into a montage of DSC archive material featuring startling catapulting highlights.

EXT. *for* INT. *Office. (As in opening scenes.) Day.*

DAVID sits on the edge of GRAHAM's desk fingering the smart ornaments.

DAVID Outdoor types always get to philosophize a bit in their documentaries, don't they?

GRAHAM *(Guardedly)* Yes . . .

DAVID I'd like to say something about environmental issues.

GRAHAM What? 'Stop chlorinated fluoro-carbons, cut down CO_2, stop deforestation; or that's the end of the world as we know it?'

DAVID . . . That sort of thing, yes.

GRAHAM Or, 'How we will be thought of in a few years' time, if there's anyone left to think, if we're not more generous with our excess food.'

DAVID . . . And how I hate pre-planned pension schemes. Might all sound a bit pompous. Who are we to say that?

GRAHAM Not in an amusing documentary, no. Pity.

DAVID Think they'll keep this in?

GRAHAM They would if we did something really stupid.

They exchange a glance, each reaches behind the desk, then suddenly and synchronously smash each other in the face with enormous custard pies.

GRAHAM We stand a chance now.

EXT. *Scottish inn. Day.*

DAVID *and* GRAHAM *face the camera. In the background DSC members come to arrangement with the hotel management about breakage.*

GRAHAM . . . The sort of high spirits we saw in there a moment ago. Is it a reaction against 'niceness'?

DAVID No, it's vandalism.

GRAHAM A statement against privilege, maybe?

DAVID Pure vandalism. But we never harm anyone else, and the damage is always aesthetically and ecologically desirable, and paid for.

GRAHAM But – you don't condone it?

DAVID Not unless I'm taking part.

GRAHAM It really is quite a dangerous club.

DAVID So the Japanese found out.

Graham pauses until he thinks the camera has cut. He turns to David.

GRAHAM You're really very good at this linking business. I'd forgotten about the Japanese.

DAVID *explains the nature of the DSC v Japan encounters over archive footage. How the Japanese visitors were given the traditional British breakfast, lunch and dinner of extra hot vindaloo, and almost emasculated by bungee rope etc.*

EXT. *Path overlooking bridge from which* GRAHAM's *bungee-jump will be made. Day.*

GRAHAM, DAVID KIRKE *plus other DSC members walk towards the bridge.*

GRAHAM A few questions people always ask . . . Have you got a death wish?

DAVID Perhaps a slightly more active life wish.

GRAHAM Are there any women in the Dangerous Sports Club?

DAVID You've already met them.

GRAHAM Yes, about five so far. I should've asked you that earlier in the documentary. What do the members' mothers, wives or husbands think of them taking part?

DAVID Mothers hate it. People lose their taste for it when they marry.

GRAHAM Are you mad?

DAVID What, about marriage?

GRAHAM No. It's another frequent question. Are you mad?

David's answer to this. (No? Slightly? Not at all? Aren't you? or whatever.)

DAVID ... So, how do you feel about a jump? It's a nice bridge.

As we follow their progress we pass MIKE, *who reads from a clipboard as they walk through shot.*

MIKE Since this will be the first time Graham has leapt off a bridge on a piece of elastic, his inner feelings should be of some interest.

The rest of this speech is in v.o. as we follow GRAHAM's *preparation for his jump from the bridge.*

MIKE (V.O.) If it is anything like his first two events, then he will feel somewhat that he may be about to leap to his untimely demise. This feeling will be pushed to the back of his mind because he knows he cannot now back out. He has seen someone else jump. Peer pressure gets to us all. He concentrates instead on explaining to himself how safe it really will be. The irrefutable laws of physics demand that all will be well. Yet still, there is that nagging doubt that, if anything did go wrong, he might not be around for supper.

GRAHAM's *jump and his feelings throughout the process, until he stands safely back on the bridge, are recorded in detail. There are cameras at a distance, on the bridge and on him. His elation at a successful outcome will be obvious. There is general jollity and congratulations as we segue into a short collage of more magnificent bungee-jumps (from the DSC archives), with jumpers actually touching the ground. This will end on a repeat of the 800-foot Arizona spectacular.*

EXT. *for* INT. *Office. Day.*

DAVID *and* GRAHAM *at desk still showing traces of custard.*

DAVID Is this where I do the 'congratulations on becoming a member of the Dangerous Sports Club' bit?

GRAHAM I haven't done the jump yet. We're shooting out of sequence.

During the above and subsequent ad lib dialogue, the camera slowly pulls back from the two and their office setting, to reveal that the entire 'office' is perched on top of the Old Man of Hoy, a cylindrical pillar of rock rising 450 feet vertically out of the sea, off the northern coast of Scotland.

Two theatrical flats make up the office walls. The scenes here have all been shot by telephoto lens from the top of cliffs on the mainland. A helicopter arrives to take them down. DAVID may have his own ideas about a more exciting method of getting off the rock, but GRAHAM will have none of this.

EXT. *Path overlooking bridge from which GRAHAM has made his jump. Day.*

GRAHAM is still elated and is modestly accepting congratulatory words and mumbles from everyone.

DAVID So, after the party you'll be a full member.

GRAHAM Yes . . . What?

DAVID You will be given your membership at a celebratory Dangerous Sports Club 'At home' . . .

GRAHAM . . . Oh that's making a bit too much of it.

DAVID hands him a black-edged invitation. It is seen in close-up. It invites you to a 'DSC At Home on Rockall'. GRAHAM is not pleased.

Cut.

Shots of the Island of Rockall. Rockall is no more than a lump of steep-sided rock sticking sixty feet out of the Atlantic Ocean some 200 miles out from the UK mainland.

The ocean swell at the base is commonly in the order of twenty feet. DSC members, all in tuxedos, leap one by one from very mobile dinghies onto the rock. With the sea hungrily clawing at their ankles, they

make the severe-grade climb up to the top. They are joined by
GRAHAM, *who arrives in comfort, in a smart motor launch.*

A wheelchair is lowered down and he is winched up into it. He joins in
polite cocktail party chit-chat on top of the rock. They have brought
suitable music with them, which plays from an old mechanical record
deck with a loud speaker horn. There is much celebration, and one or
two members may get sufficiently carried away to dive into the
pounding seas.

The end credits run over shots of further Dangerous Sports Club
eccentricities. The sixty-foot-diameter two-man bubble. Shots of
the bubble, with two members inside playing cards, as it rolls off a
200-foot cliff. A reprise of downhill ski events including some new
items, and a montage of crashes and mishaps culminates in a soaring
hang-glider flight over an Ecuadorian volcano crater.

THE END

GRAHAM (V.O.) 'Shy and thoughtful intellectual'? Well, that can go.

MIKE That's easy to cut.

THE REAL END

SKETCHES

Introduction

Without a doubt, the script format (sketches for TV and screenplays) was the area where Graham's talents really shone. It's sometimes been said of Graham that he spent the majority of time in script meetings looking out of the window and saying nothing; that he did very little actual writing – the physical act of sitting down and putting pen to paper. Whatever the degree of truth in this, it pales in comparison to what he *did* contribute. Graham's ability to add a mad twist – or sometimes even just a catchphrase ('Lemon curry?') – to a sketch far exceeded his skills as a secretary. A classic case in point can be seen in the *Python* sketch 'The Dead Parrot'. What started off as a good, if ordinary, sketch by Michael Palin and Terry Jones about a man returning a defective car (as seen in the one-off 1969 TV special *How To Irritate People*) was completely turned on its head when Graham suggested instead to make it a man returning a dead parrot. And thus a piece of timeless comedy was created.

As John Cleese, Barry Cryer, and his many other writing collaborators have said, Graham was 'a starer' and 'a walker', he was not a scribbler. 'It seems that in every writing team there is the one who is the "walker" and one who is the "writer",' Barry Cryer has said. 'Graham was a walker. He was a great walker. He should have had a speedometer on his shoes.' This may have been the role Graham fell into in his writing partnerships but on his own he did sit down, literally put pen to paper and physically write sketches and the like (I've nearly stared myself blind trying to make out Graham's spidery scrawl).

Although he is best known for his work with the always brilliant John Cleese for *Monty Python*, by late 1974 (as noted in the published sections of Michael Palin's diary) the Chapman/Cleese writing team had more or less split up – though it could be argued with some degree of confidence that they had ceased any true collaborating a year or so earlier, after the third series of *Python* (the majority of Chapman/Cleese items in the fourth series had been written earlier). Certainly by the time of filming for *Monty Python and the Holy Grail* the pair were spending more time writing apart than together and, after *Grail*, the split was *fait accompli*. Cleese began to write *Fawlty Towers* with then-wife Connie Booth while Graham went on writing solo and with many others, and for many other programmes. Some of his other writing partners include the aforementioned Barry Cryer, Bernard McKenna, Peter Cook, David Yallop, Alex Martin, David Sherlock, Neil Innes and Douglas Adams. Graham even occasionally mixed it up within *Python* and wrote a few sketches with Eric Idle – who also contributed to the brief writing team of Chapman/Cryer/Idle for the *Doctor In the House* TV series.

Not much has been said about the writing team of Chapman/ Cryer, which is odd because, outside of his relationship with John Cleese in *Python*, one of Graham's major writing partners was Barry 'King of the one-liner' Cryer. At first it may seem an unusual pairing – Graham being the 'madcap Monty Python' and Barry hailing from the old school of comedy; a man who, after all, wrote jokes for Bob Hope, George Burns, and Morecambe and Wise – but Graham appreciated a good 'set-up and punchline man' as well as the next writer and Cryer brought both to their partnership. Cryer was also a grounding influence, in much the same way Cleese was, for many of Graham's more outrageous comedic flights of fancy.

The team of Chapman and Cryer was a winning combination and, in truth, Graham spent almost as much (if not more) of his writing career working with Barry Cryer as he did with John Cleese. Together, Graham and Barry worked on dozens of projects – both produced and unproduced – including the *Doctor in the House* and *The Prince of Denmark* (for Ronnie Corbett) television series. They also did speculative work, most of which never saw the light of day. In addition to their attempted revitalization of the *Barton* character for television, Chapman and Cryer also wrote a story outline for *The Avengers* (titled 'Ah Yes, I Remember *What* Well?') and they even developed and scripted a proposed TV series in 1976 titled *Frank & Earnest*.

This last programme deserves special mention for (if all had gone according to plan) it would have been groundbreaking: the first-ever television series about a gay couple. But all did not go according to plan. Graham and Barry initially brought the script to Jimmy Gilbert (Head of Light Entertainment at the BBC, and a friend). Gilbert liked the script but was frightened off by the subject matter. Next up was producer Humphrey Barclay (at London Weekend Television and a friend, stretching back to Graham's Footlights and *Cambridge Circus* days). Barclay was more blunt in his critique. He simply thought that the script was not as funny as it should be ('Your script doesn't make me laugh enough,' he wrote). Lastly, it was shown to a producer at the BBC named Mark Shivas, who was quite candid. He lambasted the script saying that he felt that the situation surrounding the two homosexual leads was clichéd, and that the mother character was unbelievable. Although attempting to make light of Shivas's response, it made Graham quite upset, as the incidents and situations described in the script were almost exactly what had happened to him in real life. His thinly veiled anger is evident in his tersely worded reply to Shivas:

'... I am amazed that you find the [script] contains "every cliché about homosexuality" and that the mother character "seems quite a long way from believability". That character is based very accurately on my own mother and the clichéd situations happened to me, but not to Barry Cryer who is, I believe, happily married with four children, a mother, and a dog called Polly ... I would be happy to talk to you about this some time, unless you would consider it a waste of breath. If it is too much of a strain on your laryngeal apparatus, please do not bother to reply as I find that disappointing letters make me rush out and bite scaffolding, and I have already had to have one tooth capped.'

Frank & Earnest was never produced.

Somehow, in between writing all of the above, Graham also managed to find the time to sit down and co-script (with Cryer) a full stage play; co-wrote an (unproduced) screenplay based on the *Doctor in the House* television series, as well as *The Odd Job* screenplay, which *was* produced; develop a couple of sketches and some TV ideas with Douglas Adams; co-script (with Cleese) and star in the *Monty Python and the Holy Grail* film; and begin initial work on his autobiography — all of this while maintaining his normal full schedule of drinking and carousing down at the pub until all hours of the day and night with friends like Keith Moon, Harry Nilsson, and Ringo Starr. By Graham's own reckoning, at one point in the mid-1970s he wrote, or co-wrote, thirty-seven half-hour TV comedy scripts alone during a one-year period. Whether he worked with John Cleese, Barry Cryer, David Sherlock, Douglas Adams or on his own, Graham's sketch work positively brims with comic brilliance, ruthless observation and flair, and his special brand of idiosyncrasy.

With the exception of *The Severance of a Peony* (which appeared in the one and only recorded episode), the following sketches were intended for *Out of the Trees* but never produced.

High-Class Grovellers, Ltd.

A very smart Savile Row shop. A sign on the wall reads:

    'R.F. Seymore & Sons – High-Class Grovellers, Ltd.'

MR MAYNARD, *a middle-aged and fussy man, is behind a counter.*
  MR OGMORE, *a young and casually dressed man, enters.*

MAYNARD *Good* morning, sir. And how are we today?

OGMORE I don't know, how *are* you?

MAYNARD Don't come that tone of voice with me. Don't try and make cheap little jokes in here. This isn't one of your dirty little run-of-the-mill two-shilling tailors you know. This is a high-class establishment founded in the reign of *King* George the Fifth!

Hearing this, MR COOKE *comes over. He is impeccably dark-suited with a carnation in his buttonhole.*

COOKE What appears to be the trouble in this area, Mr Maynard?

MAYNARD This snotty little customer's just walked straight in here and been rude to me.

COOKE *(With a smile)* I'm sure there's a perfectly adequate explanation in this area. Where is the high-class customer in question?

MAYNARD That is he, Mr Cooke.

COOKE *(To Ogmore)* Ah. I'm so sorry. I did not recognize in the gentleman many of the qualities we normally associate with our clients. And you are the Earl of where, sir?

OGMORE I'm not an Earl at all.

COOKE What a frightful pity. Because if you were an Earl I could excuse the fact that you were not wearing a tie.

OGMORE Why should I wear a tie?

COOKE Because it makes shopping a great deal easier in establishments of this quality, sir. You are *au fait* with the gist of the term 'high-class', I presume? It means that we are discriminating.

He attends to his gloves with force of meticulous habit.

COOKE We provide the most excellent service, but not for everyone. And one of the little ways—

MAYNARD's eyes cross. He echoes in a high-pitched voice:

MAYNARD The little ways! The little ways!

He makes a sharp 'ech!' sound far in the back of his throat.

COOKE That will be all in this area, Mr Maynard. Would you kindly go and ring Lord Winteron and tell him how well he was looking yesterday—

MAYNARD retreats to the back of the shop.

MAYNARD *(As he goes)* Of course . . . Of course . . . master!

COOKE As I was saying, one of the little ways—

MAYNARD *(From back of shop)* 'The little *ways!*' Ech! Ech!

COOKE —by which we ascertain the height of the class of service we shall provide is by reference to the client's tie.

OGMORE Oh . . . we . . . I've got an American Express Card.

COOKE grabs him by the collar.

COOKE *(Shouting for help)* Maynard! Kemp! Venables . . . !

THE ASSISTANTS rush out. OGMORE is propelled to the door and thrown through it. All but MAYNARD exit. A HEADMASTER enters.

MAYNARD *(Excessive sycophancy)* Ah, hello! Good morning! As I can tell by your tie, you are the Headmaster of a famous school! Do come in . . . And how do we find ourselves today?

HEADMASTER Oh, beset by the problems of a thousand small boys.

MAYNARD Ah yes . . . the boys. How much better our schools would be without them. Pray take a seat, Headmaster, and I will advise Mr Cooke that you are here.

HEADMASTER Thank you. I am in rather a hurry, I'm off to the public courts.

MAYNARD Oh, not as a victim I presume.

He chuckles at his joke.

HEADMASTER Yes . . . I *am* actually.

MAYNARD Ah . . . well. I can't imagine a finer, nobler person to be, er . . . er . . . a crimi— a crimi—

COOKE appears, making a gesture with his hand.

COOKE Yes . . . I'll take over in this area, Mr Maynard.

MAYNARD bows and scrapes, walking backward to the rear of the shop.

COOKE Headmaster of a famous school! How absolutely delightful to see you here, sir. I was only just this very morning conversing with Lord Edrich upon the telephone. One of our *most* distinguished clients, and a thoroughly nice man – not unlike yourself, I'm sure, Headmaster.

HEADMASTER Nice of you to say so . . .

COOKE I think I would go further in this case, and say that seldom in our dealings with those whom destiny has placed in charge of our great seats of learning, has it been my pleasure to encounter one so wise – and yet so approachable and humorous.

HEADMASTER Most kind.

COOKE The pleasure is entirely mine, Headmaster, believe me. Will that be all that you require?

HEADMASTER Er . . . Just a little tiny bit more, I think.

COOKE Why of course. I find that of all the illustrious folk who we are honoured to number amongst our clientele, there is none who adds more lustre to our reputation than one who, like yourself, combines the virtues of leadership and scholarly excellence.

HEADMASTER That's fine, thank you. I feel much better.

He moves for the door. COOKE *scurries to open it.*

COOKE Will that be on the ... er ...

HEADMASTER Account, please.

COOKE Of course, Headmaster; and the very best of luck in the courts of this land.

Absolutely Everything You'll Ever Need to Know
About Anything in the Whole Universe

A television studio complete with glittery curtains and long staircase.

SFX: *Applause.*

MUSIC: *Theme music.*

HOST Welcome to Absolutely Everything You'll Ever Need to
Know About Anything in the Whole Universe. Tonight we
have a Consultant Psychiatrist—

SFX: *Awed gasp.*

HOST —whose name for obvious reasons must be Sir Ronald T.P.
Marriott!

MUSIC: *Coronation fanfare.*

*The lights sweep dramatically. The camera focuses on the glittery
curtains.*

ANNOUNCER *(Hushed tone)* And now the door through which the
Great Psychiatrist is supposed to enter is about to be opened by
the Psychiatrist's door-opener, Mr Toon . . . Yes, the door is
opening and as the Great Psychiatrist walks in, in a consultantic
manner, towards the psychiatric podium where the proud but
inadequate interviewer awaits to be impressed by this truly
most-impressive psychiatric consultant . . . Sir Ronald is, of
course, strongly tipped to be the next Psychiatrist-Royal. He's
the discoverer of the new Synapse Theory, speaks some twelve
languages, is the author of nine books and all of this before
breakfast this morning. He is the world's leading specialist in
psycho-traumatic analysis, a revolutionary new concept where
he batters his patients into a coma with a special clinical mallet,
their problems are explained to them, then they are told to
'Grow up and pull themselves together', called a 'Stupid loony

who-do-you-think-you-are-wasting-my-time' and then wheeled
out into the street . . . And here he comes . . .

*The PSYCHIATRIST walks down the staircase and greets the HOST on the
set. A CHOIR sings off-stage:*

CHOIR Welcome to Sir Ronald,
Sir Ronald Marriott,
Sir Ronald! Sir R., Sir R., Sir R.!
Welcome to Sir Ronald Marriott,
Sir R., Sir R., Sir Ronald,
Trained to sort problems!

The PSYCHIATRIST takes a seat as does the HOST.

HOST *(Reverently)* Sir Ronald, you claim a very high success rate for
your new method of treatment for all types of mental
problems.

SIR RONALD Yes, I do.

HOST I see. Some people, of course, untrained in psychiatry, have
criticized this method as being brutal. Well, not brutal, as being
severe. Well, not severe. A bit, how shall I put it – tough.
Toughish, on the patient.

SIR RONALD Oh it's quite brutal. Absolutely appalling. You should
listen to the poor loonies screaming their lungs out.

HOST They scream?

SIR RONALD Oh yes. Wouldn't you if you'd been hit on the head
with a mallet? I'll show you.

He thumps the HOST with a mallet.

HOST Ah!

SIR RONALD Now that hurt, didn't it?

HOST Yes!

SIR RONALD Would you like the full course?

HOST No thank you.

SIR RONALD I should think not. It's bloody painful.

HOST But surely that's a rather simplistic approach to your method of treatment. According to your paper it takes a long psycho-analogical workup of the patient: hypnotherapy, electro-therapy, carefully controlled use of psychotropic pharma preparations?

SIR RONALD No, I just hit them on the head – BANG! That's all there is to it. Anyone could do it, really. Cures 'em all. Never had a single one back.

HOST But – don't they complain?

SIR RONALD Of course they don't! They're far too ill. How can you complain with two or three mallet-sized holes in your head and broken limbs?

HOST Broken limbs?

SIR RONALD They struggle, you know. My God how they struggle. One woman split her own kneecap trying to fend off a friend of mine who wanted to put 2,000 volts through her. Point is, you see, this method gets them out of the psychiatric units and into the surgical wards where we can really do something about a smashed skull or a split nostril. Why all these wretched so-called psychiatrists go in for all that 'mental' nonsense, I don't know.

HOST This doesn't worry you then.

SIR RONALD No. Not since my lobotomy.

Board Meeting

MEMBERS *enter and sit quickly.*

CHAIRMAN Right, now before we read the minutes of our last meeting I'd like to ask how much money we've made recently.

TREASURER What do you mean? Today, or just since our last meeting?

CHAIRMAN Since I last spoke.

TREASURER *(Pulls out calculator)* Let's see . . . Well, since your last word, four hundred and ninety-eight million pounds. Not including the interest rate of 18.5 per cent accrued during the five seconds since I started pushing the buttons, and by the time I've finished this sentence that'll be, oooh, twenty-six million pounds, or twenty-nine million if I carry on this sentence to say the bit I'm saying at the moment, which I have, so call it thirty.

CHAIRMAN So, being the major shareholders, I say we sell out completely.

TREASURER *picks up a phone and speaks into it.*

TREASURER Sell!

CHAIRMAN Which will send the share plummeting, which we buy a hundred times as many—

TREASURER *(Into phone)* Buy!

CHAIRMAN At the cheaper price. How much have I made so far?

TREASURER Ooooh . . . Billions I should think.

CHAIRMAN Ah, a good day's business I should think.

SFX: *An alarm bell.*

BOSTON, *another businessman, rushes in.*

BOSTON Fire! FIRE!!!

CHAIRMAN Mr Boston, need I remind you that all remarks made in the cabinet must be addressed through the Chair?

BOSTON Well, this is rather important.

TREASURER *(Table-tapping)* Out of order! Out of order!

BOSTON I'm very sorry to breach the rules of procedure, but may I point out that there is a fire going on and people are probably going to get burnt!

ALL Out of order!

CHAIRMAN You must address your remarks through the Chair.

BOSTON Alright, Prime Minister and Chairman, there's a fire. I suggest that as leading prominent members of the company it is our duty to take immediate action.

CHAIRMAN Well done. Jolly good observation of procedure, Boston.

Applause all around.

CHAIRMAN Right, now where were we?

He brings out a huge War Games-type map of the world.

CHAIRMAN Oh yes, now I was America. Tim, you were . . . ?

TREASURER Russia. *(To BOSTON)* And you were the Arab States, Africa, Japan, Iceland, Malta.

CHAIRMAN Now . . . who was Britain?

A MAN raises his hand.

CHAIRMAN Yes, well you can go and make the coffee then.

The MAN exits.

CHAIRMAN Now, war. War . . . war . . . war. As I recall, Russia's sold you, United Arab Republic? Yes, six hundred million pounds worth of British nuclear weapons, air-to-ground, ground-to-air, and air-to-air, and his Russian technicians. But I see that you, Israel, have stolen one MiG fighter, so you are going to need a lot of bandages. Ah! Oh dear, the Japanese have already sold them to you. So that's ten points up to them, so we attack Russia, thereby achieving full unemployment and maximum productivity, making tons of money. Now I—

SKETCHES

The doors burst open and GENGHIS KHAN *and a* SOLDIER *sweep in.*

ALL The mighty Khan!!

MUSIC: *Dramatic*

VOICE (O.S.) Genghis Khan, the man who was elected leader of the Asian warlords, was marked out amongst men because of his curious grey eyes, his broad business acumen, his compelling fiscal ability, and the fact that he could buy the shit out of any man!

KHAN *takes his place at the head of the table. He is laconic.*

KHAN Hey. Sorry I'm late. Can't stop for long, doing a chat show. Honestly, the amount of time I actually spend on carnage and sacking the major cities is completely disproportionate to the amount of time I spend in meetings. One can hardly gain satisfaction from it all anymore. Oh well, I digress. How's the money front, boys?

CHAIRMAN Oh! Splendid, sir, piles of the stuff.

TREASURER Yes, enormous quantities . . . terrific amounts of cash!

BOSTON Unbelievable sums of cash, O Khan, pantechnicons full of crisp fivers!

Smoke has begun to filter in from the unattended fire.

KHAN Great. Right. I'll take three-quarters of it.

Starts out with SOLDIER.

KHAN Oh business worries . . . It's all so pointless, isn't it? I really ought to find more time for reading.

They exit.

The SOLDIER *bursts back in. He sticks a sword into the* CHAIRMAN *and lobs a flaming torch into the smouldering boardroom.*

SOLDIER Sorry, forgot.

TREASURER Well, I suppose you've got to admire Khan. He's got the violence of business down to a fine art.

Lawn Mower Ladies

Awful suburban PEOPLE *sitting around in awful chasm-like house with one bottle of sweet sherry.*

MR CAWDOR Well, I suppose I'm going to have to extend the garage now.

MRS GLAMIS You don't still mow that lawn by hand, do you?

MRS CAWDOR Oh no, that's just the old lawn mower out there. We've got a new one now. It's motorized.

MRS GLAMIS Oh we've got one of those rotary ones, it goes round and round.

MRS THIRDWITCH Oh we had one of those, we now have two that hover.

MR CAWDOR Yes, I think I'll do that – extend the garage a bit. Those new Jaguar XJ12s are so long.

MRS PETTYPACE I've got a hovering lawn mower that's *green*.

Awed silence.

MRS RUMPFED RUNYON We've got twenty-three green hovering lawn mowers. Don't like them very much.

MR CAWDOR There's no substitute for real leather, is there? I mean, take for instance in car upholstery. No mucking about in the new Jaguar XJ12 – straight in there with the real leather. And gosh, isn't the street lighting dim? Funny how you don't notice it though unless you happen to get really powerful headlights, like I don't know if you've seen the new Jaguar XJ12 and its headlights, because they're really powerful I've noticed.

MRS GLAMIS I'm not surprised.

MR CAWDOR What?

SKETCHES

MRS GLAMIS I'm not surprised he doesn't like his green hovering lawn mowers. I wouldn't have one if you paid me.

MR CAWDOR You may be wondering how I happen to know so much about the Jaguar XJ12, well, since you're interested – I do, in fact, have one. Arrived this morning.

MRS THIRDWITCH Of course we don't need lawn mowers now we've got a combine harvester. It's *blue*.

Stunned silence.

MR CAWDOR I think I'll just open the window – oh dear – I can't find the switch. Oh, silly me! We don't have electric windows in the house. I must have been thinking of the electric windows in the new Jaguar XJ12. Funny how quickly you get used to that sort of thing. *(Pause)* Actually, I don't mind showing it to you, you know, the Jaguar XJ12. I was just going to look at it anyway.

He exits.

MRS CAWDOR Frank's just been invited to the International Lawn Mower Conference in Munich.

EXT. *Jaguar parked in driveway.*

MR CAWDOR *goes up to his car. A* MAN *walks past, a Chartered Accountant type, looking straight ahead.* MR CAWDOR *goes after him. La Bella Machina!*

MR CAWDOR I, er, noticed you were glancing at the new Jaguar XJ12 parked in the driveway and I thought I'd mention that it's mine, in case you were wondering whose it could be – because not many people own them.

The MAN *ignores him.*

MR CAWDOR Well, come and see it any time!

He spots ANOTHER MAN *walking towards his gate, and he runs back. He pulls back to a saunter then casually walks the rest of the way, passing the* MAN *just outside his gate. He 'notices' the car.*

MR CAWDOR Good lord – look at that! Isn't that quite a car? Terrible waiting list for steeds like that.

He dashes up to the car and kisses its bonnet.

MR CAWDOR Ah! La Bella Machina!

The MAN *ignores him and walks on.* MR CAWDOR *dashes after him.*

MR CAWDOR I wonder whose it is, eh? Lucky man, that's what I say. Beautiful job, don't you think? What do you think of people who put silver mascots on the bonnets of their cars? What do you think? I mean, supposing you had, just for instance, one of these new Jaguar XJ12s – not that you would, mind you, because the waiting list is so long – unless you know someone influential – what would you think of putting something like a silver mascot on the bonnet? You know, the bonnet of a Jaguar XJ12. Charming, isn't it? Yes, leather upholstery, electric windows – it really cost me a packet I want to tell you – ooh! I've gone and given it away! Silly me. Still, a beaut – eh?

MAN I know what you mean. I can't possibly afford a beautiful car like this. I mean, here I am with a fleet of atomic-powered Silko-Glyde lawn mowers – each with a sauna bath, a cocktail lounge with three adjoining cinemas and a discotheque all rotting in the garage and next door – they haven't got a lawn, and they're such sweet people one doesn't like to humiliate them.

Disappointed silence.

MR CAWDOR Oh. You'll be wanting to speak to my wife.

Old Gentlemen's Club

Atmosphere of an old gentlemen's club filled with moribund old gentlemen.

VOICE *(Off)* Ooooooeowhrup . . .

FRINT Good lord, what was that?

COIL Tewkesbury. I think his throat must have finally got him.

FRINT Dead, is he?

COIL Looks a bit on the inert side from here.

FRINT Oh well, gorn off to meet his maker . . .

COIL That'll be a bit of a shock for him.

FRINT Will it?

COIL Yes . . . Atheist, you know. Must be a terrible thing for an atheist.

FRINT What, dying? Don't think so. They think they're here one minute, not the next. Snuff it. That's it, out like a light.

COIL No, I meant thinking that all your life and then WHOOSH! you're up front of a maker. Damn disturbing.

FRINT Not necessarily.

COIL Would be if the maker was a huge green, slimy jelly with nine yellow eyes, huge, great dripping fangs, hissing like a snake and stinking like the intestinal contents of a three-weeks-dead crocodile with enormous steel tentacles that can put 4,000 volts across your scrotum.

FRINT Yes that would be damned disturbing . . . Quite a shock to the defunct system. Why should the maker be like that?

COIL Don't think he is. At least not my maker, but Tewkesbury, being an atheist and all . . . well, that's bound to make the old fella a bit baity, isn't it? I mean, he's hardly going to say 'Hullo,

Tewkers old bean. Bit of a pity you've never believed in me. Still, never mind, have a glass of Taylor's Vintage Reserve.'

FRINT S'pose not.

COIL No. Old Tewkers is most likely to have caught him in the old, green, slimy, stinking jelly sort of mood.

VOICE *(Off)* Ooooooeowhrup . . .

FRINT Grief. Menkersdorp's copped it all over his coffee.

COIL That percolator must have had his number on it. How many's that this morning?

FRINT Nineteen, think. No, eighteen.

VOICE *(Off)* Ooooooeowhrup . . .

FRINT Sorry. Now it's nineteen. Still, we all knew Condersfoot's ticker wouldn't last the a.m. Strange thing that, me saying nineteen in the first place. Funny thing, the subconscious.

COIL Yes. Wonder if it carries on after death?

FRINT Well, the unconscious does. Look at Menkersdorp.

COIL Well, you know, it's a funny thing . . . Here we are, pretty limited life span left, I should think now . . . And yet when I look back over my life, now that it's near its end, and I think of it in all its proper perspective, it makes me seethe with rage.

FRINT Rage, old boy?

COIL Yes. I mean, I've had a pretty full life. Tried everything I wanted to, and most that I didn't . . . Take sex, for example. What was all that fucking about? Looking back on it, impersonally as if it were, I can see now why a dog looks so odd when he's at it.

FRINT What do you mean?

COIL Well, you've seen dogs at it . . . The dog . . . business end apart, seems to spend most of his time looking around with an expression of mild embarrassment and seems to be saying 'This isn't really me' and when it's all over, it might as well not have been. Sums up my sex life pretty well.

FIRTH You've got three children.

COIL Nothing to do with it, old man. Totally separate animals, I mean, do you think they give a Martlet's turd for a worn out old tube like me?

FIRTH That's a damned odd turn of phrase, Gambaccini, old tapir.

COIL Tubes. That's all we are. Everything in one end and out the other, and all you've got to say at the end of it all is, 'Well, at least you produced three more tubes, old tapir.'

VOICE *(Off)* Ooooooeowhrup . . .

COIL Another tube's bit the dust.

FIRTH I think you're a bit depressed this morning, old Quokker.

COIL Damn right. No point in living. No point in dying.

A meandering piano (or guitar) begins to doodle.

FIRTH Might as well sing a song, then.

COIL Might as well not.

FIRTH Might as well sing one, and see what we got.

COIL Might as well sing one, and see what we've not.

An Agnostic's Song For Christmas
(To the tune of 'Oh, Come All Ye Faithful')

FIRTH & COIL

Oh come all ye sceptics,
Doubtful and suspicious,
Come ye, oh come ye,
To lack of faith.

Ignore theist's teachings,
Of fantastic aspirations,
Oh come let us abhor them,
Oh come let us ignore them,
Oh come let us deplore them,
Feeble-minded gits.

Sing choirs of doubters,
Sing in vacillation,

SKETCHES

Sing all ye denizens,
Of free thought and love.

Glory to god if he is highest,
Oh come let us adore him,
Oh come let us ignore him,
Oh come let's not abjure him,
Who needs an oath?

Cardboard

A DOCTOR *examines a* PATIENT.

DOCTOR There you are, you should be having no more trouble with that foot of yours.

PATIENT But it's my arm.

DOCTOR Arm. Let's see . . .

Flips through medical dictionary until he comes to the correct page.

DOCTOR Arm, arm, arm . . . Eurgh! Ugly things, arms, aren't they? Now which arm was it?

PATIENT My righ—

DOCTOR Come on! I can't wait all day. I've got twenty-five other patients to see before I'm allowed to have breakfast and it's afternoon already. Come on, which arm?

PATIENT It's er my . . .

DOCTOR Come on you tit! Surely you must remember.

PATIENT It's my . . .

DOCTOR Which one man, which arm is it?

PATIENT I . . . I . . .

DOCTOR Left or right? COME ON!

PATIENT I . . .

DOCTOR Good heavens, have a guess. You've got a fair chance of being right.

PATIENT Right! Yes, it's my right arm.

DOCTOR You're guessing, aren't you? Come on, you should know. I could tell if it were my arm. I'd jolly well know which of my arms was ill. Of course, I'm a trained professional. Now come on, its *your* arm, you know, it's not my arm. I've got perfectly healthy arms. Look—

Shows the PATIENT his arms.

DOCTOR —you are the one with the ill arm. Now, which one?

PATIENT It's my right arm.

DOCTOR Are you sure?

PATIENT Yes.

DOCTOR I'll write that down so that I'll know if you should change your mind later. *(Writes it down)* Right . . . arm . . . Just you remember that. Now waggle your toes and say 'cardboard'.

The PATIENT does this.

DOCTOR Hmmm. Did you enjoy that?

PATIENT Well I – what is it for?

DOCTOR Oh it's just a little something I thought up myself. Fun, isn't it?

PATIENT Does it have any use?

DOCTOR Use!? USE!! Of course it has a use. Everyone sees so much medicine on TV nowadays that there's no mystique about it . . . Got to keep one step ahead . . . It's a valuable trick. D'you know, I've cured forty cases of Madura Foot – that's twenty cases of Madura Feet – two pendulous earlobes and a budgerigar with that one. Took three days to teach it to say 'cardboard' but it was worth it. Well, it's been a very nice little chat. See you the same time next week, and don't go putting your foot in boiling lead again.

PATIENT But I—

DOCTOR Good, no more boiling lead for a time. Remember, I've taken you off boiling leads. No more of it or it'll never get any better after that. Right – NEXT!

He looks down at his notes.

PATIENT But I haven't—

DOCTOR Now, what seems to be the trouble? Oh – it's you again.

Already? Not boiling lead again, I should hope. Nurse, sterilize the blow-lamp!

PATIENT No – it's my arm! *(Pause)* My RIGHT arm!

DOCTOR Oh. *(Looks at arm)* There's no lead on that one. Let's have a look at your left.

PATIENT No, it's my right arm and my elbow is swollen.

DOCTOR Ah! Tell me, do you get a tingling sensation passing from the tip of your shoulder down the back of your arm and radiating to your fingertips with a stabbing pain in your armpit every time you kneel on something wet?

PATIENT Yes!

DOCTOR That's very unusual you know.

PATIENT But – how did you know that?

DOCTOR Just a hunch, but . . . careers are built on such hunches! Mr Victim—

PATIENT McKenna.

DOCTOR —McKenna, you and your very rare injury may very well be my ticket to immortality! It will be written up in all the medical journals . . . I'll be famous! Asked to go on speaking tours! It will be nothing but wine, women and song from here on out for me! . . . Mr Humphries, I ask you . . . Are you willing to join me in the ranks of medical history? Are you willing to allow me to amputate your arm and—

PATIENT Amputate?! No, I don't want my arm amputated, I want it treated.

The DOCTOR is crushed, his dreams of medical immortality crushed.

DOCTOR I see. Well, so much for my dreams, eh? All right you selfish bastard, bathe your arm in lukewarm vinegar twice a day.

PATIENT And that will cure it?

DOCTOR No idea, but it leaves me in the clear.

PATIENT Is the swelling dangerous?

DOCTOR No. Oh no. *(Pause)* It's not at all dangerous to me, but then, of course, it's not my arm.

PATIENT But I want it cured.

DOCTOR Ooh! Ooh! 'I want it cured' . . . You don't half talk posh, don't you? Now look, it's the *arm* you've got to worry about. Forget about the swelling. Forget about that and you'll find you'll never think about it again. Now off you go, you miserable tit, and put a firm bandage on it. Not too loose or else it will do no good at all. But – not too tight.

PATIENT How do I know if it's too tight?

DOCTOR . . . You *are* a bastard, aren't you? Look, you'll know if it's too tight because your fingers will turn black and then green and then your arm will drop off!

PATIENT But I—

DOCTOR You'll soon get the hang of it. Lefty. NEXT!

The Great Insurance Trek

A MAN *in a suit staggers across the burning desert and splashes into the sea. Sharks surround him as he bobs in the water. He swims to shore and collapses onto the beach. He hacks his way through the jungle and comes to the foot of a mountain, which he climbs using his bare hands, enduring wind and rain. He reaches the other side, stumbles through more desert, past the Pyramids, and through a raging military battle. He sees a military plane and fights his way to it and takes off. A fierce air battle as he fends off pursuing planes. He's hit over London. He straps on a parachute and jumps from the burning plane, which spirals into the Thames. He parachutes to the ground, and straight into traffic. He's nearly hit by a lorry.*

Cut to an insurance office where an INSURANCE MAN *sits. The* MAN *enters. The* INSURANCE MAN *looks up.*

MAN Ahm good morning. Is this the insurance office? Well, I can see it is – my name is Kissinger. Henry.

INSURANCE MAN You're Henry Kissinger?

MAN No, Kissinger Henry.

INSURANCE MAN Oh. Well, Mr Henry – may I call you Kissinger?

MAN Yes.

INSURANCE MAN Actually I'd rather call you April.

MAN Why?

INSURANCE MAN My wife was born in April. Well, I wouldn't say she was born in April, but she's got a cousin in the artillery who was born in August – but enough of this music hall banter. I infer business-like intentions from your demeanour.

MAN Isn't there anyone else I can talk to?

INSURANCE MAN Don't worry about me, I get part-time work as a dictionary compiler. Terebinth.

MAN Sorry?

INSURANCE MAN Terebinth: a tree of moderate size.

MAN Mmm . . . Very nice. Are you sure there's no one else I can talk to?

INSURANCE MAN Yes, scumber.

MAN Mr Scumber?

INSURANCE MAN No no, 'scumber', verb. One, intransitive, of a dog or fox, to evacuate the faeces. Two, transitive, to void brackets odour brackets – figuratively, to produce something foul. Oh but beep all that – I wonder if we can put beep in the dictionary – they won't let me say it on television. Anyway, where were we? Insurance, insurance, insurance . . .

MAN Yes, you see I was particularly interested in your policy where, for a premium of only 5p, I would be covered for all risks to the sum of one million pounds.

INSURANCE MAN Yes, we've had a lot of inquiries about that. Now, can I interest you in our special Being Nibbled To Death by Okapia Policy, under which – for a premium of a mere £500 – you would stand to gain £602.49p in the event of a fatal nibbling taking place?

MAN Would I? Mmm, very interesting, Yes, now your policy here . . .

INSURANCE MAN Lophodont.

MAN What?

INSURANCE MAN Lophodont. Lopped, lopseed. Excuse me, I excuse. How about a policy protecting against having your entire family garroted by Mary Tyler Moore?

MAN No.

INSURANCE MAN It's tax deductable.

MAN No, I want this insurance as advertised.

INSURANCE MAN Certainly sir, now . . .

He gets out form.

INSURANCE MAN This insurance would be invalid for any persons
under twenty-one or over sixty-five years of age.

MAN Yes quite.

INSURANCE MAN Persons having any physical defects or infirmary.

The MAN *shakes his head.*

INSURANCE MAN Have you ever had any insurance declined or
renewal refused?

MAN No.

INSURANCE MAN British subject?

MAN Yes.

INSURANCE MAN Not an ice cream merchant?

MAN What?

INSURANCE MAN Just one of the terms, sir.

MAN Well I'm not.

INSURANCE MAN Are you, or have any of your relations, ever been a
dance band leader or the like?

MAN No . . .

INSURANCE MAN Can you guarantee that you will not consort with
fur traders, jockeys, students or timber merchants, or persons in
any way involved in trade?

MAN Well, all right, no.

INSURANCE MAN Have you got a car?

MAN Yes.

INSURANCE MAN Oh well, I'm sorry sir, that puts it right out of the
question.

MAN I'll sell it.

INSURANCE MAN So you'll be involved in trade.

MAN Alright, I'll give it away.

INSURANCE MAN Well that's reasonable enough. Oh dear, Section 12
says that 'persons connected with charity during the three years
prior to signature of policy shall be excluded'.

MAN Alright, I'll dismantle it.

INSURANCE MAN Well that seems to be all right.

MAN Right, then here's the premium.

INSURANCE MAN I'm afraid it's not quite as simple as that.

MAN What do you mean? I've fulfilled all those conditions.

INSURANCE MAN I'm afraid these are only extracts, sir. There is a full set of conditions . . .

He pulls out an enormous tome and flips through it.

INSURANCE MAN See, under General Exclusions 'persons living in houses, flats, towns or villages; persons under nine-foot four; persons with oxygen-based respiratory systems or the like'—

MAN But nobody in the world can qualify for that!

INSURANCE MAN Quite. It's one of our most pointless policies, sir. Now here's one of our simple ones. I can do this for you now.

MAN Oh?

INSURANCE MAN Yes, you give us £500, and then we give you £450 in the event of you leaving the room.

MAN But what's the point of that? It just means you're fifty pounds up!

INSURANCE MAN I'm afraid, sir, you just haven't homed-in on the whole point of insurance.

Bank Manager

Exterior of an office door. A sign on it reads:

   'City and National Bank, Ltd. Manager: Mr E. Gropvat.'

SFX: *Intercom buzzer.*

GROPVAT (O.S.) Yes?

VOICE (O.S.) There's a Mr Lemon to see you sir.

Interior of office. MR GROPVAT *sits behind a desk.*

GROPVAT Have you checked him for security?

VOICE (O.S.) Oh yes sir.

GROPVAT All right, send him in.

There is a knock on the door, and GROPVAT *opens it.* MR LEMON *stands there. A* GUARD *stands outside the door. He pushes* LEMON *inside.*

GROPVAT Ah! Mister . . . er . . .

LEMON *(Angrily)* My name is Lemon, and I do not remember ever being searched in a bank before!

GROPVAT I'm sorry Mister . . . er . . . But we do have to take every precaution these days. You do understand?

He brings out a gun.

GROPVAT Some people may think me a little over-cautious, but I think it's better to be safe than sorry. I mean, for all we know you could easily have been a thief contemplating robbing this bank, ha, ha, ha!

LEMON Maybe . . . But if I'm going to have to strip every time I want to cash a £3 cheque . . .

GROPVAT Just the latest routine security measures. I'm sorry if you were inconvenienced, but we do have to be sure about our customers. Now, what did you say your name was?

LEMON Lemon.

GROPVAT Alias?

LEMON What??

GROPVAT Just a routine trick question.

LEMON Do you mean that you still don't believe that I'm Mr Lemon?

GROPVAT Of course we do! Ha, ha, ha, of course . . . Now if I could just see your birth certificate.

LEMON But I haven't brought that . . .

GROPVAT Oh, I see . . . *(Writes)* We have some means of identification.

He produces a beard and photo.

GROPVAT Here, put this beard on.

LEMON *does so.*

GROPVAT No, still don't recognize him. Wait a minute . . .

He draws a beard on the photo.

GROPVAT Yes! That's more him. I can tell by your nose. Is it your own nose, Bugsy?

LEMON Look, of course it's my own nose. And my name's not Bugsy.

GROPVAT I'm sorry, Mister . . . er . . . But we do have to be very strict these days, you know. The modern criminal is extremely clever. Very clever. Now, about your account . . . *(Looks at sheet)* £580 minus £420 leaves – how much?

LEMON Well, er . . .

GROPVAT Ah, good, you're not clever. Can't be too careful. What is the capital of Peru?

He puts on a pair of glasses.

GROPVAT Do you recognize this man? Why did you do it?

LEMON Look, this is insulting beyond belief.

GROPVAT I'm sorry . . . I'm sorry, but it is all necessary. You do understand? *(Relaxing)* It's a funny thing about the criminal mind, you know, they often give themselves away by little things, you know . . . Ha, ha! Lovely weather, isn't it?

He looks straight ahead and speaks stiffly.

GROPVAT Ah, Inspector Crawley – in the nick of time!

LEMON turns to look.

GROPVAT Ha, you fell for it! No hardened criminal would have fallen for that! Yes, you're almost certainly Mr Lemon. *(To cupboard)* It's all right, I can handle this now.

The cupboard door opens. PADDY, holding a cutlass, is inside. PADDY shuts the door.

GROPVAT So this is your first crime, is it?

LEMON I will not tolerate any more of—

GROPVAT Do forgive me, Mr Lemon. Only routine precautions.

ROY opens his desk drawer and carelessly removes a wad of money, placing it in front of LEMON. He holds his hand in front of his face, but is obviously peeking between his fingers at LEMON.

GROPVAT I'm so glad that we were able to help you.

A pause. He removes his hand.

GROPVAT Ah! Not tempted. Good. Well, good morning. Oh, and don't forget your notes.

ROY offers up the wad of cash.

LEMON They are not mine, and I have no intention of—

GROPVAT They could all be *ours*, if you want to know.

LEMON What??

GROPVAT Sure, we'll split fifty-fifty and live in style. What do you say?

LEMON Once and for all, Mr Gropvat, I am not a thief! I'm a dentist and I have never been so insul—

GROPVAT Of course, a dentist. Do forgive me. *(Menacingly)* What is the first tooth to erupt in the second dentition?

LEMON This is too much. I'm going.

LEMON *rises to leave.*

GROPVAT Oh, I'm sorry if I disturbed you, but you do understand. *(Rises)* Good morning. Oh, use the door on the left, this one on the right is for robbers. Robbers, you see. 'R' for right. It opens straight into a lift shaft. That's it – the left one – good morning.

LEMON *exits.*

GROPVAT Oh, er, mmmmm . . . *(To intercom)* Miss Gibbon, was it right for robbers, or right for righteous?

VOICE (O.S.) Right for righteous, sir.

GROPVAT In that case, cancel my dental appointment for this afternoon, would you?

The Severance of a Peony

Couple tripping through idyllic long grass field. Then we see young couple walking down idyllic little street. Romantic music, cherry blossom etc.

They are walking down the street arm in arm when their path is partly obstructed by a large peony bush which hangs over it from behind someone's garden fence.

SHE Darling, that was wonderful.

HE What do you mean? We didn't do anything.

SHE No, the walk, silly.

HE Oh yes, the walk. Yes, well actually I had rather hoped that we would in fact . . . *(He pushes the peony bush out of the way with just a hint of irritation.)*

SHE Darling, don't be so rough – they're so pretty.

HE What are?

SHE The peonies. Look. *(She picks one)* Isn't it pretty?

Instant police siren; screech of brakes as police car slams to a halt beside them and two policemen leap out. POLICEMAN 2 is the 'brains' of the outfit. POLICEMAN 1 is the heavy.

POLICEMAN 2 *(Grabs peony from GIRL)* What's this then?

HE She picked the peony.

POLICEMAN 2 Oh, you admit that then?

POLICEMAN 1 writes in his notebook.

HE Admit? But look officer . . .

POLICEMAN 2 Don't try to flatter me, you won't get out of it that way.

HE Get out of what?

POLICEMAN 1 Calm down.

GIRL *is in tears by now.*

HE Look, please, what am I supposed to have done?

POLICEMAN 2 Not you, her.

HE Her?

POLICEMAN 2 She's committed a felony.

SHE What do you mean?

POLICEMAN 2 Theft! That's what I mean! She has taken away the personal goods of another, viz, one peony.

HE But it's only a flower.

POLICEMAN 1 Only a flower! Oh, oh, oh!

POLICEMAN 2 That is *property*!

POLICEMAN 1 Property!

HE Property?

POLICEMAN 2 Did that peony just appear out of thin air?

HE No, it came from that bush.

POLICEMAN That bush, eh? Is it hers?

HE No.

POLICEMAN 2 Is it yours?

HE No . . .

POLICEMAN 2 Is it the bush of a friend or relation of yours?

HE No . . .

POLICEMAN 2 Then it is 'another's'. Did you ask the permission of 'another'?

He indicates the house to which the bush belongs.

HE No . . .

POLICEMAN 2 Well that, my lad, is theft, which is a felony and punishable with up to thirty years imprisonment.

We can now see in the background an old lady being beaten up by four thugs and later on during the following, other innocent passers-by being attacked and robbed – other obvious felonies.

HE What do you mean, theft, felony? She just picked a flower.

POLICEMAN 2 *Stole* a flower.

HE Alright then, we'll give it back.

POLICEMAN 2 You can't lad. It's severed.

HE What do you mean, severed?

POLICEMAN 2 Well, did you intend to put it back?

HE Er . . . yes, all right, we did.

POLICEMAN 2 All right, just how would you do that sir?

HE Well, I think I'd er . . .

POLICEMAN 2 Sellotape? Nail it back?

POLICEMAN 1 A few well-placed rivets?

POLICEMAN 2 You couldn't could you?

HE Well, no, I suppose not.

POLICEMAN 2 Well, there you are. Mind you, if you'd taken the whole bush we couldn't prove you didn't intend to put it back, could we?

Background: Archbishop being strangled.

HE Alright – look this is ridiculous.

Policemen exchange looks again.

HE I'll buy a whole new bush for them.

POLICEMAN 2 Well, it wouldn't be the same bush would it?

GIRL starts to cry. POLICEMAN 1 says 'shurrup' and hits her.

HE Look . . . we'll just go and ask the owner whether he minds our having taken a peony – and if he does mind I'll pay him compensation. But of course he won't mind. Anyway the thing was obstructing the pavement.

POLICEMAN 2 Don't try and be clever with us my lad.

POLICEMAN 1 raises his fist. POLICEMAN 2 pushes it down saying 'Not yet, not yet'.

HE Haven't you got anything better to do – there are murders going on, armed robberies, rapes, arsons – and you're just worried over one bloody peony.

POLICEMAN 2 Oh! So we've got a difficult one here have we? *(Calls)* Sergeant!

A sergeant leaps out of the car and strides over.

POLICEMAN 2 Look mate, do you want to come up to the station and be 'interviewed'?

POLICEMAN 1 Can be very nasty, being 'interviewed' . . .

HE Are you threatening violence? *(He raises a finger.)*

POLICEMAN 2 Right! Send for reinforcements!

POLICEMAN 1 Right! *(Into radio intercom)* There's been a peony severance in Southwood Lane! Can we have reinforcements . . .

Note: With a bit of nifty editing it should be possible to do most of the following section using stock film.

Cut to see policemen pouring out of a door marked 'House of Lords'. They are stripping off ermine robes etc from over their uniforms and leaping into black marias.

Cut to interior of van. The sirens are going very loudly. The POLICEMAN next to the driver is talking into radio mike.

POLICEMAN IN VAN Am proceeding in an Easterly direction along North End Avenue towards the scene of a severance on the west side of South Wood Lane. I am reclining in my seat at an angle of sixty-five degrees and the siren is going er er er er er er at a level fifteen decibels above the pain threshold.

Cut to the street scene. As the police van goes through it the siren is so loud that all the passers-by are clutching their ears and some are even collapsing with the pain with their ears bleeding.

Cut to ambulance leaving hospital to pick up eardrum victims. It also has an enormously loud siren and this causes even more damage. Cut back to hospital to see another ambulance leaving. It is driving so fast down the crowded streets that it causes an accident.

We see another ambulance leaving and another police car. They both cause accidents and go up in flames. Cut to a fire engine leaving the

House of Commons. It knocks over a pedestrian. Cut to another ambulance, another accident, another fire engine etc.

Intercut into this sequence are shots of policemen, ambulance men and firemen inside their vehicles calling for reinforcements on their radios. Then cut to soldier's head talking into radio. He is in a tank moving into action. Then sound of morse code and radar bleeps.

Cut to shot of destroyer steaming into the attack. Fighter planes; guided missiles taking off; bombs descending from plane. Mushroom clouds.

Cut to shot of the whole planet, virtually exploding.

We see alien spacecraft approaching. Cut to inside spacecraft: We see strange alien creatures watching the earth explode on a TV screen and talking in vaguely Dalek-like voices. They are models.

ONE We are too late! We are too late! They have severed the peony.

ALL They have severed the peony, they have severed the peony!

TWO *(Into radio mike)* Mission has failed, mission has failed. Impossible to effect peony severance prevention.

Cut to exterior of spacecraft. We see it wheel round and return in the direction it came.

Payment for Professional Services

A WOMAN *sits at a table.* MR HUGUENOT *enters.*

MR HUGUENOT Hello, is this the doctor's?

WOMAN That's right. Hey no, wait a tick . . . Hey, no . . . No it isn't. Phew! No, this is *not* the doctor's. Ha! Thought you'd catch me out there, didn't you?

MR HUGUENOT No.

WOMAN Oh yes you did. I know when people are trying to catch me out. It's a sort of sixth sense I have.

MR HUGUENOT Really.

WOMAN Yes. I have an eye for the peculiar, a nose for the weird, and athlete's foot, so watch yourself or else I'll pass on the spores.

MR HUGUENOT Ah, so this *is* the doctor's.

WOMAN No it bleedin' isn't!!! Oop, wait a tick . . . Yes . . . yes this *is* the doctor's. Yes. I thought you said 'Royal Society for the Preservation of Free Speech, Hot Meals and a Night Out with a Naval Seaman.'

MR HUGUENOT No, I just came from there.

WOMAN Now, how much were you thinking of spending?

MR HUGUENOT . . . Isn't it on the National Health?

WOMAN You leave off that lefty-pinko socialist garbage in here! It's strictly cash on the nob, matey.

MR HUGUENOT Oh. How much do you charge for a tracheotomy?

WOMAN *(To o.s.)* Rene! How much do we charge for a tracheotomy?

RENE (O.S.) 'Arf a quid!

WOMAN It's 50p, or 60p with expenses added, snot-face.

MR HUGUENOT That's very cheap.

WOMAN Well it's more expensive if you want sex with it.

MR HUGUENOT Sex?! Sex with a tracheotomy?

WOMAN This is a bleedin' brothel!!!!!

MR HUGUENOT Brothel? But you said it was the doctor's.

WOMAN I thought that's what you were interested in.

MR HUGUENOT Look, I don't want to give the . . . the wrong impression. I wouldn't normally eschew 'a bit of the other' you know, a 'bit of skirt'. I mean, I've tried it and it's a lot of fun! *(Piously)* If only *more* people would realize the importance of frequent and satisfactory sexual release then I, for one, believe that the world would be a much better—

WOMAN Tracheotomy?

MR HUGUENOT Yes. With a blowjob, please.

MR HUGUENOT *quickly hands over the money.*

WOMAN Right. *(To o.s.)* Rene, one tracheotomy – but keep your knickers on!

RENE (O.S.) Right!

Most of the following sketches were written by Graham in the mid-1960s, and intended for *I'm Sorry I'll Read That Again*, though not recorded. 'The Rebecca Mary Barclay Corgi Show' was recorded for the fourth series of *ISIRTA* and broadcast under the title 'Gentlewoman's Protection Action Group'.

The Flesh and Entrails Dance

MUSIC: *Jim Shand-type music. Over this we hear:*

ANNOUNCER *(In a very BBC-John Cleese-Scottish-words-pronounced-as English-voice)* Good evening. And it's welcome TAE BONNIE Scotland! I hope you're ready to come AWA with me, with Jamie O'Lester and his Light Orchester . . .

MUSIC: *More of the same follows. They only know one tune – but this time with typical Scottish whoops in the background.*

ANNOUNCER OCH AYE and A' and A' . . . and very nice too. Well here in the Temperance Hall Kilferret Glasgow, we start the programme with a 'Gay McTavish' . . .

SCOTS POOF Oooooooch! Ye cheeky wee thing!

ANNOUNCER . . . written by Jamie O'Lester especially for money.

MUSIC: *Same music but with many more whoops and screams.*

ANNOUNCER . . . and very nice too. And now we have Angus McPrunepoddie to sing his composition: 'The Gordons AE SAE Muckle TAE The Lassie O' His E'E' '!

MCPRUNEPODDIE When but a wee laddie I was o sae sma'
Me mither would cackle me onto the floor
She cackled me feen
And she cackled me reet

But she's stopped cackling noo that she's
under six feet.

CHORUS Wi' A . . .
Muckle me roo and craw me tavitty
Cackle me corrack and lay me doon.

MCPRUNEPODDIE Mae faither was sich a de'ilish auld man
He took him a lassie frae the toon of Oban
But her brither was skirlin
And sae brau and sae strang
That mae faither joined mither afore very long.

CHORUS Wi' A . . .
Muckle me roo and craw me tavitty
Cackle me corrack and lay me doon.

ANNOUNCER And very nice too. It's always very jolly here in
Kilferret and colourful too, and everyone is wearing the ancient
tartan of his ancient clan – some ancient tartans going back to
Victorian times. Wha' a proud heritage . . . Now the McSmith
Dancers bring us the flavour of the HEELANDS with a BRAU
WEE fling!

MUSIC: *The same old tune again, plus whoops and death throes.*

ANNOUNCER *(Over music)* And very nice too. So it's FA' THEE
WULL from the HEELANDS from all of us here in Kilferret,
and here to put an end to the whole thing is the BBC Light
Infantry.

SFX: *Machine guns.*

Pumas Ahoy

NEWSREADER Good evening, here is the news. We now bring you an up-to-date report on the facts behind the Olympic Games controversy. Miss Edith Camel, the captain of the British Ladies team, has made a series of outspoken criticisms of the entry regulations. She complained that in the last Games the British 100 yards freestyle champion had been ousted from the final in a heat where she competed against two New Zealanders, four stingrays and a Polish hammer-headed shark. She called for more stringent stingray tests to be employed. Miss Camel further stated that while she bore no personal malice, she was suspicious of her Russian opponent, Miss Ovestavitchenka, the discus champion. Especially when one bears in mind that 'ovestavitchenka' means 'lady gorilla' in Russian.

In other Olympic news, the British shot-put champion, Miss Leslie Mammoth, has also been under criticism. While the Women's AAA said in an official statement that mammoths are extinct, they added that they are putting Miss Mammoth through a series of exhaustive tests to see if she is not in fact an extremely large elephant.

Viewers will remember the storm of controversy last year about the Australian-born low-hurdles champion, Miss Boomer, when it was discovered, after she had refused sex tests, that the handbag she carried in the 110 yards was, in fact, a pouch. Miss Boomer's trainer, Arthur Swain, the enigmatic Head Keeper of Sydney Zoo, himself complained that one of his athletes, Mrs Mary O'Keffe, had, at the Commonwealth Games, been forced to compete against seven pumas and a water ferret. He later retracted this statement when it was discovered that the water ferret was, in fact, a Russian lady who had been taking drugs and who, through a clerical error, had not been entered for the underwater rabbit chasing . . . an event introduced in the last Olympics at the request of the Soviet Union.

Finally, Miss Camel entered what amounted to an ultimatum today calling for the disqualification of all furry competitors with or without antlers. Miss Camel, scratching herself from Saturday's match, said this was for personal reasons only and that she had a slight flea infestation.

The Rebecca Mary Barclay Corgi Show

ANNOUNCER For our Woman's Hour talk today we have Clint St. Arthur Justice Fitzgibbons talking to Miss Mary Smith-Systembolungcourt.

CLINT Miss Smith-S, you are the Chairman of a Society in Cheltenham which calls itself the Gentlewoman's Protection Action Group.

MISS S Yes, that is quite correct. *(Pause)* Did you hear that?

CLINT What?

MISS S There's someone behind me, isn't there? I know there's someone behind me.

CLINT There's no one—

MISS S Go away! He's gone. Where were we?

CLINT Er . . . Oh, Miss Smith, why do you feel there's a need for a Gentlewoman's Protection Society?

MISS S Terror.

CLINT Terror?

MISS S AAAARGGH!!

CLINT What's the matter?

MISS S Something's touching my right ankle! Oh – it's my left ankle. Yes?

CLINT Terror, Miss Smith?

MISS S Yes, terror. The Good Women of Cheltenham – there are about sixteen of us – we're terrified because of the recent increase in violence and hooliganism. We are terrified of being beaten with large sticks and thrashed about the head.

CLINT Is there much of that in Cheltenham?

MISS S No, but we would be even more terrified if there were, and we'd also be beaten with large sticks and thrashed about the head.

CLINT I see. So you formed this Society to protect yourselves?

MISS S Yes.

CLINT What methods do you use?

MISS S: We have many up-to-date protection devices. Are the doors locked?

CLINT Er, no.

MISS S Have them locked, you never know who might rush in and beat me about the head. I refuse to go on until they're locked.

CLINT (Obviously lying) Er, I was wrong, yes they are locked.

MISS S I'll take your word for it, you can't be too careful . . . We use devices such as this—

CLINT Good gracious, it looks just like an ordinary fountain pen.

MISS S It is. We are all for poking it in people's eyes, and writing.

CLINT Have you anything less drastic?

MISS S Oh yes, we first started with this brooch here. You see, you just press it there and out pops a sweet little sprig of poison ivy. Brings them out in a terrible rash. Doesn't work quickly enough though, but it's useful if you're being attacked over two or three days.

CLINT I see.

MISS S Look out – don't move! There's a vampire bat in front of your face. Oh, it's the microphone. And also we have this handbag.

CLINT That handbag?

MISS S Yes. It lets out into twenty square feet of gorilla netting.

CLINT Gorilla netting. What's that for?

MISS S For the gorillas.

CLINT Are there gorillas in Cheltenham?

MISS S Very few, but there are several wild ones loose about the country. We've seen them.

CLINT Gorillas? Well, I know there'd been reports of pumas, but—

MISS S Oh dear, yes it is pumas isn't it. That's what we saw, pumas. Take that!

CLINT What is it?

MISS S Butterfly. My gorilla netting, it's no use if it's pumas.

CLINT No, I—

MISS S We also started a Gorillas Anonymous—

CLINT What was that?

MISS S —I didn't hear anything. You're imagining things, young man. Gorillas Anonymous was established so that anyone who thinks they have a gorilla chasing them can ring up and we tell them not to panic and we reassure them and then rush round and beat up the gorilla with large pointed sticks and flame-throwers. Don't do that again.

CLINT What?

MISS S You raised your finger as if you were about to strike me.

CLINT But I didn't—

MISS S Look, you've done it again. Stay where you are.

CLINT But I didn't—

MISS S Don't move. I have you covered.

CLINT Ugh.

MISS S That was a grunt – you're a gorilla, aren't you? I could tell by the way you grabbed my gorilla netting.

CLINT I am not a gorilla.

MISS S Well, you look a bit like one with those arms and legs and those teeth.

CLINT Yes, but men have arms and legs and teeth.

MISS S Don't try to talk your way out of it.

CLINT Oh I've had—

MISS S Stay away.

SFX: *Machine gun.*

MISS S Well, I'm very sorry but you shouldn't have looked so violent. We must fight against violence.

Miss Universe Competition

ANNOUNCER Welcome to the Miss Universe competition which has now reached its final stage. The number of contestants has now been reduced to two and, in a moment, we shall be seeing them both. Judging this last stage are six judges who – and here comes Miss Sweden! Five foot nine inches, one hundred and thirty-three pounds. Vital statistics: 37–24–36. WOW! Long blonde hair flowing down over her suntanned shoulders; a flashing smile and large blue eyes . . . WHAT A GIRL! I am afraid she doesn't speak much English, but when I spoke to her before the final stages she told me 'Skov bref mortig blombort' . . .

Now here comes the other finalist, Miss Mars. Resplendent in her green scales and long flowing teeth. She stands just over three-foot high. Vital statistics: 14–41–55. Wow, what a . . . er, thing! A really lovely set of mouths, firm high tendrils and a smile in her lovely mauve eye. What a lovely Martian! And now the crowd is awaiting the result . . . Miss Sweden is waving to the crowd . . . Miss Mars is letting off purple smoke . . . And here come the judges and . . . HERE IS THE RESULT! The winner is – Miss Sweden! Yes, it's Miss Sweden by 1,308 points to nil . . . and Miss Mars . . . oooh, she doesn't like that at all . . . and some of the Martians here are looking very annoyed . . . VERY annoyed . . . Some of the Martians are beginning to—

SFX: *Explosion.*

The Accountant Sketch

SFX: *A knock on the door.*

ACCOUNTANT Come in!

The door opens and headmaster MARCHBANKS enters.

ACCOUNTANT Ah, Mr Marchbanks, do have a seat.

SFX: *Marchbanks sits.*

ACCOUNTANT *(Seriously)* Now, I've looked through your accounts and I must say there are one or two queries . . .

MARCHBANKS Really? I thought I'd been particularly honest and—

ACCOUNTANT Headmaster, I'm your accountant, you can be perfectly frank with me. But it would be more useful if you weren't. Look at this *(Holds up paper and reads)* 'Additional expenses: None.'

MARCHBANKS Well, I didn't have any additional exp—

ACCOUNTANT Of *course* you had additional expenses! Everybody has additional expenses. They wouldn't believe this. If I sent in these figures they'd think I was up to something crooked. It would be the only tax return in the country with no additional expenses. Now let's see what we can think – er – find out. Ah now, your stuffed animals.

MARCHBANKS My what??

ACCOUNTANT Your stuffed lions, giraffes and bandicoots.

MARCHBANKS But I don't have any of—

ACCOUNTANT Oh, you've got a camera.

MARCHBANKS Yes, but—

ACCOUNTANT And possibly in your sideline as a photographer you may have occasion to use it?

MARCHBANKS Well, it's possible – but I never have.

ACCOUNTANT You're a photographer then. You need a background for portraits. So that's £60 p.a. for the maintenance of stuffed animals. How often do you renew them?

MARCHBANKS Well I haven't—

ACCOUNTANT Ssssh! Don't commit yourself. Er . . . Say one medium-sized animal per year. Let's say a warthog.

MARCHBANKS A warthog?

ACCOUNTANT Let's say it together.

BOTH A warthog.

ACCOUNTANT That's better. You're getting the idea. Now there's £300 for a kick-off. What about loss of ear through illness?

MARCHBANKS I haven't been ill.

ACCOUNTANT Nonsense. What about croup, trench foot, dengue, tularemia?

MARCHBANKS I haven't had those.

ACCOUNTANT How do you know? You've never even heard of half of them! You might well have had two or three weeks of dengue without knowing it.

MARCHBANKS I haven't.

ACCOUNTANT Toothache?

MARCHBANKS No.

ACCOUNTANT Cholera?

MARCHBANKS No.

ACCOUNTANT Headaches?

MARCHBANKS No.

ACCOUNTANT You must have had.

MARCHBANKS Well . . . maybe one or two.

ACCOUNTANT *(Writing)* Nine pounds twelve and six-pence for aspirins.

MARCHBANKS I've only bought one bottle this year.

ACCOUNTANT Large or small? No, don't answer that. *(Writing)* One and six-pence.

MARCHBANKS They were mostly for the children.

ACCOUNTANT Ah, the children! Your youngest child ate some valuable manuscripts! £400.

MARCHBANKS My youngest is 19.

ACCOUNTANT She dropped nail varnish all over them.

MARCHBANKS He's a boy.

ACCOUNTANT Has he got an accountant?

MARCHBANKS No. He's training to be one.

ACCOUNTANT In that case, tell him to mind his own business. Prying into my affairs like that . . .

MARCHBANKS He isn't.

ACCOUNTANT I should think not! it's bad professional etiquette. Now, er, one last thing. I want you to sing for me.

MARCHBANKS What???

ACCOUNTANT Sing 'If I Ruled The World'. Come on . . . *(Singing)* 'If I ruled . . .'

MARCHBANKS *(Singing)* If I ruled the world, every day . . .

SFX: *Banging of mallet on desk.*

ACCOUNTANT Stop!

MARCHBANKS *stops singing.*

ACCOUNTANT Mmmm. Pity. I would have given you £80 if you had been able to sing it.

MARCHBANKS *(Singing)* If I ruled the world—

SFX: *Banging of mallet on table.*

MARCHBANKS *(Singing)* If . . . I . . .

SFX: *Banging of mallet on table.*

MARCHBANKS *stops singing.*

ACCOUNTANT There. You were prevented from singing professionally by a chartered accountant. £80. Oh no, they might suspect something. Er . . . 'prevented by loss of voice', that's it.

MARCHBANKS But I haven't—

SFX: *Banging of mallet on table.*

MARCHBANKS I—

SFX: *Banging of mallet on table.*

ACCOUNTANT You see? You've lost it. All you need is a little help. Well, that's all. Oh, next time you make out your accounts, try to loosen up a bit beforehand so that there's a bit more meat in them. Try taking half a bottle of gin. Jump about a bit. It might help to free your, er, imagination.

SFX: *MARCHBANKS rises.*

ACCOUNTANT Do mind the stairs, will you? They're rather badly lit. I'll put the light on for you.

SFX: *A fall and a scream.*

ACCOUNTANT Loss of employment through personal injury! Who said accountancy was dull?

The following two sketches were earmarked for *The Canterbury (NZ) Tales*, another attempt (never produced) at a television show post-*Python*. According to Graham, *Canterbury (NZ)* was to be 'the tale of a pilgrimage (the course of mortal life figured as a journey) by air-conditioned coach to Canterbury, New Zealand. Like mortal life itself, Canterbury (NZ) is intangible, but it does cover an area of 16,769 square miles as opposed to the well-known cathedral city in Kent.'

Wrestling with It

A dressing room. Two very macho men, ROY and PADDY, sit before a make-up mirror, dressed in wrestling kit, over which are robes. On the back of ROY's robe is written 'Captain Rudolf Slaughter'. On the back of PADDY's is 'Maimer Marty "The Mad Butcher"'. PADDY also wears a straw hat and a butcher's apron.

SFX: *The distant roar of a sports crowd.*

ROY . . . I said 'This is wrestling, not a pantomime, lovey.' And so anyway he said 'Take it again from the top, dear.'

PADDY Who said?

ROY The referee. So *I* said 'You're joking, ducky. I'm not going through *that* again. It's round two or I'm off. So, knickers to you, dear!'

PADDY You poor thing. What happened next, treas.?

ROY Well . . . First round with Killer Williams—

PADDY Oh, Killer Williams! She's a bitch!

ROY I could have spat at him, I was so livid. He had me in a Market Harborough Cuttle Fish and just when I was going to convert it to a Double Ankle-Ear Hold like in the run-through – the stupid bitch goes and pulls my wig!

PADDY Ooooh!

ROY Yes. He finished up prancing round the ring like a mad thing, waving my Real Hair Frontal Topper to the audience . . . and did I see red. I was livid, love. There was me, nude frontals – was I mad? I went out of my skull . . . out of my skull. I flew at him with my fingernails . . . if they hadn't rung the bell a minute early I don't know what I might have done.

PADDY You *have* had a time. Pass the black liner, love.

ROY Mind you, you weren't all love and kisses tonight, were you dear?

PADDY What do you mean, *dear*?

ROY Well, Maimer, sweety . . . I thought your kidney chops were a bit over done.

PADDY Think so? I thought they were bona.

ROY Oh, we were just a little over the top, weren't we dear? We were going to do four lunges to the left loin, weren't we? But we had to go for the dozen, and then try to cap it with a knee in the b-e-l-l-y, didn't we? I think you should apologize to Nigel, otherwise he'll only keep it pent up inside. And you know how vicious old cat Nigel can be . . .

PADDY You know, anyway.

ROY Oooh – meeeeiaowwwww! Oh excuse me for respiring . . . *(Eyes Paddy's outfit)* Oooh, we've got our new leotard on, have we?

PADDY Yes. Do you think they clash with my eyes?

ROY Oooh no, they're gorgeous. They're so virile, love.

PADDY Not *too* virile, are they?

ROY No dear, not for you.

PADDY Oh? And what are you hinting at?

ROY Ooh, temper, temper . . . Don't our hackles rise . . . I meant they're just right . . . for you.

PADDY Ooh!

PADDY *rises and goes to* ROY.

PADDY Don't touch me! I feel so fragile. Oh zip me up at the back, dear.

ROY *(Zipping up Paddy)* Are you on again then?

PADDY Yes. I'm in the tag bout.

ROY Oh that'll be a giggle.

PADDY Very funny . . . It so happens that at this moment I feel like a wet rag. I don't know how I'll survive. *(Stands)* Is my wig straight?

ROY Yes. Only thing on you that is, love.

SFX: *A knock on the door.*

VOICE (O.S.) One minute Captain Slaughter!

ROY Ooh, I'm on! 'scuse me.

ROY *becomes very butch. He rehearses a few grunts, shouts and groans. He punches the door down and exits.*

PADDY You never know where you are with her.

Fire Brigade

Several FIREMEN *are gathered listening to the* CAPTAIN *address them.*

SFX: *Fire bell rings throughout.*

CAPTAIN Right lads, now this is what I recommend. As the crow flies it'll take us a good six, six-and-a-half minutes to reach the fire – provided we can make use of the through roads – but this time of day, in this traffic, I put it more at a good couple of hours. So, it's a question of either catching the first bus in the morning, or taking the fire engine.

MEN Right!

CAPTAIN But this bus stops right outside the door, whereas if we take the fire engine it means going round into Edgware Road where we parked her, turning her around, backing her up, bringing her round to the front, then turning her around again which takes five minutes.

General consensus from the MEN.

CAPTAIN Now, there *is* a milk train at five-to-six in the morning, but the hoses, bit of a problem there.

General consensus from the MEN.

CAPTAIN Although we could come back and get them after we've been to see how bad the fire is. Now, I've drawn up a graph here . . .

He pulls a chart out and refers to it throughout.

CAPTAIN This is the bus, this if we go by milk train, this one is the fire engine, and this is if we go by moped. Now – the bus. Straight on it outside the door, but vis-à-vis bus travel, we sacrifice the quickness element at the level crossing waiting for the milk train to go past. But if we opt for the milk train it's a quick ten-minute sprint to the station. And if we miss the bus, and take the milk train, we lose the hoses. Now, in addition, it's going to take a good fifteen minutes to explain all this which means that we miss the bus anyway. If we strike out the bus that means that we save five minutes discussion time. So, if we rule out the bus we can catch the milk train. Now, the possibility of mopeds.

MAN We haven't got any mopeds.

CAPTAIN I'm coming to that, Wilson. Now, mopeds, top speed thirty miles an hour, but I've got a friend who can tune 'em up nicely, touch forty. But it's a good three-hour job, which from the point-of-view of rapidly springing into action is a bit shaky, and anyway, my friend is on holiday. And, as you pointed out, we haven't got any mopeds anyway. So . . . the fire engine it is.

SFX: *Fire bell stops.*

CAPTAIN Well, that certainly changes the complexion of things. Right, now lunch . . .

The following two radio scripts went unrecorded, and it's unknown what Graham might have intended them for.

The Radio Shop Sketch

CALLER (V.O.) Good evening, David. This is Marcus James of Surrey.

HOST (V.O.) Good evening, Marcus. You had a point to make?

CALLER (V.O.) Yes, I would like to ask what we are doing with a Madeira cake mountain in Frankfort at 49¢ a milligram, when my wife has to wait 10 months to have her nostrils attended to.

HOST (V.O.) That's not quite the question we were—

CALLER (V.O.) *And* David *and* furthermore, do they think that the average man—

MR ARMAGEDDON: Turn that rubbish off!

MR DAVIS switches off, the VOICES stop.

MR ARMAGEDDON People like that should be drummed off the media!

DAVIS What, squire?

MR ARMAGEDDON Drummed off the media. That man shouldn't be cluttering up the wavebands when there's vital issues to be aired.

DAVIS Well, he was only an ordinary bloke, wasn't he?

MR ARMAGEDDON Oh. Pardon my holistic error! Excuse me while I nip down to my well of personal experience and revitalize myself in the stream of common consciousness! Ah! Ah, yes, that's better. Oh yes, I see it. Yin and Yang. Action and reaction

... That bloke's drivel was as a counterbalance for my own clarity of thought when I said 'Turn that rubbish off.'

DAVIS You always like this?

MR ARMAGEDDON Why should I be categorized as being 'like this' merely because I'm telling it like it is?

DAVIS Look mate, I don't know what you're on about, but I'm here to sell fucking radios.

MR ARMAGEDDON Oh I see! You don't know what I'm 'on about' but you *do* sell radios. The qualification about 'coitus' I take as being a reference to your state of mind more than the radios which, I presume, despite recent advances in technology, to be as yet asexual.

DAVIS Look, Guv, I'm here to sell radios, that's all.

MR ARMAGEDDON My poor fellow, does that summarize your lot? 'I am a seller of radios' period. I would like to take issue with your limited vision of yourself. Now, my good fellow, what are you doing here?

DAVIS Selling radios.

MR ARMAGEDDON No no no. What are you doing here on earth? What is your *prime* function?

DAVIS ... Sell more radios.

MR ARMAGEDDON That at least would be ambition. No, again my meaning eludes you. You sell radios, right?

DAVIS Yes.

MR ARMAGEDDON Now, what do radios do?

DAVIS Play music.

MR ARMAGEDDON Yes, and ... ?

DAVIS News bulletins.

MR ARMAGEDDON Mmm. And ... ?

DAVIS Well it's entertainment, isn't it.

MR ARMAGEDDON Is it? We'll let that pass. Now, we had reached a

point where your description of a radio's function encompassed
music, news and, for the nonce in parentheses, 'entertainment'.

DAVIS Are you from an 'ome of some kind?

MR ARMAGEDDON 'An 'ome'?! 'An 'ome.' I see. Now you postulate
my voluntary commitment to some asylum or psychiatric
outpatients as a possibility. Far from it, young man. What I am
driving at are bigger issues. Radios are for *communications*.

DAVIS I suppose so.

MR ARMAGEDDON: Well 'supposed', at least. Now, young man, do
you not see, is it not clear now? Your life is not fettered to the
humdrum of this counter. You should conceive your life as that
of a 'bringer of tidings, a purveyor of communications'. The
very fabric of our human soul. You could, if you choose, with
reason, liken yourself to Hermes himself, the patron of
merchants and messengers. Yes, young man, a veritable Greek
God. 'I sell fucking radios' indeed! You mock yourself. Now,
suddenly, doesn't everything, a purpose, become clearer to you?

DAVIS Well, that does sound pretty good, doesn't it.

MR ARMAGEDDON Good. Splendid fellow. Now, having been at pains
to establish some kind of rapport, please, could you mend this
radio?

DAVIS Right, sir. That's the radio?

MR ARMAGEDDON Yes.

DAVIS What's wrong with it?

MR ARMAGEDDON The socket for the power plug has come adrift.

DAVIS That sounds simple enough. You bought the machine from
us?

MR ARMAGEDDON Yes.

DAVIS I don't think so, sir.

MR ARMAGEDDON What?!

DAVIS We don't stock that model, I'm afraid.

MR ARMAGEDDON I did buy it here.

DAVIS No sir. A 2E, yes, but this is a 2EL. We don't stock them, sir.

MR ARMAGEDDON You did.

DAVIS Never have.

MR ARMAGEDDON Really. So, hard-won rapport is cast to the winds. Well, it just so happens that I'm ahead of you this time. I have had trouble of this kind before, not only in this shop but in this country in general. Avoidance of responsibility is as English as toasted muffins.

DAVIS Toasted what, sir?

MR ARMAGEDDON I shall ignore that. You will not destroy my flow. I have a sales document headed 'STUDIO SOUNDS'. This is Studio Sounds, is it not?

DAVIS Yes sir, but there are several Stu—

MR ARMAGEDDON 142 Greencroft Place, London, England. The World, the Universe?

DAVIS Yes.

MR ARMAGEDDON It states quite clearly 'Sold on the 8th of January, one cassette recorder number 2EL.'

DAVIS Could I have a look at that, sir? Oh yes. Oh I see. Yes, there's been an error.

MR ARMAGEDDON Good. So if you would effect the repair . . .

DAVIS Repair? No, can't do that, sir. You see, there's the error. It says 'number 2EI' not 'L'. That's an 'I'.

MR ARMAGEDDON No. Good try, but I'm afraid not. There is no such thing as a model 2EI, or 2E1. That, my lad, is an 'L'. Here is the maker's catalogue.

DAVIS Well, no one in this shop would have written 2EL. We don't sell them. Never have.

MR ARMAGEDDON Well they *did*.

DAVIS *(To o.s.)* Burt!

BURT Yeah?

DAVIS We've never sold 2ELs, have we?

BURT No.

MR ARMAGEDDON I see. I see how it goes. This gentleman, Mr Fang, was here with me at the time and was witness to the sale.

FANG Yes. I came with this gentleman and I took this Polaroid of him buying that recorder in this shop.

MR ARMAGEDDON Now, wriggle out of that.

DAVIS All right. Look, we're very busy at the moment. I can't take one of my electronic engineers off whatever they're doing just to do a little thing like that – but I'll tell you what, you leave it with us and I'll do my best for you.

MR ARMAGEDDON When would it be ready?

DAVIS Mmmmmm . . . Nine months.

MR ARMAGEDDON No. Now look here, I rang this shop before bothering to come down here with recognition of your obstructive policies, and your Managing Director, Mr Kyles Plate, said this – may I use your machine?

SFX: *Cassette loading.*

MR PLATE Yes sir, just bring it in and we'll fix it up in a jiffy as you're an old customer!

MR ARMAGEDDON *presses* Stop *on the machine and the* VOICE *stops.*

DAVIS Oh, why didn't you say you were an old customer?

MR ARMAGEDDON You mean that bringing in the recorder, the receipt, a manufacturer's catalogue, a witness of the sale *and* a Polaroid flash of the event was insufficient evidence? And, had I not had the foresight to record my conversation with your Managing Director, I would have completely wasted my time?

DAVIS Frankly, yes sir.

MR ARMAGEDDON So I surmised. Now, I have to warn you and all your staff that this shop is surrounded by armed men. Kindly inform all your workmates that I wish to have a word with them.

DAVIS Sorry mate, tea break.

SFX: *Machine-gun fire.*

DAVIS All right. All right . . . *(To o.s.)* Come in everyone!

General disgruntled murmers of people assembling.

MR ARMAGEDDON Now. I am loath to use firearms, but my experience with British industry in general has forced me into this position. Your job, each one of you, is to sell hi-fi equipment, and to provide a reasonable after-sales service as written out in your guarantees. This is not a tricky job. It does not require years of painstaking research, hours of book learning, or supreme physical fitness. You are paid a reasonable wage, otherwise you would, presumably, not be fools enough to be here at all. Am I right?

Grudging murmers of assent.

MR ARMAGEDDON Now, given that, why will you not enhance your own lives, and those of people around you, by rendering the services to which by your presence you lay claim?

Grudging murmers of very grudging assent.

DAVIS Why should we?

MR ARMAGEDDON I beg your pardon?

DAVIS Who do you think you are?

MR ARMAGEDDON Ah, you again. Just read the name at the top of that sales docket.

DAVIS *(Reading)* 'Mr Armageddon'.

MR ARMAGEDDON Correct. And . . .

SFX: *Prolonged bursts of machine-gun fire. The shopkeepers are laid waste.*

MR ARMAGEDDON Better luck in your next incarnation! Mr Fang, Let us leave.

Falling About Routine

The wind howls. The crunching of feet on snow, of pick-axes being plunged into ice. The scream of someone falling, descending in volume as they plunge into the breach.

TIM Well, we're up here anyway. All in one piece.

JIM Not quite at the top yet . . . one more pitch over there.

TIM But you can walk around that.

JIM Climb's not finished 'til you've done that, though.

TIM Oh. Difficult climb on the way up. What grade climb was it? A seven?

JIM Ha! Seven? No, two.

TIM Only two? But Eddy told me it was a grade seven.

JIM No no no, that's the way we're going down.

TIM Oh. Is it?

JIM Wonderful view that way down. Absolutely miss it if you come up by that route. Don't stand on the rope!

TIM Sorry. Certainly get a sense of achievement anyway . . .

JIM DON'T MOVE! Now, slowly move your left foot back. Now the right one. NOT TOO MUCH! Now, the left. Don't turn around. Try to stop shaking. Now the right. Right, you'd better sit here.

TIM What did I do wrong there?

JIM Well, you were on an ice-cornice on a corrie edge with sagittal crenations.

TIM Oh, was I? Can I help with the rope?

JIM Hah! 'Help with the rope' . . . No, I think you'd better not.

TIM Interesting climb on the way up . . . Are you sure it was only a grade two?

JIM Yes, quite. The way down's a good deal more interesting though.

TIM Why? What happens there?

JIM Well, once you're over the Banker's Safe and through the Skittle Alley it may be a bit tricky on the Devil's Mantelpiece, you know, with all this ice around.

TIM What's the Devil's Mantelpiece?

JIM Oh, it's a one-in-three inclined ledge about four inches wide on an absolutely sheer face. So it's no good trying to work your way down. You've just got to stand on it. Slide down about, oooh . . . fourteen or fifteen feet, then you come to a projection of rock called the Butler's Hunch – ruddy great jug handle – grab it with one hand and pull yourself to the side. Ha ha ha . . . On second thoughts, with all this ice about you'd better grab hold of it with both hands or you might find yourself taking the quick way down. Ha ha ha ha ha!

TIM Is it going to be very difficult then?

JIM Oh, you get the knack after a time, of course. Austrian party went down there in '48. All four of them. Then there was Rudy Friedell last year . . .

TIM But after that it's all right, is it?

JIM Oh well, then you've got Harper's Lift. Blood Gully. Ha ha ha! Nasty mess there in '57. Blood all over the place. I don't know, all over the . . . No, '58 it was, that's right. Then you've got the Blue Spider Crevasse.

TIM Would you like some mintcake?

JIM No thanks. The ol' Blue Spider's pretty straightforward though. You've got a nine-foot jump onto a ledge about as big as my hand. The only thing is, you've got to make a half-turn in mid-air – you know – to land on the ledge with your weight well forward. If you land with your weight backward – BINGO! Ha ha ha ha! Oh yes. Did I ever tell you about a chap called Pongo

Carstairs? Got an England rugger trial just after the last war. Anyway, Old Pongo was going to make the jump down the Blue Spider when someone bet him a fiver he couldn't do one and a half turns before he hit the ledge. Well, old Pongo was always a bit of an exhibitionist . . .

SFX: *A falling scream in the distance.*

JIM There goes another one. Gym shoes, I wouldn't wonder. Where was I? Ah, Mohler's Coffin, yes! The main thing about that is that you've got to go over headfirst because the holds underneath the rock aren't big enough for feet. You heard about the German party there in '49, did you? Ha ha ha! This'll kill you . . .

SFX: *Wind noises get louder.*

JIM One of the . . .

TIM Er, can you walk from here?

JIM What? Oh, yes. Very boring though. Well, it's blowing up a bit rough. It isn't going to make it any easier, you know.

TIM Are you sure you won't have any mintcake?

JIM Quite sure, thanks. Come on, we'd better be off. Put your klettershoes on then.

TIM My what?

JIM Your klettershoes.

TIM But I've only got leather with nails.

JIM Leather with . . . leather wi— hahahaha! Well, leather with nails! Devil's Mantelpiece in nails, eh? You *are* going to have something to tell the boys when we get down. *If* we get down. Hahahahaha! This is going to be worth watching.

TIM Is it really grade seven?

JIM At least. Nothing to it really, though. On second thoughts, let's walk down. The pub opens in an hour. Don't mind, do you?

TIM No! Ha ha . . . Of course I was looking forward to—

JIM Oh, well, if you'd rather climb down . . .

TIM NO!! Honestly. I'd almost rather walk. Only I've got this
blister . . .

JIM A blister!? Why didn't you say so?! Come on then, I'll carry
you. Must be down in time for opening, anyway, tell the boys
about our climb! Ha!

They start off.

JIM Did I ever tell you the one about . . .

LIFE AND TIMES

Introduction

'Alcohol is commonly used as an aid to social intercourse. If you're onto a cert, the last thing you need is something nagging away at the front of the brain ... What you need is another pint.'

Dr Graham Chapman

At times, events from Graham's life read like the plots of a particularly wacky sitcom: he attends a posh party, removes his trousers and briefs down to his ankles, then sits serenely smoking his pipe as though nothing is wrong (Graham Pulls it Off) ... He's hired to host a celebrity charity event, ends up in a brawl, is forcibly thrown out, barred from re-entering, and develops an impetigo-like infection (Incident at the Hard Rock Café) ... An ordinary airplane flight suddenly becomes a reluctant life-saving mission when one of the passengers is taken ill and he's the only doctor on board (Little White Pills) ...

It's easy to classify Graham simply as someone who was habitually drunk and out of control; as a man who openly courted trouble and weirdness. To some degree this is true, but what he really was, was one of the last of the truly dangerous people. He lived his life the way he wanted to without one concern for what anyone else thought. While that sort of behaviour often landed him in trouble, today Graham's antics would be viewed in an entirely different light. There would be talk of 'rehab' and 'anger management', perhaps a mandatory visit or two to the Betty Ford Clinic or, worse, prison. Jokingly writing 'I've always wanted to be a pederast, but people make it so difficult for you' on a questionnaire '20 Questions (Minus 10)' would more than likely elicit a visit from the police these days.

*

The world's greatly changed in the years since Graham's death, and it's debatable as to whether or not he would have been able to remain a comic rebel without having to resort to caricature. Of course, we'll never know. Thankfully we still have these remnants to remind us that there once was a time when dangerous men walked the earth.

Graham wrote this tongue-in-cheek bio for *News*, Rediffusion Television's weekly programme guide (Issue no.439) for the week starting 27 February 1967. At the time he was one of the stars of *At Last the 1948 Show*.

Graham Chapman's Biography

by Graham Chapman (from February 1967)

Graham Chapman, who describes himself as 'amazingly humble', was born on 8 January 1941, educated at Melton Mowbray Grammar school, and later at Emmanuel College, Cambridge, where he studied medicine.

While at Cambridge he joined the Footlights Club and appeared in their 1962 revue with John Cleese and Tim Brooke-Taylor. He also appeared in *Cambridge Circus* at the Lyric Theatre in 1963, and went on tour with the revue to New Zealand and Broadway. While in America he took part in *The Ed Sullivan Show* and *The Jack Parr Show*.

During the time he was appearing in the revue, he was also working at St Bartholomew's Hospital, and qualified as a doctor in June 1966.

Graham has appeared in cabaret at the Blue Angel and the Edmundo Ros Club. He worked on *The Frost Report* with John Cleese, and has written for *The Illustrated Weekly Hudd* and the radio show *I'm Sorry, I'll Read That Again*.

Graham Chapman used to play rugby football, at which he was 'brilliant but disinterested'. His other pastimes are rock-climbing and mountaineering, which interest him but he is 'too timid to be brilliant', and politics in which his leanings are 'towards a determined apathy, but I would like to be Prime Minister – if I weren't so amazingly humble'.

Written in 1973, *Incident at the Hard Rock Cafe* is the amalgamation of two of Graham's lecture-tour transcripts and certain working notes from his autobiography.

Incident at the Hard Rock Cafe

I'd been asked to MC a charity concert at a place called the Hard Rock Cafe in London. It was to be a very special evening, as this concert was to mark the first appearance by Paul McCartney and his band Wings. 'This sounds interesting,' I thought. 'And not too taxing' as all I would have to do was announce the other acts filling-in before The Big Moment. I had never met Mr McCartney – but I had once sat behind him in a viewing theatre while listening to the music he'd composed for the film *The Magic Christian* – and here, clearly, was an opportunity to meet the front pieces of the said Mr M. while engaging in good works.

Consequently the Hard Rock Cafe was filled that evening with the most *excrementally trendy* people you could ever wish not to meet. An undeservedly rich, immodest, exhibitionistically-conceited, vacuous, mean-minded, illiberal, self-important set of micro-cephalic twits. They regarded themselves as something apart from mere mortals – and should have been. Their twittering vapidities reached a noise level several decibels above the pain-threshold of a Tyneside ship riveter. They were all talking, although no one was listening, and all they wanted was for people to look at them. One idiotic son of a millionaire watch salesman had thought it amusing to bring his one-year-old daughter and have her eardrums pierced by famous musicians. It was an appalling occasion, really. And I wasn't looking forward to my part in it.

I announced the first group. No one was bothered, so I stood on an even higher box, had the sound turned up, and bellowed at them. Three or four people turned around. The first band went on – I can't remember their name – and they were very good. Their loudness completely drowned the screams from the one-year-old. The rest of the room was unaffected, surrounded by a sound-shield of self-importance. One or two of them may have enjoyed the music, but were most likely too afraid to show it in case it wasn't quite cool enough. I was also rather annoyed that the crowd were so fashionable that they didn't even notice – or pretended not to notice at any rate – the topless go-go dancers who'd been employed for this evening. The trendy crowd were *way* above that level.

Well, the poor girls came off after their ... act ... having just been totally ignored, and they were rather distressed about this. I had sympathy for them because I overheard one of the girls worrying that she had to go out and do their second (what was laughingly called) 'set' and she'd seen her son's headmaster in the crowd and wanted to give a good impression. I resolved that, for their second appearance, they'd at least have a space on the dance floor so that their act could be seen, and they could leave happy. So I went up and made an announcement that the dancers were about to come out and to please clear a space on the floor. Well, they did clear a space, fortunately, but through the artificial cordon I'd created came a very very very large, and extremely trendy, black lady wearing a modest dress consisting of vertical stripes of black and white ostrich feathers and an enormous hat.

She strode hippopotamously across the empty floor, straight through this cordon I'd created, and stood there ignoring the go-go dancers again. So I gave her a quick little pat on the bottom with my foot as she passed. She immediately cried out 'Get him Cosmo!' and suddenly a tiny Sicilian sort of gentleman of about four-foot-eight leapt at my throat with his fingernails! I tried to just brush him off, but he wouldn't let go. Of course the bouncers at this occasion, it being a very important evening, had been told 'At the first sight of trouble – out!' and, as I was the taller of the two, they assumed that I'd been the aggressor. Therefore I, as the MC, was promptly ejected by two very very large gentlemen.

Outside the club I tried to explain to them that I was the MC and that I had a function to perform inside the building, but they clearly didn't understand that – in fact I don't think they understood much at all. A slight problem in the brain area. But no problem at all on the muscle side. They refused to let me back in, so I left dejectedly, with a slightly bloody shirt.

I did receive a very nice apology the next morning from the organizers but, sadly for me, this portion of my neck became infected with a rash. A sort of impetigo-like rash. Clearly the Sicilian's fingernails were not too clean. So I went round to see an old friend of mine, a doctor, who shot me full of penicillin. Unfortunately, that week we were filming for the *Python* TV series, and so I had to get up at about six o'clock every morning to inject myself. I mean, clearly I couldn't expect my friends to come out and give me a shot of penicillin every morning.

While a penicillin shot is unpleasant at the best of times, it *was* easier after about three or four slugs of gin, and by the end of the week the rash was getting better. But I'd run out of water and syringes, so I had to try and find some time off to get these things from a nearby pharmacy. While film directors are not pleased to have their artists wandering off, I did manage to persuade the director, Ian MacNaughton, to allow me ten minutes off – however, he *insisted* that I be dressed for the next piece of filming. I'd already been dressed as one of those strange creatures – I won't call them women – that we did, so I was already in a dress, with breasts, of course. As it was raining that day I had on a pair of Wellington boots and, as my next piece of filming was a head-and-shoulders shot of the Colonel figure, on top of all of that I wore a colonel's jacket, a tie and, of course, a moustache. I then looked around for an umbrella, as it was now raining rather badly, and the only available one in the unit happened to be a pink one.

So I wandered into the nearest Boots pharmacy dressed like this and asked for sterile water and syringes for injection. They were not keen. I explained to them that I was, in fact, duly qualified – a fact that they duly doubted – and so duly looked me up in the medical directory – as well as in the telephone directory. Sure enough they found my name in both and so were obliged to give me the articles I'd requested. Although I think their opinion of the medical community was somewhat *tarnished* by the incident, I still got the stuff.

Although the origin of this Q&A is unknown, it's a fair guess that from the type of questions and his candid replies it was intended for a gay men's magazine, most likely around the mid-1970s, a period when Graham was quite outspoken about his homosexuality.

20 Questions (Minus 10)
with Graham Chapman

Q What is your favourite colour?

GRAHAM Chinese.

Q No, your favourite colour?

GRAHAM Oh, I'm sorry . . . Yellow.

Q What do you look for in a girl?

GRAHAM In a what?

Q A woman. What qualities do you find attractive?

GRAHAM Oh, I don't know . . . A nice penis, I suppose, and allure. Spelled 'a lure' so I can use the girls as bait to attract good-looking young men.

Q Would you do a nude scene in a film?

GRAHAM I've done a nude scene in a book. It's called *Monty Python's Brand New Bok*. I had to stand on a big white sheet of paper in a warehouse and be photographed. None of the others would agree to it. I knew from the moment I took me knickers off exactly where everyone would look. It's natural and I didn't particularly mind. Some people were even kind enough to say how nicely formed it was, so I guess I'm lucky in some areas.

Q Do you have any hobbies?

GRAHAM Well, of course I masturbate, if you'd consider that a hobby, but I certainly never play golf.

Q Have you ever been hurt by any of your fans?

GRAHAM Not by any fans. I was bitten once, but that was on the penis.

Q Your latest film, *Monty Python and the Holy Grail*, is about a search, really, a search for goodness, for perfection which fails. The characters in the film are, eventually, consumed by their own personal greed.

GRAHAM Gosh, it sounds like a very important film.

Q Tremendously. Is it true that you got into show business by answering a newspaper ad?

GRAHAM No, that isn't strictly true. What I did was I rang up several museums and got nowhere, they couldn't offer me anything in terms of show business. So then I rang up the London Library, but they couldn't help me either, especially as I wasn't even a subscriber. Then I put an ad in a newspaper shop window explaining that I was an utter pervert and that seemed to do the trick. I got a lot of offers. Well, naturally, some of the offers were rather strange.

Q Do you have any secret desires or fantasies that you'd rather not talk about in this interview?

GRAHAM I think I've done them all actually, except I've always wanted to be a pederast, but people make it so difficult for you. I love children, but it's a punishable offence.

Little White Pills

Medicine is nice as a hobby but it does have its downside, especially if anyone ever discovers that you are, in fact, a doctor. For instance . . . I was coming from Los Angeles to London one time, on a long haul of a flight. I was sound asleep, and quite happy – until about an hour out of London when I felt a tap on my shoulder. I woke up to find that the air hostess was standing over me saying 'Excuse me, but we understand that you're a doctor.'

I said, 'Surely there must be *another* one . . .' She replied, 'Afraid not – you're it.' So I asked her what had happened and she said, 'Well, there's this lady that's stopped breathing.' I didn't look forward to the next few minutes at all.

I said, 'Yes. Well . . . I had better go and have a look, I suppose.' I didn't really know what I could do, but still . . . So I went back to the rear of the plane and, sure enough, there was a lady there surrounded by a few stewards who were desperately trying to give her oxygen, but it was quite plain that she was taking in nothing at all. I was a bit . . . tense, shall we say. Especially as I was being observed by the rest of the aircraft.

So I shooed away most of the people and made it look as if nothing was happening, particularly. The air hostess who had first contacted me then began to give me some sort of vague history about the lady 'possibly being an asthmatic or something' and 'perhaps that was a possibility'. Well, hmmm, yes, possibly. But all I knew for certain upon examination, as they say, was that she was definitely not breathing. A thought occurred to me upon seeing the woman seated next to her, that perhaps the lady had had some peanuts and that one had become stuck. So I got behind the seat and gave a great push all around the lady, and she *did* begin to breathe again. But not for very long, unfortunately. Clearly there was something else amiss.

Fortunately, because of my having taken along a whole caseload of medical equipment over to Tunisia for the shooting of *Life of Brian*, I had some *salbutamol* tablets in my bag – amazingly fortunate – so I popped one of those into her mouth during one of the occasions when I'd gotten her started [breathing] again, and she immediately began to breathe and then continued to breathe. Great relief all round. Of course, her first question to me was 'What the *hell* did you give me?!'

I was given a Pan Am Junior Flyer's Badge for that.

The origin of this short and oddly touching piece is unknown, but considering the date (1976) it was most likely intended for inclusion in *A Liar's Autobiography*.

Sunday, 24 October 1976

Woke up at 11.00 a.m. in order to go number one's. Climbed back into bed and examined the sleeping body in it for any signs of identification. It appeared to be someone I didn't recognize, but vaguely remembered from the night before. I patted the dog and it made a sort of noise-my-dog-usually-makes sort of noise, which was a relief because the thought of sleeping with someone else's dog is abhorrent to me.

I looked around the room for familiar landmarks, and having found three – including a ball gown with a pair of tattered pantyhose draped over one shoulder, five pairs of other people's trousers, and someone I didn't know asleep in the corner using a shoe for a pillow – decided that it was statistically unlikely for it to be anybody else's house. An empty gin bottle and a pipe confirmed my worst fears: I was at home. Shit.

The Chapman Years

by Tony Hendra

I met Graham at Footlights – in fact I think we were both inducted or initiated or whatever Footlights did to you – at about the same time – the autumn of 1960.

I was in awe of Graham, who was the funniest of the new boys, with Cleese a close runner-up. Graham was a natural, one of those people who make you laugh the minute they emerge from the wings before they've said anything. Rather in the mould of Peter Cook – strong, mad, idiosyncratic – but unlike Cook, with a charming, disarming diffidence offstage. He struck me as very masculine, a pipe always clenched in his jaw. I, on the other hand, was rather precious with a taste for academic musical and literary parody and a piercing Peter Pears-like tenor.

Graham took the initiative about us working together. I think we'd appeared together with Cleese or Tim Brooke-Taylor but that may have been later. There were a couple of weekend nightclubs in Cambridge run by undergraduate entrepreneurs and they occasionally included 'cabarets' or comedy sets as a break from dancing. Several Footlights members singly or in teams made beer money at such gigs.

I was hugely flattered. Appearing with Graham was great because I was pretty insecure about my comic abilities; his were so well-formed I could relax a bit and be the straight man. We did mostly our own material with some borrowed from other Footlights guys. Everyone did this to round out their slim repertoires to the required twenty-five minutes.

We became good friends, eating and drinking together frequently and spit-balling new comedy bits. On 14 February of that year – 1961 – I received a heartfelt Valentine from my big, masculine, pipe-smoking partner. I was naive enough to be deeply puzzled; Graham laughed it off as a joke. Not until years later did I realize it was no joke.

Graham and I did Cambridge gigs intermittently throughout that

"I think you're <u>TERRIFIC</u> !!"

I mean it, too! (you are my
Valentine and all that jazz!)
— with luv (xxx)
from
Graham

14th Feb '61.

M. CHAGALL - Les deux têtes
The two heads

P.S. See you Wednesday night, then — so glad
you can come. Will be eating out if you're in time to
come with us for Rose Tire — 7.35 in case you feel the eating injun

year and the next, including May Balls at the end of each year in June. Both of us – Graham more than me – worked fairly promiscuously with other Footlights guys: Cleese, Brooke-Taylor, Oddie. May Balls were clean-up time for undergraduate cabarets – you'd sometimes do three or four a night.

When we worked together we did several solo bits each. The two-handers I remember were a bit called 'Autostop' in which I was a hapless Brit student hitch-hiking through Germany – Graham played the mani-acally polite German Mercedes driver who refuses a ride. We would finish with a hugely energetic piece called 'I Buffoni', an Italian opera take-off in which we killed each other several times – but never terminally enough to stop us singing florid 'deathbed' arias. Graham couldn't sing for beans but his death-throes would bring the house down.

In spring 1962 we were both in the annual Footlights revue *Double Take* which put a curb on cabaret work (except the May Balls). Then we all went off to Edinburgh for the Fringe. Both of us graduated that year and in the autumn of 1962 Graham became a medical student at St Bart's in London, and got us several gigs in London including a big dance for St Bartholomew's Hospital students. My recollection is that, for some reason, an agent called Mrs Braham was present. She was at least sixty, five-foot nothing and the shape of an enormous meatball. Everyone called her 'Ma'. She said we were 'quite talented' and offered to handle us. What did we know? She got us a tryout at the Blue Angel in Berkeley Square and early in 1963 a two-week engagement there. As I recall, this was extended a couple of times so we spent a month or more at the place. It was a great room to play – intimate but with a big stage so we could do our, by now, quite physical humour. Unfortunately, it was often frequented by various Guards from the palace down the road – Hooray Henries all, invariably blind drunk and the most arrogant hecklers I've ever come across.

Graham became quite good at dealing with these morons and once threw one of them off-stage when he tried to climb up on it. One tends to forget that gentle Graham was formidably large and strong.

We played other places for Ma Braham – including the Edmundo Ros Club not far away. Edmundo was a fave of both the Queen and Princess Margaret – so the drunk Hooray Henries frequented it too. Seems like we couldn't get away from that damn palace.

It was hugely exciting though, and we were by now pretty good: funny, physical, smart. Ma Braham believed we had a big future on TV. However, at this time I was doing a term of teaching in London at St Paul's School – part of a diploma of education course. We'd finish at the Blue Angel at 2.30 or so usually after a couple of drinks – we often drank for free. I'd get home to Notting Hill Gate around 3 a.m. then had to be up at 7 a.m. the next morning bright-eyed and bushy-tailed to handle a class of snotty – but highly intelligent – teenagers.

My report card on that term was not good; not only were most of the lessons conducted through a post-whisky fog, but I had to make it all up as I went along not having much time for preparation. I didn't care because I thought we had a brilliant career ahead. Graham's schedule was even worse – sometimes he had to be up at 5 a.m., so he was doing rounds and stuff on two hours sleep – and not long after he announced, with enormous regret I think, that we'd have to pack it in. He really wanted to be a doctor and he had to decide between Bart's and laughs.

Bart's won.

Graham Pulls it Off

by David J. Sherlock

When *Python* was at the height of its popularity, all English university towns and cities with accessible public televisions in pubs, bars and hotel lounges would be besieged by student fans. Sometimes the crowding in some bars was so bad that, for everyone to see what was happening that week, they would climb onto tables and seats, or even onto someone's shoulders, just so they did not miss a word. This was in the old days before video recorders, so even the famously wealthy were reputed to return home every Thursday from wherever they happened to be in the world just so they could be in front of a TV set.

It was rumoured that George Harrison never missed a single show, originally screened late on Sunday nights and then again on Thursdays. There were also tales of certain nameless 'old hippie neighbours' of the generous Mr Harrison who, scorning the use of 'evil television', would 'religiously moonshadow' themselves over every Thursday to 'George's place' to watch *Monty Python*.

Pythonmania gripped the nation for a while. I remember the team receiving letters about the show including one from a bishop who described how appalled and disgusted his congregation had been by one particular episode (it may have been the one involving the Church police). The letter said the Pythons had 'angered and distressed his flock' and everyone in his diocese was 'talking about it'. He ended the letter with the advice to 'continue doing it' – it was obviously keeping him in work!

Some people, however, loved to say, '*Monty Python*? I just don't see what's funny. No, I never watch it.' This included some of the old-school British comedians who considered the Pythons to be upstarts from the universities who had never served a proper apprenticeship by treading the boards.

Graham Chapman was one of these reviled writer/performers from Cambridge University. As with each of the Python members, he was already well known as a writer of TV and radio shows. At the start of his career both he and John Cleese had written for a BBC radio show called *I'm Sorry, I'll Read That Again*. John also performed in the show and was fast becoming the star.

The BBC were insistent that *Python* was to be recorded live. The 'boys' were insistent it wasn't. It was. Quite a few of the anti-Python brigade used to enjoy saying, 'Of course, what I hate about it is the canned laughter.' The canned laughter was, in fact, a group of near-hysterical teenage fans of Cleese who were always present at recordings of *I'm Sorry, I'll Read That Again* and who had followed him (as fans do) to the *Python* studio. Their cackles can be heard distinctly, especially during the first year. Luckily those particular fans melted away after the first season.

By the second year, Graham found himself working mainly for television. At one time he was working on two other major TV shows: a serialized comedy show about student doctors,* and a domestic sitcom called *No, That's Me Over Here*, directed by Marty Feldman and starring a well-known and very talented comedian called Ronnie Corbett.

Ronnie and his wife often gave lavish, well-attended parties for all sorts of exotic showbiz personalities. We were all invited to one of these parties one Sunday night. In those days, Sunday was the only time everyone in the business could meet because the theatres were closed. The large Tuderbethan house, with views over a beautiful golf course, was full of the famous and the funny. Graham, myself and Graham's young ward John Tomiczek arrived, accompanied by our tall, dark, handsome chauffeur Andrew. Heads turned, but then heads usually turned when Graham went to parties.

We were made very welcome by our hosts and, some gins and tonics later, we went to join the happy throng who were assembled in a baronial living room which, I believe, had a minstrel's gallery. (Yes, *that* sort of a place!) At the grand piano a lady was warbling a song from the current revival of *Showboat* (most of the cast were in the audience), and at the end the assembled audience applauded politely.

---

* *Doctor in the House.*

Then, suddenly, a New York choreographer appeared. He grinned and began to perform an agonizingly bad striptease, to reveal a string tank-top complete with paunch. People muttered and examined their shoes. The guy realized his mistake and just as suddenly motioned for the pianist to finish. As he did so, there was an audible gasp. People were staring aghast at Graham seated in his chair (on the arm of which I was balanced). He had pulled his trousers and briefs down to his ankles and was serenely smoking his pipe as though nothing was wrong!

Although the silence must have lasted for only a few seconds it seemed to last for ever, then, from behind us appeared Danny La Rue, the famous female impersonator, and Ronnie Corbett's partner. Danny was dressed in an impeccable suit (complete with matching tie and handkerchief). With a flourish, he quickly withdrew the handkerchief from his top pocket and carefully placed it over Graham's naughty bits. 'Now you see it, now you don't!' he said with all the aplomb of a stage magician. Taking his cue, Graham pulled up his trousers and promptly declared it was 'time for another drink'. He'd made his point. The spell was broken, and hysterically relieved party noises once again filled the room. When we got to the bar our host was still asking 'What happened? I couldn't see . . .' After a decent interval, we left for home.

Danny had saved the day, but we were never invited back. Much as Ronnie was fond of Graham, he feared what Graham might try as an encore.

Some time later we heard that as the guests were discussing the incident, the wife of a great friend was heard to remark, 'Well, I thought it was *very* well formed . . .'

SPECIAL SECTION

ONLY FOR PURCHASERS OF THE DELUXE EDITION

Note: If you have not purchased the Deluxe Edition
you should not be reading this.

Letters to the Editor

Dear Sirs,

Why must we have all this violence on television? I am sick and tired of it. Every time I switch it to the late news I see people having their noses split open with garlic crushers; young innocent children having their toes sawn off by power drills with rotary saw attachments, and old ladies being slowly lowered into scalding hot wood preservative. Surely the time has come to stamp out this violence. We need a real deterrent. I suggest it's that the insidious boys that perpetuate these atrocities should have their brains sucked out with high-powered vacuum cleaners.

Yours,

Mrs Crapargument

PS Haven't the heads of television got anything better to do than write replies to boring letters? (SAE included)

Dear Sirs,

Why doesn't the Lord do something about all the violence in this world?

Yours sincerely,

The Reverend J Pottinger

Dear Sirs,

Why can't we have more violence on television? I am sick and tired of every time I turn on my television I see terrible opinion shows and other times filthy garbage. How much longer do we have to put up with religious programmes and Des O'Connor and Cliff Richard? A good old broken bottle in the face and a mouthful of knuckles would be much more natural.

Yours,

E. McDermott
(near Glasgow)

Dear Sirs,

Coming as I do from Glasgow, I feel I must reply in the strongest possible terms to that last letter. If the demented person who wrote it would come round to my place I wouldn't be at all violent and would definitely not slit his face up a treat.

Yours sincerely,

Chief Chris Steeltoecap (Retired)

Dear Sirs,

Why must we have so much violence on television? Why can't people make their own entertainment as we did in the old days? Why must I be forced to watch television when I could be making conversation or building wardrobes? I bet you a thousand pounds you don't broadcast this letter on your marvellous programme, Points Of View, with the urbane and witty Robert Robertson at the helm of what must surely be one of the best things that ever happened.

Yours,

Mary Whitehouse
(no relation)

Dear Sirs,

I am sick and tired of being sick and tired of people who are sick and tired.

Yours,

Sick and Tired
(Mr SA Tired)

Dear Sirs,

I have been dead for the last fifteen years. How glad I am that I wrote this letter in advance.

Yours,

James Nameontelevision

Third on left of nearest entrance,
Garden of Peace
Stoke-on-Trent

Ideas for Gay News Radio Pilot: '20 to 1 Favourites'

Theme music (Graham Collier)

GIRL ANNOUNCER Hello and welcome to 20 to 1 Favourites, London's first radio show for gay people. We've been asked a lot why we're putting on a show specially for people who prefer their own sex – after all, apart from that one factor we're indistinguishable from ordinary decent upright citizens. Or are we?

Cut to: Vox pops. People say things such as 'Homosexuals should be shot', 'These unfortunate people are to be pitied', 'Well they're disgusting, ain't they? Oughta be put away' etc. (the real pick of the worst answers).

ANNOUNCER We know why we need a gay radio programme, don't we boys and girls?

Cut to: Vox pops. Funniest answers to: 'Should there be a gay radio programme?'

OLD LADY Oh yes. The news is so grim, they should put on something cheerful.

CRUISER Do you fancy a coffee back at my place?

HIP WEST INDIAN Yes, why not man. Dig it – a gay radio show, yeah!

ANNOUNCER That survey was taken from an average cross-section of the British public on a Saturday night in the Earls Court Road.

SFX: Canned laughter.

Jingle (a take-off of the 'Daily Mirror' one that plays on radio Luxembourg).

ANNOUNCER And now, brought to you from the resources of Europe's largest independent gay newspaper – we bring you once a week, every week, the latest coverage of what's going on at the front.

NEWSREADER Gay News Radio bulletin. Dateline: Thursday, September 26th. Michael Mason reporting. A GLC councillor and Liberal Party candidate, Dr Rundle, claimed last week that prejudices against homosexuals have been disappearing in the last year. He was addressing a meeting of the Richmond Campaign for Homosexual Equality [CHE].

SFX: *Bleep-bleep-bleep jingle between news items.*

NEWSREADER A GLC ruling resulted in all listings for CHE and Gay News being dropped last month from the free information pamphlet 'Use It!' Councillors feared that young people might see the CHE address and get corrupted.

Jingle

ANNOUNCER Gay News is available, price fifteen pence, from newsstands throughout the London area, or direct from 62a Chiswick High Road, W4.

Sound of phone ringing, leading into a sketch set at a gay switchboard office. Bright cheerful do-gooder Operator picks up the phone and has ludicrous silly problem. Opportunity for regular situation comedy every week, while still giving the switchboard another plug each time.

JINGLE If you're down in London Town and happen to be gay
There's a great information service open every day;
They'll tell you who and what and when and how and
why and more
On eight-three-double seven-three-two-four!

Sound of motor bike roaring up and stopping. Rider (obviously under-age) starts chatting up another guy (obviously a little older) waiting for last bus, trying to get him to come home.

If possible use dialogue actually written in a piece 'Gay News' published some time back in which every conceivable legal loophole making their

317

relationship illegal crops up (under 21, in armed services, in public place, Scotland, etc.).

At the end of the piece, heavy footsteps echo up to microphone as someone whistles 'Dixon of Dock Green' theme in background.

POLICEMAN So remember gentlemen, when consorting with other gentlemen of similar disposition, do make sure neither of you is under twenty-one, in a public place, in Scotland, Wales or Ireland, in Her Majesty's armed forces, or in the same room as anybody else. You know it makes sense. Right. And don't forget, if you're out tonight and you're on your bike – no consorting with other gentlemen of similar disposition. Evenin' all.

Footsteps recede into distance as 'Dixon' whistling fades up and out.

12 Days of Syphilis

A naughty family game

All you need to play this exciting family game (also suitable for people who aren't interested in families) is a pair of dice, a loaf of bread, a tin opener, a carpet (all of the latter items are unnecessary). All four players stand in separate corners of the room – or all six players if you count the chimney sweep – or all 29+ players if it is a large round room – or 29 if it is a small round room – or all 525,200,000,000 players if you are playing in an unenclosed area.

RULE ONE:
The first player hops over to the board on one leg and, upon reaching it, asks 'Who has the dice?' If there is no reply, the game is over. If there is a reply such as 'I have' then approach the answering player and say 'May I have the dice, please?' If the answer is 'Here you are, hen' then carry on to the next part of the game. If the second player replies 'Come and get it' or 'Shove it —— face!' or some such thing, then the game is over. Unless you are bigger than he is – or, if you have a knife/gun or any formidable weapon.*

Having received the dice, or taken them by force (two points for the former, ten points for the latter), hop back to the board on one leg and bare your teeth at anyone showing signs of getting bored because of Rule One (above). The player then throws the dice out of the window, or at any unarmed, smaller or weaker player. All the players leave the room and the game ends.

* Careful here. The second player may have a gun to your knife, etc. But that will become obvious as the game progresses.

The Complete Works of E.P. Snibbet, Esq.

with an introduction by Lantan Hart-Beamish

1st Collected Edition 1972

The great E.P.'s family originally came from Barwell near Hinckley in Leicestershire. Surprisingly little is known about his parents. His father was of English extraction, and his mother was of English extraction. But his great-great-uncle Edward lived in Hinckley and was of English extraction. His maternal aunt Elizabeth is Queen of England and is of German extraction. He began writing, and turned to writing rather late in life at the age of nine, but soon was soon to become established as a mundane, run-of-the-mill nonentity in his own right.

I, however, am six-foot-two and live in Chelmsford and am of Scottish extraction. My mother's extraction is of Welsh extraction, but all the extractions on my father's side (except for one extraction) are Scottish extractions and that exceptional extraction is a Welsh extraction. Oh extraction extraction extraction! A million zillion more extractions than you can list here!

Lanton Hart-Beamish
Nineteen Hundred and Seventy Deathbed

Apologia:

Sorry about the introduction.

Signed,

Methuen & Co. Ltd.

by Ethel Methuen for Mr Methuen in his absence.

(Sorry about that. I wish I could have apologized personally.[1])

Mr Methuen Snr. (deceased)

---

1. Sorry about all the apologies in the *apologia*.[2]
2. Sorry about saying 'apologies' and 'apologia' so close together.[3]
3. I've done it again. Sorry.[4]
4. Sorry about saying sorry.[5]
5. Damn.

The Condensed Letters of E.P. Snibbet, Esq.

On or about the morning of the 12th of July, 1967
To: The general public:

BUM!
TIT!!!

(The use of the word 'bum' here was probably in the sense of to 'bumdeedle', or the act of humming loudly:

> '. . . 'eard 'im and 'e was a bummin' ausaay
> loike a buzzard-clock.'
> > – Tennyson. SOD
> > (Shorter Oxford Dictionary)

And 'tit' is, of course, a small horse.)

To: The gentlemen of Barwell
Circa 3rd August 1935

Tosser Harris is a wanke

(Incomplete. Believed to have continued to be 'wankedoo', a white gum tree of Western Australia.)

(Written on a page torn out of a textbook.)

To: Tracy Roberts
Circa 3rd August, 1936

See you tonight down behind the bus shelter. And that Trevor is a wanker and had better watch out for his hindquarters or I'll put the boot up his arse!

(Presumably the person referred to, 'Trevor', was a boot maker, or a saddler who bought and sold work-horses.)

Small Fragment of a Manuscript (Recently Recovered)
by E.P. Snibbet, Esq.

My Hobbies

by E.P. Snibbet, aged 9

My hobby is football and I like to play it and things like that a lot, right. Me mates and I always get down the match, right, on Saturday, right, and things like that a lot too. When I leave school next month, right, I am going to go down and see if I can get signed on and things like that. Terry B got in and he is very awful at it, right, and things like that. It is going be a wake, right, because I can get twice as many in the net as he can, right, and things like that. Ask anybody, right, now piss off and things like that.

The End.

DNA: The Thread of Life!

Good evening. Over the course of the last 164 television programmes I have been trying to tell you a little bit about that thread of life which we scientists call *DNA*. Now DNA is the genetic unit, that is to say that it is a kind of *code* that controls the way in which each individual cell is formed. It's rather like having several building sites all linked together by a vast telephone exchange all controlled by an enormous, invisible, traffic policeman which we scientists call Police Constable Harris.

We have now found a way of altering this DNA molecule in real life. We can, as it were, take DNA and turn it upside-down. Or to put it another way, upside-down it can we turn take DNA. This means that we scientists can now change this very template of life and thus alter the shape of life itself! (Thank you.)

Now, obviously, this is quite important in the field of germ warfare because we can now produce an almost infinite number of new diseases. We can make *germs* – G.E.R.M.S. – or *bacteria* to order. Here in Britain, we have recently made a major breakthrough by producing a new extremely large germ; a germ so huge that it can actually kill a man by acts of physical violence. We have nicknamed this germ 'The Extremely Large Germ', but more correctly we refer to it as The Big Strangler – named after Doctor Big Strangler, the biologist. Soon The Big Strangler will also be able to kill people by simply kneeing them in the head. And we hope soon to develop a particularly virulent bacteria which can drive tanks, and a sophisticated form of cholera which goes to the opera twice a week and can choose a decent Claret.

Quite likely written for St Mary's Hospital, Paddington, for a student Rag Week in 1980.

A Foreword about Charity

by Dr Graham Chapman, author of

A Liar's Autobiography and *Monty Python Ltd Owes Me a Few Quid*

If you have bought this publication then you have made a contribution to the NSPCC and St Mary's Hospital Mother-and-Baby Research Fund. If you have not, then you should not be reading this. If you are *still* reading this and have made no contribution, however small, then you should by now be feeling pangs of guilt. This is a perfectly normal response and the negative feelings can quickly be relieved by a process known in medical terms as 'giving'.

Neglected and/or unassuaged, these feelings of guilt, though seemingly insignificant when set against the total vista of problems a person may face, nevertheless persist and form a focus, or 'guilt-nidus', which may be forgotten only to emerge many many years later as old age and even death. The Charity-Avoidance Syndrome* (as it has become known) may not only prove troublesome (as outlined above in its chronic form), but may also manifest itself in an acute form where the 'avoident's' failure to pay the 'avoidee' results in a transitory attack of the characteristic *thick lip*.

Although it can not yet be regarded as scientifically proven, there is powerful statistical evidence to show that Charity-Avoidance may play an underlying ectological role in a diverse number of

---

* Not, as is commonly believed, named after Professor Sir Benjamin Charity, whose personal hygiene problem was pure coincidence.

complaints ranging from *tineapedis*, sexual impotence and joblessness, to the bizarre (but no less common) Bad Luck on the Horses Syndrome. 'Avoiders' have also reported profoundly unsettling 'daymares' in which the potential sleeper finds himself a total insomniac until disbursement. Only with the help of huge charitable donations can the medical establishment hope to make any progress against this crippling and pandemic disease.

Not too long ago, before the charitably induced advent of antibiotics, the best the beleaguered physician could do was to try and kill as many germs as he could with whatever he had and, in those days, this often meant going for them with a rolled-up newspaper. Now all that is just so many metaphors under the bridge and the fact that *Erysipeloid of Rosenbach* can, today, be cured is taken for granted by a general public which, but for its earlier charitable donations, could well be dead.

Lots of Love,

Dr Loony-up-the-spout-with-a-cream-bun-cheques-accepted-only-with-a-banker's-card-Smith-Smythe-Smith-Loomis
(SOP)

A Typical Day

by God

8.20. Did not wake up.

6.40. Thought of the line '8.20, did not wake up.'

6.41. Did not go to sleep.

6.41.30. I know that I know everything and do not need to think up lines.

6.41.31. NB *Must* stop talking to self.

6.41.31.5. I am perfectly ~~sane~~. I am ~~perfect~~. I ~~am~~. I.

6.41.31.51. Oh fuck it.

8.20 Zzzzzzzzzzzzzzzzzzzzzzzzzzzzzzzzzzzzzzzzzz.

Graham wrote the majority of this biography, up to the November 1988 section. It was most likely a standard bio he kept on hand whenever he needed to supply something to the press.

Graham Chapman's Biography

1941   Born in Leicester on 8 January. Father a policeman, mother not.

1953–59   Melton Mowbray Grammar School.

1959–62   Emmanuel College, Cambridge. Studied Medicine. Member of Footlights Club. *Double Take*, Footlights Revue directed by Trevor Nunn. Other cast members include John Cleese and Tony Hendra.

1962   St Bartholomew's Hospital, London. Clinical Medicine.

1963   Joins the cast of *Cambridge Circus* Footlights Revue in West End. Footlights Revue tour of New Zealand, then Broadway, three weeks, off-Broadway, three months.

1966   Wrote with John Cleese for *The Frost Report* BBC-TV series. *I'm Sorry, I'll Read That Again* (BBC Radio). Qualified as a Doctor. Did not marry. Met David Sherlock. Wrote for *The Illustrated Weekly Hudd* BBC-TV series, *Tom Jones Show*, *Cilla*. Wrote with Barry Cryer and Eric Idle situation comedy series *No That's Me Over Here* for Ronnie Corbett.

1967   *At Last The 1948 Show*. Second series *The Frost Report*. Writing only. *At Last The 1948 Show* second series. Wrote for Marty Feldman BBC-TV series *Marty*.

1968   Second series *No That's Me Over Here*. Film scripts, *The*

Magic Christian, The Rise and Rise of Michael Rimmer and *Rentasleuth* (released as *Rentadick*). First TV episode of *Doctor in the House* with John Cleese followed by three more with Barry Cryer and five more with Bernard McKenna and one or two with Eric Idle. First series *Monty Python's Flying Circus*.

1970   Third series *No That's Me Over Here*. Second series *Monty Python's Flying Circus*. Eleven more *Doctors* with Bernard McKenna.

1971   *And Now For Something Completely Different* film. *Monty Python's Big Red Book*. Became legal guardian to John Tomiczek.

1972   Third series *Monty Python's Flying Circus*. More Ronnie Corbett shows (*No That's Me Over Here, Now Look Here, Ronnie!*) with Barry Cryer. Co-founded *Gay News* newspaper. Script doctor (with B. Cryer) on *No Sex Please, We're British*.

1973   *Python* UK stage tour. Canadian stage tour. *Brand New Monty Python Bok*.

1974   Fourth series of *Monty Python's Flying Circus*, without J. Cleese. Now simply called *Monty Python*. *Python* stage show, Theatre Royal, Drury Lane, with J. Cleese. *Monty Python and the Holy Grail*. Wrote stage play, *Oh Happy Day*, with Barry Cryer.

1975   More *Doctors* (with B. McKenna and D. Sherlock). Filled in, between acts, for The Pink Floyd at Knebworth.

1976   *Monty Python* stage show at the City Center, New York. Filled in a bit for The Who at Hammersmith Odeon.

1977   *Out of the Trees* BBC-TV. *Prince of Denmark* (sit-com) for Ronnie Corbett. Stopped drinking alcohol.

1978   Produced, co-scripted and acted in *The Odd Job* film. *Monty Python's Life of Brian* film.

1979   Co-produced (with Eric Idle) *The Life of Brian* soundtrack. *Montypythonscrapbook*. Guest appearances on

The Big Show NBC-TV. Appear for a week on *The Hollywood Squares* NBC-TV.

1980 *A Liar's Autobiography* published in hardback. *Monty Python* stage show at The Hollywood Bowl; now a movie. *Monty Python's Contractual Obligation Album.*

1981 *A Liar's Autobiography* published in paperback. 2nd March: First 'comedy lecture' at Facets Multimedia, Chicago. Began lecture tour of twenty-three US college campuses.

1982 Guest appearance *Saturday Night Live* NBC-TV. *Monty Python's The Meaning of Life* film. Screenplay for *Yellowbeard*, an adventure comedy film. Completed filming in October in Mexico for Orion.

1983 *Monty Python's The Meaning of Life* film, book and soundtrack released.

1984 Contributes interview chapter for *The Courage to Change*, a book on alcoholism by Dennis Wholey.

1987 Guest appearances on *Still Crazy Like A Fox* CBS-TV. Host four episodes of *The Dangerous Film Club* TV series for Cinemax. Wrote (with D. Sherlock) and shot pilot episode of *Jake's Journey* (sitcom) CBS-TV. Hal Ashby directs. CBS passes, but The Disney Channel picks up the option. House burgled. Among the items stolen are a computer with partially-completed manuscript, *Gin and Tonic* (A.K.A *A Liar's Autobiography Part II*), on it.

1988 Undertakes a lecture tour of US college campuses. June 11: Helps MC *Artists Against Apartheid's 70th Birthday Tribute to Nelson Mandela* concert, Wembley Stadium, London.

1988 November: A routine visit to the dentist turns tragic when a cancerous spot is discovered on his tonsils. Begins cancer treatment. Revives *Ditto* film project, rewriting script with D. Sherlock. Signs production deal with Ron Howard's Imagine Entertainment. Records *A Liar's Autobiography* for

Dove Audio (owned at that time by old friend Harry Nilsson).

1989   Cancer treatment appears to be working and Graham is released from hospital. September: Reunites with the other Pythons for a cameo in *Parrot Sketch Not Included* (aka *20 Odd Years of Python*), a twentieth anniversary salute to the team. There is talk of future Python activities, but this proves to be Graham's final public appearance.
October: Suffers a sudden relapse. Dies of throat cancer in Maidstone Hospital, 4 October, just one day shy of the team's twentieth anniversary. Terry Jones calls it 'The worse case of party-pooping I've ever seen.'

This piece, and the Index, was originally intended for A Liar's Autobiography.

What You May Have Missed by Skimming Through this Book

— Why I advised Elton John to go to my trichologist.

— How Germaine Greer remained unliberated at Cambridge until she wasn't screwed by anyone, but kept bragging about being screwed by everyone.

— What Wilfred Hyde-White *really* said to Terry Southern in the presence of Peter Sellers.

— What happened the day I invited J.B. Priestley to tea in his own home.

— What the severed prick was doing in the leading debutante's handbag at a Cambridge May Ball.

— What Mrs Rose Kennedy suggested to me in the middle of New York.

— Why the Queen Mother told me to piss off.

— Why John Cleese stayed at a naughty boarding house.

— Why David Bowie and I fought over a chair in a gay club.

— Why Harry Nilsson bit the dog.

— Why Keith Moon was dropped in a hotel lounge.

Author's Note: All of these incidents actually happened, but I've realized that the only way people are likely to believe them is to pretend that I'm lying.

– Graham

Index

(of People Who May or May Not be Included in this Book)